TIMON OF ATHENS
Shakespeare's Pessimistic Tragedy

ROLF SOELLNER

TIMON OF ATHENS
Shakespeare's Pessimistic Tragedy

With a stage history by Gary Jay Williams

Ohio State University Press : Columbus

Library of Congress Cataloguing in Publication Data

Soellner, Rolf.
  Timon of Athens, Shakespeare's pessimistic
tragedy.

  Includes bibliographical references and index.
  1. Shakespeare, William, 1564–1616. Timon of
Athens. I. Williams, Gary Jay. II. Title.
PR2834.S6   822.3'3   78-10884
ISBN 0-8142-0292-6

Contents

To My Parents

Preface

Charlton Hinman's observation that "critical responses to *Timon of Athens* have not always been characterized by moderation" should have a sobering effect on any critic of the play. But since most violations of moderation have been committed by those who dislike *Timon*, I may be forgiven if I have lapsed occasionally into fervor when defending its merits. I have tried to write a comprehensive critical analysis of the play in its dramatic and cultural contexts. I have felt no need to take up the so-called authorship question; few people now doubt that *Timon* is wholly Shakespeare's. Three other questions much debated in the past are merely marginal to my purposes: when *Timon* was written, what its sources are, and how to explain the defectiveness of the only text we have, that of the First Folio. Such thoughts as I have on these subjects are in the Appendixes.

After completing the manuscript, I had the good fortune of meeting Gary Williams, of the Catholic University of America, whose interest in the play and fascination with it parallel mine. He kindly accepted my invitation to contribute a stage history—the more welcome an addition to this book as he speaks with the rare authority of a man who has directed *Timon* on the stage.

My approach has made it necessary to discuss some key passages of the play in more than one chapter; the reader in search of their total interpretation may consult the Index of Lines. The edition of *Timon* quoted and referred to is H. J. Oliver's in the Arden Shakespeare (London: Methuen, 1969); plays other than *Timon* are cited from *The Riverside Shakespeare*, text ed. G. Blakemore Evans (Boston: Houghton Mifflin, 1974). For illustrating the intellectual background, I have sought to quote sixteenth- and seventeenth-century sources in preference to secondary, modern ones; but I have cautiously modernized their punctuation and spelling. I have followed the same procedure with the Bible, which I quote in the Genevan version (London: Christopher Barker, 1599).

It remains for me to acknowledge the magic of bounty received in writing this book. Two grants-in-aid from the Humanities College of the Ohio State University helped me to travel to research libraries. The personnel of these libraries—the British Library, the Folger Shakespeare Library, and the Newberry Library—was most generous and helpful. For reading and criticizing parts or all of my manuscript at various stages, I am indebted to my colleagues Lee Cox, John Gabel, Robert Jones, James Kincaid, and Edwin Robbins. Maurice Charney of Rutgers University gave me the benefit of his learning and intimate knowledge of the play. Thelma Greenfield of the University of Oregon read what I thought was my final version and convinced me for my own good that it still needed considerable revision. Last but not least, I am grateful to Weldon Kefauver, director of the Ohio State University Press, for his consideration and encouragement, and to Robert Demorest, the editor, for guiding the manuscript through the press.

1

Facing the Depth

Pass by and curse thy fill

    Timon of Athens opens on a casually ominous note. A poet and a painter meet and, after mutual greeting, the poet asks: "How goes the world?" Whereupon the painter answers: "It wears, sir, as it grows." Shakespeare's audience was familiar with the idea that the world was now in the last stages of its life; therefore, the poet can treat it as a cliché: "Ay, that's well known." But this hackneyed notion could still conjure up the fearful image of a doomed humanity as it did effectively in medieval Christian eschatology and as it does again in the blind Gloucester's cry when he meets his wracked and tortured old master Lear: "O ruin'd piece of nature! This great world / Shall so wear out to nought" (4.6.134–35).

    The painter's offhand reminder of the world's impermanence is followed by the poet's alarmingly cynical portrayal of man and society in the allegory of Fortune he is about to present to Timon: it depicts a world of fortune-seekers where "all deserts, all kinds" greedily congregate at the foot of Fortune's hill. The one man—a person "of Lord Timon's frame"—whom the goddess wafts upward to her throne is obsequiously adulated by those below; but when Fortune displays her proverbial fickleness by rejecting her erstwhile darling and he slides down the hill, the odious sycophants abandon him, "Not one accompanying his declining foot" (1.1.90). This satire on greed and ingratitude is a fitting overture to the strident displays of meanness and the breaking of societal bonds in the play. This may be a shrinking and decaying world, but what is dramatized is the sickness and degeneracy of man. "The strain of man's bred out / Into baboon and monkey" says the cynic Apemantus when Alcibiades and his followers arrive at Timon's hospitable house and exercise their pliant joints in courtesy (1.1.249–50). Apemantus's inverse Darwinism is an apt expression of the feeling of the human regression the unfolding play conveys; one is reminded that most Renaissance moralists thought that men too were shrinking and degenerating along with the universe. The cynic's remarks bristle with biting invectives against the hypocrisy and depravity of this human world.

The initial cynical statements, borne out as they are by the accompanying action, are mild compared with what is to come: in the second part of the play, a virulently pessimistic voice is raised and spews forth hatred and disgust, the voice of Timon the misanthrope, a man who has rudely awakened from his long dream of universal friendship and love to the reality of his destitution and his friends' villainy. He is now misanthropy personified; he cannot be moved from his fixed hatred by finding gold, which would permit him to be rich and honored again, nor by the subtle plea of Alcibiades to help him against Athens, nor by the Athenians' desperate supplication to save them from Alcibiades' army. While his countrymen strenuously seek to extend their sojourn on the ultimately doomed globe, Timon becomes an insistent apocalyptic voice, a prophet of gloom, a preacher of destruction, and a destroyer of himself.

Episode after episode demonstrates the meanness and venality of men, the relentless insistence varied only by the disturbing inversions of irony, sarcasm, and grotesquerie. There is no substantial relief. Too much, I think, has in this respect been made of Timon's faithful steward. His role, after all, is relatively minor, that of a warning voice against Timon's extravagance and of a choric commentator on his fall. Flavius loses all claim he might have of being the moral center of the play when he takes the gold proffered to him by the misanthrope with the uncharitable advice to hoard it and to show charity to none. Even though he and Timon's other loyal servants attract some sympathy, we realize that they are reduced to ineffective lamentations that heighten the pathos of Timon's ruin. There is no prominent and totally likable exemplar of honesty in Athens because Apemantus, who might provide it, enjoys too much his job as castigator of vices. The milieu in which Timon's monumental hatred develops is permeated with corruption, and the incidents that release his curses are evidence of a general detestable ingratitude. As much as these curses jar our sensibilities, we must admit that they are amply motivated.

Timon begins with a potentially disquieting note, continues with stronger accents as the action progresses, and comes to a climax in the most wildly nihilistic speeches ever penned. The most memorable lines of the play are pessimistic. This is not merely a declarative pessimism; it penetrates, as I shall show, into the structure, the characterizations, the imagery, and the themes of the play. It is far from being dispelled by the rather short Alcibiades business of the ending. E. K. Chambers says justly that *Timon* constitutes "the ultimate summing up of the remorseless analysis of human nature" that Shakespeare undertook in his tragedies.[1]

This pervasive darkness of the atmosphere has been a major stumbling block for the just appreciation of the play. Coleridge, as J. P. Collier reports, saw the problem:

> His admiration for some parts of the tragedy was unbounded; but he maintained that it was, on the whole, a painful and disagreeable production, because it gave only a disadvantageous picture of human nature, very inconsistent with what, he firmly believed, was our poet's real view of the characters of his fellow creatures.[2]

Even more strongly, Andor Gomme complains in our own time about "the characteristic *Timon* whine, which has proved so prominent a pointer to what is most unattractive in the play: the unexplained mood of cynicism which seems to inform the whole movement of the verse."[3] Although few indeed have been as outspoken as Coleridge and Gomme, the history of criticism shows that, consciously or unconsciously, commentators have been influenced by their human but entirely uncritical resistance to the play's pessimism. These are facts with which a critic of the play has to come to terms, and it is best to face them at the outset. A brief look at the history of the play's reception with focus on the reaction to its pessimism is therefore in order.[4]

We may profitably begin with the method of criticizing Shakespeare favored during the neoclassical period: altering his plays. It is not surprising that an age that could not endure a starkly tragic *Lear* would also seek to lighten the load of *Timon*. Thomas Shadwell's brightened-up version entitled *The History of Timon of Athens, the Manhater* was performed for the first time in 1678 and held the stage into the later eighteenth century; this version had eight printed editions between 1678 and 1732. Shadwell kept so little of what he called "the inimitable hand of Shakespeare" and intruded so much of his own that his boast should have been not that he made Timon into a play but that he made it into a non-Shakespearean one; he altered characters, speeches, and ideas quite irreverently, and he supplied others incongruous with the drama's ethos. No single overriding principle can be discerned in these changes, but many were clearly dictated by Shadwell's belief that the play had to be made more "noble" and less depressing. Thus, for instance, he dropped the Fortune allegory and the derogatory comments on human nature by the strangers and servants in the first three scenes of the third act. Apemantus became a benevolent warner rather than a scurrilous cynic. The general villainy of Athens was much reduced by the conflation of Timon's friends with the ungrateful senators. Most perversely, Shadwell provided a romantic entanglement for Timon, making him desert his betrothed, Evandra, for a meretricious coquette only to realize his mistake at last. The loyal Evandra followed him even into exile and death. Timon expired grandly on stage: "Thou only! dearest! kind! and constant thing on earth!" His faithful fiancée joined him promptly. Of course, Timon's doting on the coquette made him look ridiculous, and the faithful companionship of Evandra deprived him of much of the reason for his quarrel with the world.

The tendency to allay Shakespeare's pessimism is also observable in Richard Cumberland's version, *Timon of Athens, Altered from Shakespeare* (1771), which David Garrick, in spite of reservations, put on the stage. Cumberland, it is true, was somewhat less violent in his changes than Shadwell; as he said, he retained "many original passages of the first merit," and he lightened the play's mood primarily by omissions. Apemantus's role was much reduced; not only were his obscenities removed but he was also absent from Timon's banquet and thus had no occasion to utter his cynical prayer and his comments on the dance as a hypocritical exercise of fortune seekers (in fact, there was no masque and no dance). Sempronius, the most odious of Timon's friends, did not appear, and some of Timon's misanthropic speeches, such as his address to the walls of Athens, were deleted. Worst, Timon had a noble daughter, Evanthe, who joined Alcibiades in warning him against his prodigality. Alcibiades too was a much ennobled man who naturally fell in love with Evanthe and became engaged to her. No prostitutes for him. The ending of this version was, if anything, worse than Shadwell's: Timon, trembling between sanity and insanity, died a Lear-like death in the presence of his family; unlike Lear, however, he still managed a fatherly blessing.

Not until 1816 was something approaching Shakespeare's *Timon* performed when Edmund Kean, who like Garrick cherished the play, acted in the title role. Kean's romantic portrayal of the misanthrope, of which we have a vivid but probably not too accurate account by Leigh Hunt, assured the play at least a *succès d'estime*. George Lamb, the author of this version, informed the reader that "the present attempt has been to restore Shakespeare to the stage, with no other omissions than such as the refinement of manners has rendered necessary." Naturally this refinement necessitated the elimination of the prostitutes and the sexual innuendos. But Lamb was somewhat less than ingenuous; he also added a few non-Shakespearean touches, most notably by having Alcibiades mete out justice to Lucius and Lucullus, Timon's odious creditor-friends. Poetic justice was thus restored, Alcibiades ennobled, Timon vindicated, and the play grossly sentimentalized. And so, in some manner, it has been until recently; directors and actors have flinched from the play's pessimism and introduced modifications to alleviate it. (See Gary Williams's Stage History in the Appendixes.)

Eighteenth-century literary critics generally avoided facing the full pessimism by moralizing on Timon's failure and by disregarding the moral to be drawn from the Athenians' villainy. So Dr. Johnson: "The catastrophe affords a very powerful warning against ostentatious liberality, which scatters bounty, but confers no benefits, and buys flattery but not friendship."[5] However, a new direction came in with the Romantics, who had a tendency to sympathize with the wronged hero, idealize him, and identify him with Shakespeare, and Shakespeare with themselves. *Timon* now was widely admired; however, what was acclaimed was not the stage play but the somber document read as Shakespeare's spiritual autobiography whose mood resembled romantic melancholy, *Weltschmerz*, and *dégoût du monde*. William Hazlitt found Shakespeare in earnest throughout; this was his only work in which "spleen is the predominant feeling of mind." Timon especially appealed to Hazlitt because he faces misfortune "with a lofty spirit of self-denial and bitter scorn of the world."[6] Charles Lamb saw in him an ideal being whose free and generous nature is too trusting for the world.[7]

The reading of *Timon* as Shakespeare's somber confession was most eagerly practiced in Germany, where philosophical idealism and melancholy romanticism were married and where they engendered the greatest of the pessimistic philosophers. It is hardly accidental that several of the strongest admirers of the play in the nineteenth and twentieth centuries have come from Germany, Friedrich Schiller, Karl Marx, Gerhart Hauptmann, and Bertold Brecht among them.[8] For Schiller, the enthusiasm for *Timon* was part of a passing pessimism during his Mannheim years, before he met and joined the more optimistic Goethe. During these years, he himself attempted a tragedy of a misanthrope, entitled *Der Menschenfeind*, which he did not finish. In an essay of 1774, Schiller recommended *Timon* for performance on the German stage, saying that he knew no work of Shakespeare that presented greater truth about man, appealed more strongly and eloquently to the heart, and taught more wisdom of life.[9] The German critic most influential on interpretations of *Timon* as a somber spiritual autobiography was Hermann Ulrici, for whom the play was the fragment of a great confession from Shakespeare's last London years. There had been guesses before that the play might have been one of Shakespeare's last and that it was not fully complete; Ulrici spun these notions into a romantic fantasy about its being left unfinished by a depressed and despairing Shakespeare, whose feelings on his departure from London and from the theater resembled Timon's when leaving Athens. Shakespeare had seen his art profaned and despised by a rude populace as society became increasingly degenerate. Bitterly resenting the commercialization of his deepest thoughts, he hurriedly sketched a play that allowed him to give vent to his nausea. When he became calmer, he abandoned the project; and even though he later tried to complete it, he could not recapture his original mood and therefore gave up.[10]

An interesting variant of Ulrici's hypothesis of *Timon* as a late-Shakespearean spiritual testament was devised by the Dane, Georg Brandes, whose *William Shakespeare* (1895) influenced more than one generation of Shakespeare students. Brandes painted a broadly gloomy picture of the late Elizabethan and Jacobean England of which, he argued, the play was a reflection. The Essex affair, in which the wisest and meanest sage of mankind turned against his former benefactor; the anxiety about the approaching death of the queen and the grief for her after it; the new king's lack of political wisdom; the religious tensions and conflicts; the moral depravity of the court, with its unworthy favorites and unscrupulous scramblers for office; even the affairs and poisoning activities of Lady Essex—all served Brandes to draw a picture of an age that amply deserved a Timonesque scorn. He characterized the Shakespeare of the *Timon* period as an aging, broken man in a nation that was drifting toward its predestined doom, the conflagration of the Civil War. Brandes claimed that Shakespeare condensed all his bitter experiences, all his disappointments about man's ingratitude to man, and all his sufferings into this play. To purge himself of the excruciating spiritual pain that threatened to destroy him, Shakespeare created this drama around the huge, despairing figure of the misanthrope, who became a dark secretion of his own bitter gall.[11]

It is perhaps not surprising that when the conjecture of Shakespeare's writing *Timon* in depression and despair crossed the Atlantic to what was then the heartland of optimism, it was seized upon to support the dislike for the play's theme and major character. Henry Hudson surmised in 1855 that Shakespeare wrote the play when his normal judgment was suspended by a melancholy, self-brooding earnestness; only thus could it be explained why he took up a subject so unsuitable for dramatic treatment—with a predictably deplorable result.[12] This hypothesis was often accompanied by another hypothesis: Shakespeare, it was claimed, left the play unfinished because, so to speak, he despaired of the possibility of making poetic profit from his despair. This is patently unlikely, and it should be said to the credit of Edward Dowden, who among the nineteenth-century English critics is most associated with the notion that Shakespeare wrote his tragedies *de profundis*, that he held the playwright to have been in a reflective rather than a desperate mood when he composed *Timon*, near the end of his career after his irascible impulses had subsided.[13] Yet the notion of the play's being a direct record of the author's depression has crept up among later critics. Even the generally sane and judicious E. K. Chambers suggested that Shakespeare may have been neurotic and ill when he wrote *Timon*, "under conditions of mental and perhaps physical stress, which led to his breakdown."[14]

Since C. J. Sisson's keen strictures,[15] critics have become shy of romanticizing about Shakespeare's sorrows (although playwrights may still profitably engage in this fantasy). Shakespeare was too impersonal an artist to let us infer what events made him happy or unhappy, and the chronology of his plays, such as we can establish it, shows no simple emotional curve. In the case of *Timon*, we not only lack the biographical facts to determine Shakespeare's state of mind at the date of composition, but we are also in doubt about the date itself—various years in the span of about ten having been proposed. We must remain shy or becoming psychotherapists no matter how much the play nudges us into saying something about why Shakespeare wrote it. We must also remain aware of the influence of our own temperament and outlook on life when we face the great misanthrope. Harry Levin has argued that the problem with *Timon* is that Shakespeare undertook an erroneously conceived task that he could not help finding uncongenial.[16] Levin does perhaps prove that Levin finds the task uncongenial; his presupposition (the same as Coleridge's) that Shakespeare was predominantly optimistic about life is as unprovable as any other.

The most ardent champion of the play has been strangely unaffected by its pervasive pessimism: George Wilson Knight. For him *Timon* is Shakespeare's culminating tragedy, a work with a "movement more precipitous and unimpeded than any in Shakespeare; one which is conceived on a scale more tremendous than that of *Macbeth* and *King Lear*, and whose universal tragic significance is of all most clearly apparent." This significance lies for Knight in the hero's allegorical journey from an earthly paradise with a magnificent "erotic" display to a realm of loneliness and universal loathing, in which he "fronts his destiny, emperor still in mind and soul, wearing the imperial nakedness of his hate."[17] Few lovers of the play will be altogether able to soar with Knight beyond optimism and pessimism and beyond all good and evil; the "humanism" he sees in Timon is an odd term to apply to the abstraction the character becomes under his enthusiastic pen. To admire without reservation both Timon's indiscriminate giving and boundless hate is to go outside ordinary human standards; to do so would hardly have struck Shakespear's audience, whose moral measurements were still influenced by Christian humanism, as human or humane—interchangeable words in their time. Yet it should be said that Knight offers a counterweight to the plethora of unsympathetic interpretations and that he sees details brilliantly: the glorious sensuousness of the earlier part, the pyrotechnics of Timon's passion, and the grandeur of his rejection of the world.

For most critics, at any rate, the question of why Shakespeare gave Timon so somber a hue has imposed itself. The only answer that can be given with assurance is that dramatic considerations required a gloomy atmosphere and tone; if Timon's misanthropy was to be motivated, there had to be good reasons for it. Shakespeare certainly set himself a difficult task in representing misanthropy tragically. Misanthropy is an emotion more palatable in an at least slightly amusing context, more comfortable to view as a human oddity than a tragic affliction. We can smile at Molière's Alceste, who despises the artificiality of society but is hopelessly in love with Célimène, one of society's most artificial products. The satiric situation allows us still to smile, even if with embarrassment, when Gulliver prefers the odor of his horses to the embraces of his wife. Also, literary misanthropes are generally not all-out pessimists but pejorativists, as we ourselves are at one time or another; they are more like Apemantus, the critic of society, than Timon, the all-out hater. Gulliver, it is true, has touches of the darkest hue, but he is in a land of horses when he becomes a misanthrope, not in a realistically portrayed society. Alceste's inconsistency and the absurdity of Gulliver's situation allow us to distance ourselves from them as characters while we respond to the satirical message. It cannot be quite so with a tragic hero like Timon; we must enter more deeply into his mental processes. And for many it seems easier to enter the mind of a murderer like Macbeth than that of a misanthrope, to sympathize with a man who hates Jack, John, and Peter and kills them than with one who suffers from the abstract and life-denying affliction of misanthropy.

Shakespeare decided to make Timon's misanthropy into a humanly plausible experience and a tragic phenomenon by dramatizing it as a reaction to an ingratitude that hits Timon like an avalanche. For this purpose, Timon had to be an idealist; but Shakespeare did not make him into a flawless hero—his gullibility is too visible—and this, I think, was dramatically the right decision. To have done otherwise would have detracted from the stature of his misanthropy, which is, paradoxically, an improvement on his philanthropy. If the later Timon were not in some sense greater than the earlier, he would not command amazement, awe, perhaps even respect for his uncompromising rejection of the world; the tragedy would lose interest just when it proceeds to the heart of the matter.

Given the subject of tragic misanthropy, Shakespeare surely also made the right decision to present Timon's misanthropy as a total microcosmic and macrocosmic pessimism. Had he let Timon hang on to any consolatory notion, trust in a person or belief in a nonhuman order and beauty, he would have run the risk of creating not an essential misanthrope but a sentimentalist or disappointed idealist. Of the former danger, the eighteenth-century adaptations with their Evandras and Evanthes bear witness. Of the latter, Schiller's failure with *Der Menschenfeind* is an indication: Schiller tried to balance his hero's misanthropy with a Rousseauistic admiration for the order and harmony of nature, which men have done their best to pervert. Shakespeare's conception is surely more fascinating psychologically because it is unrelieved and is cosmically extended into a horror of nature as a whole. In toning down the light on Timon the philanthropist and in generally painting with dark pigments, Shakespeare showed his sense of dramatic coloring and gradation. The focus on Timon would have been disturbed had he made Alcibiades or any other character into a shining hero. The world Shakespeare created for this play is a fitting one: a corrupt, upside-down world, a place of insidious evil and ruthless ambition where the bitch-goddess Fortuna is adored and feared. The tragedy of the extremist has its appropriately extreme setting.

But we are still faced with the question of why Shakespeare chose a subject that required such somber colors. Not, I think, by accident and mistake. Timon is the end and climax of a series of partial misanthropes: Jaques, Hamlet, Thersites, and Lear. Shakespeare evidently wished to create a hero who took cleansing the body of the infected world totally seriously. And, as Chambers says, the play is "continuous with the development of pessimistic thought that is traceable along the whole line of tragedies."[18] All Shakespeare's tragedies have nadirs of disillusionment and despair, such as Othello's "This was Othello," Macbeth's dismissal of life as a walking shadow, and Lear's "Never, never, never, never, never." There is a special pessimistic momentum in the later tragedies, beginning with *Lear*. It is thought-provoking that in both *Lear* and *Timon* Shakespeare took stories that were not tragic in his sources and gave them a very dark configuration. Also, both *Coriolanus* and *Timon* present particularly corrupt societies, if not societies in dissolution. So, of course, does *Troilus and Cressida*, but only the two tragedies establish very close connections between disintegrating societies and the heroes' fall. Both Coriolanus and Timon are placed in tragic predicaments because they pay tribute to the ostensible ideals of their society; both try to break the societal fetters but fail to achieve freedom.

If we locate the pessimism of *Timon of Athens* in Shakespear's personal experience and world view, we transcend the limits of legitimate criticism, although it is possible that this is part of the explanation. Certainly an incorrigible optimist would not have looked so deeply into the well of despair. In any case, it is fair to conclude that the opportunity of deepening the pessimistic aspects inherent in all tragedy drew Shakespeare to the Timon story, of deepening them not merely emotionally but also, perhaps primarily, intellectually. The play proves Shakespeare's exposure to, and interest in, the pessimistic ideas that were in the air. And this interest, unlike his personal feeling and temperament, can be demonstrated.

I shall argue that *Timon* is more deliberately anchored in a pessimistic intellectual tradition than has generally been supposed. But Ulrici, Brandes, and others provide examples on how not to proceed in this matter. We cannot relate the play to political, cultural, and religious failings of the Jacobean age that have left no discernible reflections in it;

for that matter, F. P. Wilson has warned us not to simply identify Jacobean and pessimistic.[19] Certainly the societal debacle
nourished pessimism, but did not create it. We must seek to
understand the *Timon* atmosphere in the context of a general
European crisis to which literature responded without neces-
sarily concerning itself with particular events. Trevor-Roper
points out that the artists reacted to this crisis with cynicism,
despair, and disillusionment, and he quotes Gerald Brenan's
dictum that the Baroque age "was a tight contracted age,
turned on itself and lacking in self-confidence and faith in the
future."[20] Trevor-Roper mentions Donne, Sir Thomas Browne,
Quevedo, and the painters and sculptors of the Spanish
baroque as examples. Shakespeare, too diverse and individualistic to be placed wholly into one category, belongs at least
partially here, most signally with *Timon*. The play is imprinted with the strains of the age.

For the spread of pessimism in England we should not look
merely to such major Renaissance propagators as Machiavelli and Montaigne; there were older and more domesticated
voices. Christian humanism had not made the *contemptus
mundi* obsolete but had absorbed it. The notion of the decay
of the world, a concomitant of Chrisitan conceptions of the
Fall and the Last Judgment that keeps coming back to haunt
mankind, reached a high point in the late sixteenth and early
seventeenth centuries.[21] Two of the very sources Shakespeare
used for *Timon* were impregnated with *contemptus mundi* and
decay-of-the-world rhetoric: Pierre Boaistuau's *Theatrum
Mundi* (translated by John Alday in 1586, and repeatedly
reprinted) and Richard Barckley's *A Discourse of the Felicity of
Man* (1598; rpt. 1603, 1631). In humanistic fashion, the
Theatrum combines a lament for the miseries of existence and an
onslaught against the vices of mankind (in the first part) with a
praise of the dignity of man (in the second part); but the praise is
too short and superficial to mitigate the fierce thrust of the
pessimism. Barckley's odd mélange of Christian piety and
historical anecdotage is imbued with a distressingly somber
outlook on man and the world: the post-lapsarian universe is for
him dominated by disorder instead of order and discord instead
of harmony, so that it resembles "a chain rent in pieces, whose
links are many lost and broken and the rest so slightly fastened
that they will hardly hang together."[22] No Tillyardian chain of
being for Barckley!

Barckley also demonstrates how easily the new pessimism
could infiltrate and strengthen the old. One of his sallies
against man and society has a familiar ring to readers of
Renaissance history and literature:

The time is so changed and men's manners with them so corrupted that the precepts heretofore given by wise men for the

commodity of life grounded upon virtue and honesty will not
serve their turn; friendship is grown cold, faith is foolishness,
honesty is in exile, and dissimulation hath gotten the other
hand. That is effectively done which is commonly spoken: he that
cannot dissemble cannot live. Machiavel's rules are better followed than those of Plato, Aristotle, or Cicero. . . . So long as
thou hast no need, thou shalt find friends ready to offer thee all
manners of courtesies; but if fortune begin to frown upon thee,
and a tempest chance to arise, they will find quarrels to leave thee
and cover their infidelity with thy fault.[23]

Notwithstanding the dissociation from Machiavelli, these
lines are a paraphrase of a famous passage in *The Prince*.[24] It
evidently appeared to Barckley that Machiavelli could have
been talking about the England of Barckley's own time, and
it appears to us that both could have been talking about the
Athens of *Timon*.

It may finally be noted that the very location of the play
supported, for Shakespeare and his audience, an emphasis
on man's corruption and degeneracy. Ancient Greece, particularly post-Periclean Athens, furnished the Renaissance
with spectacular examples of what happens to states when
men become vicious and beastly. As T. J. B. Spencer points
out, Shakespeare and his fellow writers took the unsympathetic Roman view of the Greeks, even darkening it—a
tendency well demonstrated in *Troilus and Cressida* as well as
in *Timon*. In popular consciousness, Greek and crook were
practically synonymous. The satirists and moralists vied with
each other in depicting the Greeks as "licentious, luxurious,
frivolous, bibulous, venerial, insinuating, perfidious, and
unscrupulous. . . . Timon and his circle lived like Grecians."[25]
This, of course, is moral rather than local coloring; Greek
materials—*Timon* is no exception—were still treated as an
appendix to the matter of Rome.

The location of the play and some of Shakespeare's sources
account at least partly for the somber view of man and
society that permeates it. They do not account for the deepening of the tone toward tragedy, if indeed it is a tragedy. As the title of my study indicates, I think it is.
But since some have denied this, the play's status as a true
tragedy will require a defense.

2

At the Boundary of Tragedy

Nature's fragile vessel

That a number of critics have found *Timon* lacking in tragic qualities is symptomatic of the general feeling that it is in some manner different from Shakespeare's other tragedies, that it lies, to use Willard Farnham's phrase, at the frontiers of tragedy. But, to my mind, it is still clearly within these. This is not, I think, an academic argument, because a critic's attitude toward all aspects of a work is influenced by what he judges the whole to be.

Although critics generally realize that there are no universally accepted definitions of tragedy, they sometimes act as if there were and disregard the lesson of the history of criticism, which records considerable changes of opinion about what plays to call tragedies. Well into the nineteenth century, most critics, whose judgments were formed by the standards of Greek tragedy, or rather some select Greek tragedies, were averse to using the term for Shakespeare's. And when Shakespeare was accepted into the canon, it was at first for a small number of plays. Bradley's singling out of *Hamlet*, *Othello*, *Lear*, and *Macbeth* made it fashionable to think only of these as true tragedies, and some even excluded one or the other of them. There are few now who would deny that *Romeo and Juliet* and the Roman plays are also tragedies. But *Timon* is still in most critics' limbo if not somewhere in an upper circle of hell; and this, I think, is unfortunate.

This is not to say that it is in the same league as *Hamlet*, *Othello*, *Lear*, and *Macbeth*; but I think that it belongs to the next group, being in kind no less powerful than *Antony and Cleopatra* and *Coriolanus*, Shakespeare's other late tragedies. If it has not been so ranked, by and large, this has been due to an overemphasis on the defectiveness of the text and to preconceptions on the need for tragedy to uplift and edify, preconceptions, I believe, that are restrictive and really quite arbitrary.

Parenthetically, we may note that there is no basis in fact for the widespread belief that the case aganst *Timon* as a tragedy can be supported by the irregularity of its placement in the First Folio. This belief is based on the editors' putting *Timon* in a place originally intended for a longer play, as shown by a gap in the pagination. Even though the editors put *Timon* among the tragedies, they did so, it is claimed, because they had no play available other than this hybrid; to indicate that it did not really belong there, they "denied" *Timon* the status of a tragedy by entitling it *The Life of Timon of Athens*. But such designations are used quite haphazardly in the Folio. Who, for instance, would wish to argue that "The Life and Death of Julius Caesar," as this play is called in the table of contents, constitutes an appropriate description? The case against *Timon* grows even weaker when one realizes that the most-difficult-to-classify play of all, *Troilus and Cressida*, was originally scheduled for the place into which *Timon* was put; a canceled leaf, found in several Folio copies, shows on the one side the last page of *Romeo and Juliet* (the preceding play) and on the other the beginning of *Troilus and Cressida*, which was later supplanted by a printer's ornament. Perhaps the most glaring example of the editors' nonchalance about genre is their inclusion of *Cymbeline* among the tragedies. No argument on genre can be supported by reference to Folio titles and classifications.

My argument for *Timon* as a tragedy rests on a negative and a positive demonstration. I shall first try to show that the claims for its being something else—a morality play, a satire, a domestic drama, or a pageant—stem from a partial or simplified reading. I shall then point out the essential elements Timon shares with plays that we have come to recognize as tragedies. Each of these is in some features different from the other, and we can therefore grant *Timon* some idiosyncracies if it meets many of the criteria that have been thought characteristic of the genre. No one play meets them all.

Although my argument is primarily formalistic, it cannot be altogether divorced from a qualitative judgment. I actually have no objection to somebody's calling *Murder in the Red*

Barn a tragedy along with *Lear*, but for good reasons only the latter claims our critical attention: it is superior in what it says about life as well as in its formal articulation. Unless we feel that a play illuminates the human condition more deeply than an ordinary serious drama, we are not apt to argue that it is a tragedy. A moral judgment of this kind, of course, is subjective, and I cannot claim universal validity for it. Only if *Timon* excites greater interest than it has in the past and is more widely felt by audiences and critics to have meaning for our time is it likely to become generally accepted as a tragedy.

Of the claims that *Timon* belongs to a genre different from tragedy, the one easiest to refute is that it is a "morality."[1] True, its outcome is in a sense predictable; but then, in what Shakespearean tragedy is it not? For that matter, all tragedies make us anticipate their general endings since these must rest on some inevitability. The dramatic strategy of *Timon* is not as simple as some would have it; the outcome is not altogether anticipated by the poet's allegory of Fortune, and certainly the moral is not contained in it or the play would be both cynical and banal. Although the allegory anticipates the major turn of the action (leaving out, however, the Alcibiades movement), it makes of Timon a mere favorite and victim of Fortune, and, for better or worse, he is something more. It is also true that there is some stylization in the character portrayals, but none of the characters are really "subtilized virtues and vices." The only moral emphasis that is simple and unequivocal is on the villainy of Timon's friends—an instance of Shakespeare's painting "livelier than life." Granted that the "vices" that oppose Timon, taken *en bloc*, represent something like "Commercialism" or "Exploitation," not a single one represents a clearly defined particular vice, such as Pecunia or Luxuria or Dissimulatio. And there is certainly no character that embodies a definite pattern of virtue: Timon the philanthropist is also prodigal; Apemantus the philosopher is also vain and envious; Flavius is loyal but also interested in gold. We do not have the feeling of a clear moral orientation to which Timon could and should adjust himself. Alcibiades is no model of virtue; he succeeds in making himself the master of Athens because of his ambition and cleverness, not because of any moral quality. Nor does the action suggest that the characters have to make the kind of moral choices facing the characters of moralities. The play does not indicate a spiritual framework or prepare us to expect either salvation or damnation of its hero. It is therefore nonsense to say that a salvational ending is "denied" and to call *Timon* an antimorality.[2] *Timon* heightens life; it does not organize it according to didactic principles. Its apparently simple pattern is made complex and ambiguous by ironies, and its presiding deity is the enigmatic and unpredictable Fortuna.

More to the point is the designation of "satire" or "tragical satire." Critics who subscribe to this classification belong to two schools, those of O.J. Campbell and of Alvin Kernan, and Kernan's is the more defensible position. The difference turns on the critics' attitudes toward Timon, on whether he is the object of satire or the satirist. Campbell opts for the former alternative and denies that Timon has our sympathy to any extent. The nature of his outbursts, he claims, is such as to arouse our strong disapproval; they represent everything that the Renaissance moralists and Shakespeare believed to be false, presumptuous, and ugly, and attacked as such.[3] I would grant Timon some sympathy; but naturally this is a subjective area. In any case, his outbursts do not characterize him as the butt of satire; violent as they are, they are saturated with arguments that reflect major ethical preconceptions of Shakespeare's age. Campbell's claim that *Timon* was written in the new manner of Ben Jonson's *Sejanus* as a tragical satire is also untenable. Jonson's moral viewpoint is so much simpler; he permits no ironies or ambiguities and gives us a clear bearing toward all major and even most minor characters. His Sejanus is a monster quite unlike Timon.

Alvin Kernan has the better case when he finds both Apemantus and Timon satirists and considers Timon's as, in some ways, the higher kind of satire. He grants Timon a Lear-like grandeur; but whereas he sees Lear passing through the stage of satirical outrage to tragic perception, he notes that Timon persists in unyielding hatred. Timon, so to speak, is killed by the nature of satire, which, if pursued unrelentingly, becomes self-destructive.[4] However, we should not stipulate that a tragic hero must attain a "tragic perception" like Lear's. For that matter, critics often exaggerate the extent of Lear's self-knowledge and its significance for his tragedy. Undoubtedly he gains a fleeting understanding of his and man's nature that goes beyond Timon's, but the major impact of this attainment on the tragedy is that it is useless for practical purposes since it comes too late. Timon gains a clear and sharp understanding of the sycophants and usurers around him and generalizes it into the nature of man and the world. This knowledge may be faulty as a universal insight, but this does not matter for the tragic quality of the play; what does matter is that Timon finds it as impossible to live with this knowledge as does Lear with his.

Kernan's statement that both Apemantus and Timon are satirists requires modification. Although Timon speaks occasionally with the accent of a satirist, only Apemantus does consistently so; only he is true satirist, a recognizable relative of Elizabethan-Jacobean satirists. His criticism of society has the ring of what Marston calls "cynical satire." Timon, like Shakespeare's other tragic heroes, has an idiom of his own, an idiom that has the ring of tragedy. This is unmistakable in such phrases as "nature's fragile vessel" or "the sweet degrees that this brief world affords." It is audible even when his speech becomes muscular and harsh and resembles the satirists'. "Cut my heart in sums. . . . Tell out my blood" (3.4.91—93) castigates the moneygrubbers but also rings with the pathos of victimization. Tragic pathos often suffuses the satire and irony: "Strange times, that weep with laughing, not with weeping" (4.3.490). Still more often the satire disappears in the apocalyptic, Lear-like amplification. As much as this idiom absorbs the cynic's satirical arguments, it transcends the tone and purpose of satire. Biting, harsh, and insulting as Elizabethan satire is, it never rises to the all-inclusive destructive denunciation to which Timon leaps immediately: "Burn house! Sink Athens!" (3.6.100). All the stops are out:

> Crack the lawyer's voice,
> That he may never more false title plead,
> Nor sound his quillets shrilly. Hoar the flamen,
> That scolds against the quality of flesh,
> And not believes himself. Down with the nose,
> Down with it flat, take the bridge away
> Of him that, his particular to foresee,
> Smells from the general weal.
>
> (4.3.155–62)

Timon is a pessimist, a nihilist, a prophet of annihilation; above all, he is a misanthrope. Among Shakespeare's heroes, who are all extremists, he is the most extreme; to call him a satirist is to put him into a frame from which he breaks.

That Timon is killed by the nature of satire sounds better in the study or the classroom than when seeing the play or reading it as theater of the mind. What is self-destructive is Timon's misanthropy, which is an extreme reaction to the villainy and ingratitude of his friends, and this misanthropy is fed by his recognition of the general venality of Athens, which he generalizes into that of man. Timon's death derives with tragic logic from his character and circumstances; it does not matter that it occurs offstage if one attends to classical models, as Shakespeare appears to have done. Timon's death certainly dominates the catastrophe in tragic manner.

To call *Timon* a satire is to put the cart before the horse, the satire before the tragedy. This has been recognized by those who, like Sylvan Barnet, use the term "satiric tragedy," which, however, contains the unfortunate implication that what is satirized in the play is tragedy.[5] And to group Timon together with Troilus and Cressida under this heading is to link two plays that are profoundly different in spite of the similar moral climate they have. Troilus is satirized clearly and obviously even in his greater moments, such as when he expresses his disillusionment with Cressida and womanhood, and he is undercut by Ulysses' comments. Unlike Timon, he never gains the strength and final definiteness that makes the tragic hero seek and find death. It seems to me therefore unwise to separate Timon from Shakespeare's tragedies by labeling it a "satirical tragedy" or a "tragical satire." Certainly satire is one of its defining elements, but there are other components that equally claim attention.

One of these is the particular domestic quality of the play—in fact, "domestic tragedy" was Dr. Johnson's label for it. The action turns on the misfortune of a citizen of Athens, and the fall of his great house provides some of its pathos. Clifford Leech, who notes these facts, would look upon Timon as "not the last and least of the tragedies, but the doubtful harbinger of the romances."[6] Leech is undoubtedly right in observing the play's domestic quality—one that he says is not like that in Heywood's dramas; he is wrong, I think, in associating it with Shakespeare's romances (and, for that matter, with Webster's, Tourneur's, and Ford's tragedies). First, domestic elements in Shakespeare are not restricted to the comedies or romances; they are strong also in Othello and Macbeth. Othello's jealousy is of the sort that can afflict any ordinary citizen, and Macbeth's subjection to his wife's ambition is a domestic matter. Second, Timon is no more an altogether private man than is any other Shakespearean tragic hero. Senators go in and out of his house, and his prestige is such that they offer him the leadership of the state when besieged by Alcibiades. I find him an imposing enough figure to make this credible and not to see it à la Leech as a mere concession to the Renaissance postulate that the tragic hero must be a great man. The significance of Timon for Athens is surely comparable to that of Othello for Venice. Domesticity is linked to matters of state in Timon just as it is in Othello: it is significant that the hero's house stands in a particular city-state, Athens, of which we form a distinct impression; by contrast, we learn nothing of Leontes' Sicily.

Like Antony and Cleopatra and Coriolanus, Timon emphasizes the "social dimension of tragedy," as Larry Champion has noted.[7] The heroes of all three plays have undergone, or undergo, a profound conditioning by the shaping influences of their states. It is true that these influences are primarily sociopolitical in the other two tragedies, socioeconomic in *Timon;* but Coriolanus's Rome at least associates economics with politics: Coriolanus is of the patricians' party, and this makes him callous toward hunger, poverty, and the plebeians. In both tragedies, the hero's predicament is closely linked with the ills of society. Timon is a large landowner with aristocratic manners and tastes; his ruin entails the fall of a great house and rich estate. As much as his disaster is self-generated, it is in part also due to the false, materialistic value system he has absorbed from the commercial villainy that reigns in Athens.

In one respect *Timon* does move closer to Shakespeare's romances: in the large role given to spectacle—to the banquets, the masque, music, and dancing. The very settings are spectacular: Timon's splendid house, the walls that symbolize the large city, the wild, wooded land that contains Timon's cave, and beyond them the universe evoked in Timon's apocalyptic imagination. Whatever one may think of M.C. Bradbrook's claim that *Timon* is a "dramatic show" or "experimental scenario,"[8] her pioneering insistence on its staginess is wholesome in view of so much criticism that dwells on its dramatic insufficiency. *Timon* excels in contrast, variety, and dramatic spectacle; incidents and scenes are given an emblematic heightening. Yet, as much as its spectacle appeals to the senses, it is integrated into the action and the dialectics of ideas. The two banquets, for instance, not only contrast lavish spending with austerity and harshness but also have a multiple significance for the reversal of images and themes and thus lead the imagination from one phase to the next. This latter function is quite like that of the two appearances of the witches in *Macbeth*. Neither in *Macbeth* nor in *Timon* does anything ever happen for a purely operatic effect.

J.M. Nosworthy, who has also found staginess characteristic of the play, attributes this quality to Shakespeare's intention of writing a "spectacular tragedy." Rightly, Nosworthy grants that *Timon* is not unique among the tragedies in this respect: *Macbeth* scintillates with such theatrical effects as fog, witches, cauldrons, a banquet, and songs.[9] And surely the banquets and battles and the antithesis of Roman might and Egyptian sensuality in *Antony and Cleopatra* also foreshadow the spectacularism of the romances; so do the large crowds of soldiers and citizens with their loud noises of clanging swords and civil uproad in *Coriolanus*. The development of drama pointed in the direction of overwhelming the mind by strong effects on the senses and the imagination, in the direction of the Baroque. Shakespeare's *Timon* and other late plays participate in this trend in their own way without offending the intellect.

We have so far characterized *Timon* as tragical-satirical-domestical-spectacular, a hyphenization that views with Polonius's "tragical-comical-historical-pastoral." In effect, all of Shakespeare's plays are hyphenated things; *Hamlet*, for instance, could be called "tragical-historical-satirical-psychological." *Timon* follows an even more complex recipe. We must yet add that other adjective that keeps recurring to the hyphenization that characterizes the play: pessimistic. Pessimism, of course, is as much a matter of reaction to what is presented as it is inherent in the play: what may strike one reader or viewer as a deeply discouraging statement about mankind may register only mildly on another; but experience has proved that the play manipulates its audience toward pessimism, a manipulation some have resented.

In this pessimism lies the major problem for the play's appreciation as a tragedy. Unlike the other tragedies, we are told, *Timon* does not "end with some sort of resolution, with a certain degree of nobility attained through suffering, and with a catharsis experienced by the audience"; and it is therefore not a tragedy.[10] We had rather leave aside this vexing matter of catharsis, the most unmeasurable of all demands made on tragedy; but we cannot do so completely since it is interrelated with the claim that the hero must be noble and that there must be a "resolution" in the ending: there can be no catharsis (Aristotelian, Augustinian, Hegelian, or otherwise) without some uplift. Tragedy, we are urged, reconciles us in some manner to the universe or teaches us something about the working of retributive justice or edifies us about the dignity of man. Dorothea Krook puts this stipulation as follows:

> We feel, extraordinarily, liberated from pain and fear (Aristotle's "purgation" of the emotions of pity and terror); not depressed and oppressed; but in a curious way exhilarated; not angry and bitter but somehow reconciled: our faith in the human condition not destroyed or undermined but restored, fortified, reaffirmed. . . . In the greatest tragedy, I suggest, what in the end is reaffirmed is something more than the dignity of man and the value of human life. We are made to feel that, through the affirmation of man and the life of man, there is at the same time being affirmed an order of values transcending the values of human order.[11]

If such affirmation of a transcendent order via the assertion of human dignity is *de rigeur* for tragedy, *Timon* does not qualify; its hero does his best to prove human indignity, and rather succeeds in it. But then, how many Jacobean tragedies would qualify? The pervasive corruption of society, the quirkiness of fate, and the impotence of the good in Webster's tragedies are not recommended reading for those who want their faith in mankind restored. To derive an even moderately optimistic lesson from *Lear* requires a particularly benign reaction in view of the cataclysmic ending.

The claim that tragedy asserts the dignity of man and some kind of cosmic order is a characteristically twentieth-century notion and may have to be reassessed in the changing intellectual climate of our time. Much more pessimistic formulations were sometimes voiced in the nineteenth century. Schopenhauer put the case most strongly when he saw in tragedy "the representation of the terrible side of life: the unspeakable pain, the wail of humanity, the triumph of evil, the scornful mastery of chance, and the irretrievable fall of the just and innocent."[12] Since tragedy showed that the self-mortifying efforts of a few were always thwarted by the wickedness and perversity of most, Schopenhauer thought that tragedy proved the futility of giving reign to the free will; resignation was the only answer. For Nietzsche, as much as he disapproved of Schopenhauer's pessimism as one of sensibility and therefore of weakness, the "Künsterisch-Tragische," which he opposed to it, contained a recognition that the abyss of life has to be faced with a "Pessimismus der Stärke." Nietzsche wished to substitute for Aristotle's *catharsis* an identification with the force of creation—equivalent to the Dionysian impulse, if I understand him right—a drive that even includes the will to destruction.[13] I do not wish to suggest that *Timon* is Nietzschean or Schopenhaueresque but that its pessimism does not disqualify it from being a tragedy.

Quite to the contrary, the Elizabethan and Jacobean dramatists thought that a tragedy ought to be pessimistic about man; although it was the fashion to speak about tragedy in moral commonplaces, nobody seems to have considered the representation of human dignity its province. Tragedy held the mirror up to nature, as Hamlet says, but the image reflected was dark. In the Prologue to *Antonio's Revenge*, John Marston warned that his "sullen tragic scene" and "black-visaged show" were not for him who was

> Uncapable of weighty passion
> (As from his birth being hugged in the arms
> And nuzzled 'twixt the breasts of happiness)
> And winks and shuts his apprehension up
> From common sense of what men were, and are,
> Who would not know what men must be—[14]

the implication being that what men were and are is something unpleasant and that what they must come to is death. This horror of what men were and are penetrates the Timon tragedy.

A pessimistic moral for tragedy was suggested to the

Renaissance by the ubiquitous commonplace of life as a play, the *theatrum mundi*, which always has a melancholy message: life is a lamentable or ridiculous performance under the aegis of Fortune, who assigns the roles and directs the action. It is generally a tragedy the catastrophe of which is death. The frequent use of this commonplace by writers of tragedy shows that it was very much in their minds. It could be used with an explicitly Christian script that recalled that the danger in the game of fortune was to sell one's soul to the world. It could also be without theological implications and with classical-pagan exemplification. An emblem by Lebey de Batilly, for instance, envisages the *theatrum mundi* as an arena-style theater, the actors of which are a row of young heroes in the arena who pass torches from one to the other in the manner of a relay race; life is here a race toward death. On a platform behind the men, statues symbolic of the auspices and the goals of the race are erected: Fortuna, Hercules (for Virtue), and a Terminus figure with some goal posts.[15] So, one might say, the race is run by Timon and the torch is passed to Alcibiades.

The analogy to the emblem directs our attention to the significance of Fortune in the Timon tragedy. The immobile Fortuna statue of the emblem, of course, conveys no impression of the sinister implications and menacing ironies associated with the word *fortune* in Shakespeare's play. The world of *Timon* is a nightmare of meanness and greed; Shakespeare shows what happens when men make Fortune into a deity. Even the philanthropic Timon pays her tribute since he makes giving away his treasures his sole occupation. "Fortune, not reason, rules the state of things"—the apt characterization of the French court by Chapman's Bussy d'Ambois—also applies to the Athens of *Timon*. Shakespeare's play is a tragedy of fortune in a wider sense than that of presenting the fall of a great man—the classical Renaissance formula. The hero's change of fortune is associated with a fundamental change of attitude toward the world and with an equally radical change in the attitudes of his friends toward him. Fortune dominates this world in a crude and materialistic way to which we are not accustomed in Shakespeare but which is not so unlike that of Chapman's tragedies (and, for that matter, in this respect at least, of Jonson's *Sejanus*). As in Chapman, virtue is doomed here.

The suddenness and radicality in Timon's change and, with it, in that of the play have been seen by some critics as a violation of tragic structure, as evidence that *Timon* is too obtrusively didactic to be a tragedy. It should be said that for Renaissance theorists the change of fortune was the defining element of tragedy and that some insisted on its suddenness. Aristotle in the *Poetics* had merely found a *peripeteia*, a "change of fortune in the action of the play to the opposite state of affairs," characteristic of the complex plot of tragedy, the type he most approved.[16] Julius Caesar Scaliger made this *peripeteia* prescriptive in his definition of tragedy: "Tragedy is the imitation of an action that involves the fortune of a distinguished man, with a turn toward a disastrous ending. . . ."[17] Daniel Heinsius, demanding a *peripeteia* for tragedy, defined the term as a "sudden change of fortune to its opposite."[18] From Heinsius's position, then, the suddenness of Timon's change would have been a virtue, and its radicality, the change to an opposite direction, is in line with what theorists since Aristotle have demanded. The later Shakespeare seems to have been tending toward a conception of tragedy based on sudden spectacular changes. Antony abruptly turns from Egypt to Rome and Rome to Egypt. Coriolanus leaves Rome for Antium, hating now the city he formerly loved—a *volte-face* comparable to Timon's. Unlike the misanthrope, of course, Coriolanus conquers his hate.

Preconceptions about tragedy have made some critics insist on an *angnorisis* by the tragic hero; Timon has been faulted for not having one. Aristotle actually merely associated the *anagnorisis* with the *peripeteia* of the complex tragic plot; he understood by it simply the discovery by the hero of the disastrous outward turn of events, not a process of self-search. Nor did the Renaissance theorists, as far as I know, require the tragic hero to come to an understanding of his psychological and moral condition; this postulate comes out of the didacticism of our own age. In Aristotle's and the Renaissance theorists' sense, Timon has an *anagnorisis* when he realizes that he has been duped by his friends. It is true, of course, that some of Shakespeare's tragic heroes go further in the acknowledgment of their own responsibility for their fall than does Timon in his: "Unwisely, not ignobly have I given" (2.2.178). But to claim that these heroes achieve full insight is to exaggerate. In fact, the heroes of Shakespeare's other classical tragedies, that is, his Roman ones, are at least as deficient in searching their souls as is Timon. Brutus probes his psyche only before the murder of Caesar, Antony never feels sorry for the bloodshed his actions have occasioned, and the reasons for Coriolanus's saving Rome are problematic; they include certainly no acknowledged regret for what he has done. Shakespeare may have felt that a tragedy with a classical subject matter should not explore the human soul too deeply.

Much more important for tragedy than the hero's attainment

of self-knowledge is his subjection to suffering—a desideratum that, strangely, is not explicitly demanded by Aristotle. Timon's anger at mankind certainly is the manifestation of an intense suffering, and the pathos of his fall is underlined by the servants' choric comment. We feel that the suffering of the hero in tragedy should not be senseless, that there should be some meaning we can read into it. This wisdom can be, but need not be, adumbrated by a recognition of the hero—I agree here with Dorothea Krook: "The important implication . . . is not that the tragic hero, the vessel of the suffering, shall receive the knowledge issuing from the suffering, but that we, the reader or the audience, shall receive it."[19] *Timon* is one of the tragedies that allow us to be much wiser about the causes of the hero's downfall and suffering than the hero because the *hamartia* he commits entails a failure to understand himself. As the Greek tragedians and Seneca showed, him whom the gods wish to destroy, they first make blind or mad.

Like Shakespeare's other tragic heroes (Brutus is an exception), Timon is highly passionate; Shakespeare's tragedies still bear a faint imprint of the humanistic genre with its warning against excessive passion. The passion of Timon, like that of other tragic heroes, is articulated and given significance by being set in a relationship to similar but not identical passions of characters who function at least partially as foils. What Laertes and Fortinbras do for our understanding of the ways in which the grief of Hamlet and his desire for revenge express themselves is accomplished by Apemantus and Alcibiades for the wrath and misanthropy of Timon. The low-burning anger of Apemantus and the quickly aroused but also quickly controlled temper of Alcibiades show up the self-harming fury of Timon. The more vulnerable personality, he is also, not the least because of the magnitude of his passion, a man of larger sympathies and capacities. In tragic terms, Timon's wild misanthropy is his claim to greatness.

This greatness is one that isolates the tragic hero, and Timon, more than any of Shakespeare's tragic heroes with the possible exception of Coriolanus, is a lonely figure. Northrop Frye classifies *Timon* along with *Othello* and *Coriolanus* among the tragedies of isolation *par excellence*.[20] In *Timon*, the isolation theme, as recent critics have recognized, relates particularly strongly to social issues. G. K. Hunter notes that Timon is an outcast of society as are also in some manner the heroes of the other late tragedies, Macbeth, Antony, and Coriolanus.[21] Cyrus Hoy calls *Timon* a tragedy of alienation—a useful, if modern, term.[22] And R. A. Foakes makes the valuable modification that in *Timon, Coriolanus,* and *Antony and Cleopatra,* the heroes are "unable to adapt themselves to a world of relative values which sanctions the flexible man [like Alcibiades] in place of the man of absolutes [like Timon]."[23] But Foakes thinks of Shakespeare as accepting this changing world and new flexibility more complacently than I do. Shakespeare certainly shows that Timon's isolation is not merely self-created. Misanthropy, of course, is by definition an isolating passion, but philanthropy should be a fusing and a synthesizing one; if it fails in that, the meanness around Timon is at least as much to blame as his own foolishness.

The isolation of the philanthropic Timon is the one we moderns know best: the loneliness in the midst of the crowd. Timon, the giver, is a loner even when among his admiring friends. His most ironic, tragically ironic, sentiment is that of the first banquet: "I have often wish'd myself poorer that I might come nearer to you" (1.2.98–99)—at the very moment when he glories in opulent togetherness, he feels most alone. When in the same speech he compares his friends to instruments hung up in cases, instruments that "keep their sound to themselves," he unwittingly characterizes himself and his longings as much as his friends. They mask their true selves deliberately, and in the process they stifle the free development of his own self even though outwardly they encourage it. His wish to be poorer and thus to come closer to them expresses a hidden desire to put everything at stake in order to break out of his dimly felt isolation and become free. But Timon's remains an "unsounded self" to the very end.[24] Only death brings him health and freedom.

As E. A. J. Honigmann has noted, the theme of loneliness is mirrored in the other characters: it reappears in Apemantus, the professional outsider; in Flavius, whose separateness is evident even when he laments, together with the other servants, the fall of his master; and in Alcibiades' long silences in the earlier parts of the play. These characters do speak with Timon and interact with him in some manner; but they have no close personal relationship with him, and they are quite unrelated to each other.[25] This lack of interaction of the secondary characters, which has been criticized and attributed to the play's incompleteness, emphasizes the non-coherence of the society portrayed. The prevailing tragic pessimism is reflected even in the dramatic structure.

But can a pessimistic tragedy, we are asked, produce a *catharsis*? Let us leave aside here the question of what Aristotle really meant by this term—purgation, purification, or clarification—and whether he wanted it to be that of the hero, the dramatic characters in general, or the audience. Let us adopt the common conception that the hero's tragic predicament and fall must produce a feeling of pity and fear (or awe) in us that we can relate to our own lives. Does then Timon have this effect on us? Actually, every reader must answer this question for himself, but I shall keep the editorial "we" here for persuasion's sake. Timon, it must be said, alienates more than attracts us. He never seems much like us, and even if we are rather pessimistic about man and the world, misanthropy in such force bothers us. Yet we are not without some pity for him. This pity, I think, is of a special kind, different from that which we accord to Hamlet, Othello, or Lear but resembling what we feel for Macbeth in some respects and for Coriolanus in others. Macbeth is really not much like us either. Do we really think ourselves capable of murder except in self-defense? Macbeth, of course, overcomes our antipathy by his sensitive moral imagination that makes us aware of man's potential greatness. Although Timon lacks Macbeth's poetic apprehensiveness, he has qualities that we admire in other contexts, and he achieves a rhetorical triumph in his protest against man. He has a total commitment to the two causes to which he dedicates his life, and he shows an uncompromising courage in throwing off the fetters of the society that is bent on his ruin. We feel some pity for him, if for no other reason than that he is born into the exploitive society of Athens. This is a pity similar to that which we feel for Coriolanus for having been born a Roman, a patrician, and the son of Volumnia; Timon, like Coriolanus, is cut off from life-nourishing springs. We feel pity for Timon also because he has something in him that would be admirable if it found a different outlet, a tremendous human power that bestows on him a paradoxical glamor even when he is at his worst. The alienation and pity Timon engenders in us are mixed with awe. His misanthropy is an awesome phenomenon to watch. Much like the fear of Macbeth, it is heightened beyond the human scale and enlarges our comprehension of what man is capable of feeling. He pursues his pessimism with a total consistency to the very end to which we dare not or, shall we say, must not go.

For Shakespeare's audience, there must have been a special catharsis similar to that which the satirists provided.[26] Since the Jacobeans were accustomed to think of the fall of Athens, like that of Nineveh, Jerusalem, and Rome, as due to the kind of vice and sin rampant in their own London, they would have applied the purge he gives to Athens to their own city. On the Globe stage, surrounded by the theater walls that symbolized the city walls as well as the frame of the world, Timon's invective, which resembled the fulminations of the preachers of doom and gloom, had a particularly powerful relevance. But I do not think that we are barred from this kind of moral *catharsis*, and a modern performance might well bring it out. Many of our modern ills resemble the Athenian or, better,

Jacobean ones Timon attacks. Pessimistic and apocalyptic strains have risen in volume and insistence in contemporary fiction and poetry. What is presented on our stages as tragic (although we have become shy of the word) is not the dignity of man and the consoling cosmos but the insecurity, fragility, and smallness of man and the menacing inscrutability of the universe.[27] As we have become greater pessimists because we are plagued with much of what *Timon* depicts as hateful, we find the tragic misanthropy of Timon less repelling than have preceding ages. If we are to experience a feeling analogous to the play's catharsis for Jacobean England, we must imagine a modern Timon standing in our lands, denouncing the towns and cities for the evil they harbor, and we must feel this evil in us and around us, but also in some measure in him. And if this Timon despairs of a mankind that has created and suffered such conditions, we must feel his predicament—and ours—as tragic. I do not think that this is too difficult an imaginative exercise.

Yet the critic who pleads for accepting *Timon* as a tragedy, not merely because of an embarrassment about what else to call it but because it truly belongs to this genre, must realize that he will find little echo if its literary and dramatic qualities continue to be underrated. I shall argue in the following chapters that the play's structure, characterization, imagery, and thematic development bear the imprint of Shakespeare's craftsmanship and genius, an imprint by no means inferior to that of his other tragedies. Regardless of sporadic deficiencies in the text, which are undeniable but have sometimes been exaggerated, *Timon* has an over-all imaginative unity and a grand tragic design. It is subtle, rich, and deep.

3

The Turn of Fortune's Wheel

Not one accompanying his declining foot

The poet's opening allegory of Fortune falls neatly into two halves: the ascent toward good fortune of a man of signal stature and his subsequent decline. Some commentators have taken this polarity not merely as predictive of the outward fortunes of Timon but as a fair account of the structure of the play. Mark Van Doren, who denies that *Timon* has a plot in the Aristotelian sense, says, "The play is two halves, casually joined in the middle; or rather two poems, two pictures in swan white and raven black."[1] That the actual structure is not so simple proceeds already from Van Doren's leaving the Alcibiades movement out of account. In terms of the Fortuna iconography, the action of the play does not make me think of the hill but of the old wheel Boccaccio imprinted on medieval and Renaissance conceptions of tragedy. One, in fact, seems to have suggested to Shakespeare the other. In the Pyrrhus speech of *Hamlet*, the actor asks the gods to take all power away from the "strumpet Fortune," and to "Break all the spokes and fellies from her wheel, / And bowl the round nave down the hill of heaven, / As low as to the fiends" (2.2.495–97). In *Lear*, the fool taunts his master by burlesquing the world's customs concerning hill and wheel: "Let go thy hold when a great wheel runs down a hill, lest it break thy neck with following, but the

great one that goes upward, let him draw thee after."
(2.4.71–74).[2]

The structure of *Timon* is more complex than the rotation
of a wheel, but it could be said that roughly the main plot
together with the Alcibiades subplot make a full circle.
Timon is at the top when the play opens; he falls during its
course, and Alcibiades now moves upward. The careers of
the two complement each other in the kind of circle formed
in *Richard II* by the descent of Richard and the ascent of
Bolingbroke, although, of course, descent and ascent are not
brought into causal relationship in *Timon*. In any case, the
progress of Alcibiades is a structural movement; its significance transcends, for instance, the casual take-over of
Denmark by Fortinbras at the end of *Hamlet*.

Although the wheel rhetoric does not determine the structure as such, it provides emotional coloring for it.[3] This becomes transparent if we remember that traditionally Fortune's clients were depicted as being at one time on one of
four positions of her wheel: they were either rising, or presiding, or falling, or they were thrown to the ground or
sometimes into a grave. This was symbolized by a figure in
four different positions: climbing at the left, standing or
enthroned on top, falling at the right, and prostrate under-
neath. The respective mottos for the positions on the walls
of medieval churches were: *regnabo, regno, regnavi, non regno*
or *sum sine regno*.[4] This cyclical motion was surely in Shakespeare's mind when he dramatized Timon's course as a kind
of reign and Alcibiades' victory as a replacement of Timon
as the figure of prominence. In the first act, Timon behaves
as if he ruled from a throne; his "I could deal kingdoms to
my friends" (1.2.219) is a *regno* proclamation. He stays in this
position throughout the first two acts; at the end of the
second, although already beset with creditors, he still proclaims "Ne'er speak or think / That Timon's fortunes 'mong
his friends can sink" (2.2.234–35). His precipitate decline
takes place in the third act, where the servant's simile of
the sun-like decline of a prodigal's course (3.4.12–14) predicts the end of the downward motion. Simultaneous with
Timon's fall, Alcibiades comes into prominence; his defiant
declaration "Soldiers should brook as little wrong as gods"
(3.5.118) is a *regnabo* announcement. Timon's *regnavi* stage is
over when he declares, in his last words, "Timon hath done
his reign" (5.1.222). His ultimate *sum sine regno* stage is
reached with his death and "low grave" in the fifth act.
Finally, Alcibiades' entry into the city puts him in a *regno*
position where, king-like, he will use the olive with the
sword.

This indication of a wheel-like movement is accompanied

by a swarm of ironies. Timon feels on top of the wheel or hill in the beginning of the play, and the flatteries of his friends seem to put him there. But the steward knows otherwise, and Apemantus hints in the second scene that Timon's sun is setting (1.2.141). Fortune's ironies reach into Timon's *regnavi* phase since he rejects the potential new prosperity offered to him by his finding gold and drives away the Athenians who flock to him as if his cave were a court.

If Timon's fall is not quite what the world understands by this term and is in some sense a victory, Alcibiades' rise, although genuine, is fraught with uncertainties. The young general rises on the wheel almost at the very moment when the senators seek to condemn him to the *non regno* position by exiling him, and he becomes the master of Athens in the end; but he is in a more than usually insecure *regno* position since it rests on a compromise with the senators. The rise of Alcibiades was in any case apt to inspire apprehension since his was one of the tragedies in Boccaccio's *De casibus virorum illustrium*, taken over by John Lydgate for his *Fall of Princes*. He was one of the world's signal fools of Fortune.

If we look at the structure in the light of the fortune pointers, we see it as tripartite. The first movement focuses on Timon, the spender and giver, and occurs in Athens; Timon here feels on top, but we know that he is on his way down. The second movement begins when the world seeks to put him in the *regnavi* position in the woods and continues with the world changing its mind and vainly visiting and wooing him; it ends with Timon's announcement that his reign is over. At the point where Timon's friends write him off, Alcibiades seems forced into the *non regno* placement; instead he rises to make himself master of Athens. His ascent is the third movement.

These dramatic movements correspond to the basic structure the Renaissance humanists had extracted from the comedies of Terence and transferred to neo-Latin and vernacular comedies and tragedies. The evolution of the formula and its early use by Shakespeare have been described by T. W. Baldwin;[5] Ruth Nevo has shown its relevance to the ways in which Shakespeare's tragic heroes progress through their plays (she does not, unfortunately, include *Timon*).[6] The formula prescribed an articulation into five acts as well as the general three-phase movement. Regularly constructed Renaissance dramas move from a *protasis*, in which the background information is given, the characters are introduced, and the action begins (acts 1 and 2); through an *epitasis* (acts 3 and 4), in which the plot is entangled, errors are committed, and a crisis or a series of crises occurs; to a *catastrophe* (act 5), the happy ending of the comedies or the turn to disaster and the final reordering in the tragedies. This, I shall show, is the structural pattern of *Timon*.

Note must be taken of the tendency of modern critics to see the play's structure as rather different from that of the other tragedies. Wilson Knight, as we observed, senses a quasi-allegorical design.[7] Maurice Charney speaks of a "moral fable."[8] H. J. Oliver finds a contrapuntal technique the secret of the play's construction: Shakespeare sets off against each other the reactions of one man to different situations and the reactions of different men to similar situations.[9] On Harold Wilson, the play makes "a spatial impression like a painting or a tapestry that unfolds in a succession of tableaux"; it is thus "splendidly complete"—but only as "an imaginative conception or as a symbolic poem."[10] Muriel Bradbrook, however, sees the play as a dramatic pageant and emblematic show.[11] There are good reasons why such claims are made, but they are relevant not to structure but to texture and thematic quality, which will be discussed at later points in this study. When, as in the case of Wilson, the implication is that *Timon* is eccentrically structured, I believe that the claim goes too far.

We shall appreciate Shakespeare's conventional structuring better if we apply Baldwin's and Nevo's analyses to the play—in Baldwin's case, this means applying the structural analysis of the Renaissance humanists. Going over the plot in this manner will provide the opportunity of noting that some of its alleged inconsistencies disappear in a structural reading and that the play is much more sequential than has been alleged. Our overview will also allow us to see how the scenes fit into the acts and how they are constructed as units of dramatic significance. But the emphasis will be on the digestion of the play into acts and on what Nevo has called the inner movement, that is, the stages of the hero's progression from the seminal situation to its logical conclusion, a progression that is flexibly attuned to the five-act articulation.

We must not assume that the act divisions in modern editions, divisions that date back to Capell and other eighteenth-century editors, are in every way correct. In the case of *Timon*, I think, they have done some outright harm to the appreciation of the play's structure, and I shall suggest revisions dictated by dramatic logic. The most disturbing separation is that of the fourth and fifth acts; it has a way of jarring one's feeling for the continuity of the action and of obscuring the distinction between *epitasis* and *catastrophe* since it puts the separating line between the visit of the steward and that of the poet and painter to Timon's lair, followed by the senators. A quite notable break, however, does exist between the departure of the senators after their failure to receive help from Timon and their reappearance in Athens, that is, between the present 5.1 and 5.2. One must assume that some time has elapsed between the senators' departure and their reappearance, whereas no such interval is evident at the point of the customary act division. The two later scenes are separated also by a shift in location—strikingly so after the long stretch of action at Timon's cave. Logic and common sense demand putting the act division at this point.

Presumably only the shortness of what is left induced Capell not to begin the fifth act here, and it must be admitted that these 112 lines are indeed not enough for an act. Shortness is not the only problem; there is something unsatisfactory about the dramatic movement: the pace is too fast and the action not sufficiently consequential. Here, and only here, do I find myself in agreement with those who say that we do not have all of the play we should have. However, I do not think that this is by itself a proof that the play as a whole is incomplete. It is quite likely that in *Macbeth* too some passages or even scenes of a longer original version have not come down to us; yet who would say that *Macbeth* is "incomplete"? Shakespeare seems to have had the habit of writing plays too long for the stage, plays that had to be subjected to cutting for production. It is possible that this happened to *Timon*; if so, something else must also have gone wrong. Lack of finish does not seem to me a persuasive explanation because the action is brought to a clear and logical, if somewhat hasty, conclusion; I suspect some special corruption in the text, a corruption also responsible for the deficiencies of the text in general. (See "Text" Appendix). In any case, to call this a truncation or mutilation of the fifth act would be to exaggerate. The scene shifts now to the homefront in Athens as expected after the ending of the fourth act (in our realignment); the senators await the return of their ambassadors to Timon and, with their arrival, learn that Timon has rejected their plea for help against Alcibiades. The young general becomes now the focus of the action; he makes himself the master of the city and initiates a reconciliation. Timon's death is reported, his epitaph read by Alcibiades. These are surely developments that make an appropriate *catastrophe*.

Besides the major realignment of acts four and five, I propose a somewhat less important change of the boundary between acts three and four. The third act, I think, should be extended through what is at present the second scene of the fourth, and the new act should begin with Timon's appearance in the wood. Throughout the following discussion, I shall indicate the placement of the scenes in the proposed rearrangement in brackets after the conventional numbering. Divided thus, the play's structure follows closely the Renaissance formula abstracted by Baldwin and unfolds the tragic movement in the fashion outlined by Nevo.

The *protasis* fulfills the Renaissance theorists' requirement for being, in Giraldi Cinthio's words, "the part that proposes that which is to be treated by the whole play in such a way as to arouse great attention in the spectator."[12] The first act, which according to Giraldi must contain the "argument," introduces all the major characters and numerous minor ones in a way that intimates the tragic situation. The first scene, one of the best of its kind in Shakespeare, is a masterpiece of dramatic movement and compression and conveys an atmosphere of anticipation. The Fortuna poem presented to Timon both illustrates his present eminence and foreshadows his later dethronement. In a few quick strokes, the greed, fulsome flattery, and odious hypocrisy of the society around Timon are sketched, the insouciant spender and philanthropist is introduced, and the cynic Apemantus is given the opportunity to satirize Timon and his friends. It might be argued that Alcibiades, who speaks only two lines, is not given sufficient prominence for his later star role. But if not in reading, at least on the stage, Alcibiades' importance proceeds from his large retinue, the "twenty horse," that is, cavalry soldiers (240), and from the sound of a trumpet (stage direction), the only musical note after the "trumpets" that announced Timon's entry earlier.

The second scene, the tableau of the great banquet, continues the portrayal of Timon and the parasitical society around him. There is music, entertainment, and much fawning, acerbically commented upon by Apemantus. We learn, as we may have suspected, that Timon's decline has already begun: the steward announces in his soliloquy that Timon's coffers are empty and his land is pawned to his false friends.

The first act thus presents the seminal tragic situation. It shows, to use the analysis of the first act of Renaissance drama by the humanist Willichius, "the first tumult already as it were growing [*gliscens*], the occasion of the play, and the argument."[13] This is the first phase of the hero's tragic progression, in Nevo's terminology his "predicament," that is, what marks his situation as potentially tragic. Timon differs from most of Shakespeare's heroes in having no inkling of what may be in store for him and in being completely content; but then, blindness to his friends' natures is part of his predicament, and we have been shown the threatening result allegorically. We suspect that the intense absolutist will ruin himself absolutely. Apemantus's pessimistic Fortuna moral appropriately concludes the act:

Thou giv'st so long, Timon, I fear me thou wilt give away
thyself in paper shortly. . . .
O that men's ears should be
To counsel deaf, but not to flattery.

(1.2.242–51)

The second act of the *protasis*, according to Giraldi, must
show how "the thing contained in the argument should begin
to progress toward the end."[14] Nowhere does this happen with
greater speed and more persuasive logic than in *Timon*. The
action gains momentum immediately when in the first scene
—essentially a monologue of sixty lines by a creditor of Timon's—the first claim for payment of the philanthropist's debts
is raised. The speaker views Timon's generosity coldly as mere
improvidence and extravagance and dispatches a servant to
Timon's house with his demand. Since this creditor is a senator, we get a sense that greed is leagued with politics in
Athens, a feeling that is later confirmed when Alcibiades
clashes with the senate.

The long and complex second scene succeeds in combining
a fast-paced action with a look at a lower stratum of Athenian
society, represented by the servants of a variety of masters,
that is, of Timon, of his creditors, and of a prostitute. The
exits and entrances of the numerous characters, which include Apemantus, the steward, Timon, and Alcibiades, are
aptly managed. First, the steward soliloquizes on Timon's
financial blindness; then the creditors' servants appear, followed immediately by a sanguine Timon in Alcibiades' company, seeking to refresh himself for the hunt that is to follow.
As the servants press upon Timon, the steward tactfully draws
away his master; but the servants find their own diversion
when Apemantus and the fool appear. This provides a humor-
ous interlude and takes the steward's account of Timon's
financial condition off the stage; we already know the tenor.
We are shown Timon's reaction to learning the extent of his
indebtedness when he reappears with the steward after the
servants and the others are sent away. We note his first
touches of anger. He interrupts the steward's tale and voices
the suspicion that this loyal servant has taken advantage of
him but has to admit that Flavius has tried to warn him before. Then he learns of the senators' refusal to come to his
help, and he goes so far as to declare these old fellows ungrateful. This disturbance of his optimism, although temporary and slight, is significant dramatically because it prepares
us for his later and greater anger. When his ill thoughts have
subsided, he expresses his renewed confidence that his fortunes will never sink among his friends and that these will
come to his rescue. The steward wisely doubts this, and since
we orient our moral bearing by his, we expect the worst.

Thus the ending of the *protasis* lives up to the Renaissance formula's requirement that it must show the external conflict brewing without attaining full vigor. This is the stage that Nevo calls *psychomachia*; it is here generally that the turmoil in the soul of the hero begins as he realizes his dangerous situation and gains an inkling of the nature of the choices he has to make. Shakespeare, however, muted the conflict in Timon's soul so as to make his awakening from his delusion about the goodness of his friends gradual; Timon does not gain full consciousness of his situation and therefore does not have a marked psychological conflict until the third act. To this degree, the characteristic Shakespearean movement of tragedy is modified here, and it is presumably because of the mildness of Timon's *psychomachia* that the act is rather short. When it ends, however, we are fully aware of his situation, of his need to revise or abandon his belief that everybody around him is an ideal human being and to learn something about the reality of evil.

Only when the *epitasis* begins can the external conflict be joined and the hero's passion rise to its peak. The *epitasis* is the part of the structure that, as Giraldi said, must bring "the nexus or rather the knot of the argument, which contains all the turbations [*sic*] and travails of the action." Specifically, the third act is to present "the impediment and the perturbations."[15] And so it is in *Timon*. The impediment to Timon's happiness is manifested by the cumulative villainy that erupts in the first three scenes. Lucullus, Lucius, and Sempronius form a kind of ascending scale of nastiness. Lucullus's "I knew it would come to this" attitude, if awful, is the simplest, and his attempt to bribe the servant is crude and stupid. Lucius's transparent pretense of being out of money and thus missing the chance of reaping honor by rescuing "such an honourable gentleman" (3.2.56) makes ingratitude a bit more odious by joining it with hypocrisy. It remains for a character whom we have not known before, Sempronius, to add insult to hypocrisy and ingratitude when he pretends to be offended because he, the first to have borrowed from Timon, is solicited last. Some critics have puzzled over why the rejection of Timon's offer by Sempronius is dramatized here and not that by Ventidius, who has most reason to be grateful to Timon because the latter has released him from debtors' prison. But by adding a new name and a spectacular villain in Sempronius, Shakespeare heightens our sense of Timon's large circle of false friends. When Ventidius is subsequently mentioned as also having refused Timon, this heartlessness becomes an offhand ratification of the general turpitude.

The moral significance of each of the three scenes is driven home by a mirror commentary that reflects the friends' wickedness and Timon's plight. This is done with dramatic variation: the first commentary as well as the third are put in the mouths of loyal servants and conclude the respective scenes; the second is contained in a conversation of two strangers that frames the scene. The first servant, Flaminius, speaks in verse, contrary to Shakespeare's general (but frequently broken) rule of having persons of lower station speak in prose; Flaminius's honesty after the sly crudity of Lucullus is eloquent. Conversely, Sempronius's more elegant villainy rises to blank verse, whereas the servant's commentary is a contrasting ironical prose speech that breaks into verse at the end when his thoughts turn to his deserted master. In these cases of masterful mingling of prose and poetry, we certainly need not think that Shakespeare did not finish what he wanted to write.

The strangers' comments highlight Lucius's hypocrisy in the second of the three scenes; but here the moralizing is undercut by irony. The first stranger's perfect conditional phrase "Had his necessity made use of me, / I would have put my wealth into donation" (3.2.84–85) anticipates Sempronius's excuse, "But his occasions might have wooed me first" (3.3.17). The stranger is quite safe from having to put his conditional kindness into practice, and not only among Athenians do imagined benefits provide satisfaction for the non-giver. The stranger's concluding maxim that policy sits above conscience has an ironic application to the speaker himself.

The three mirrored portraits of villainy are succeeded by a vivid action that dramatizes the prediction of the servant in the preceding scene: "Who cannot keep his wealth must keep his house." Timon, beleaguered by his creditors, is now a virtual prisoner in his own home. Besides two servants of Varro, whose name was mentioned by the senator who called in his credit, and the servant of the odious Lucius, "other servants" appear, two of whom, Titus and Hortensius, are singled out by name; it is almost as if an army, the kind of skeleton army of Shakespeare's stage, were laying siege to a fortress. As the servants clamor, the steward rushes through them, and Timon makes a brief appearance. He is for the first time enraged; but he controls himself. Surprisingly, he gives the order to invite his friends for another banquet.

The development of Timon's hatred, as we noted, is delayed by the beginning of the third arc of the action with Alcibiades pleading, banishment, and decision for revenge. We shall look at Alcibiades and the scene closely later and note here only the effect its placement (3.5) has on the total structure. In terms of plot, its intercalation into the main action allows the time needed for extending the invitations to Timon's friends and their appearing at the banquet. Critics sometimes think it a fault of the play that we see Timon at one moment as a philanthropist and at another as a misanthrope; but we may assume that his rage is already boiling when he is offstage during the Alcibiades scene. Incidentally, the placement of this latter scene also conveniently explains the general's absence from the banquet as due to his banishment. He could not be present, of course, without considerable loss to his dignity, and dignity is needed for his future position of conqueror.

The emergence of Alcibiades as the hero of the subplot is an unexpected turn of events, but it is hardly more surprising than the sudden transformation of apparently minor characters into movers of the action elsewhere in Shakespeare, such as when Antony in *Julius Caesar* becomes Caesar's avenger or when the Duke in *Measure for Measure* turns into the director of the play's plot. It is often said that the connection between subplot and main plot in *Timon* is thematic in that it pivots on the theme of ingratitude: the Athenians turn against Alcibiades in the same heartless way as they do against Timon. The viewer of the play, however, is more likely to focus on a dramatic connection, not on the ingratitude as such but on the two men's reaction to it, their outbreak of anger. The scene in which Alcibiades faces the senate is so positioned as to form a link in a chain of anger: it is preceded by the first indication of Timon's rising temper and followed by its explosion. In the interposed scene, Alcibiades goes from one emotional stage to the other in his own way. He is not depicted as a hothead, and he argues at first with restrained passion—he has, of course, less cause than Timon for being angry since Alcibiades' friend, for whom he pleads, has indeed broken the law by killing a man in a duel. Only the unprovoked banishment from Athens decreed upon Alcibiades by the senators (angry men themselves) makes the general's temper flare up. He will not take injury without revenge and he decides quickly on purposive action against Athens. The situation is such as to produce a dramatic contrast between the two angry men. The spectator is in suspense about how Timon will react to the evil he has encountered and expects some sort of emotional climax, an expectation ambiguously fulfilled. Timon's pelting of his guests with stones makes a marvelous scene in the theater but is merely a symbolic gesture of revenge; its meaning is quite lost on the guests, who amiably conclude that Timon has gone mad.

As much as Alcibiades outplays Timon on the stage of the world, in which actions count more than words, Timon upstages him in the theater, in which dramatic gestures count sometimes more than actions. Of course, Timon has learned from a good actor, Apemantus, who like Alcibiades is an absentee at this banquet. Timon speaks now a mock grace as Apemantus did at the banquet of friendship and mutters Apemantian asides about his friends' villainy. Timon is not only an actor here; he is also the director of a play-within-the-play, a function in which he is superb. He directs the mock banquet to contrast mimetically and even musically with the earlier entertainment. A blaring trumpet now takes the place of the ingratiating oboes and lutes and heralds the dissonance and confusion of the scene.

To end the third act with this episode, spectacular as it is (and all modern editions end it here), is to obscure the plan on which Shakespeare designed the *epitasis* and to interrupt the flow of the action. The phase that begins with Lucullus's refusal to aid Timon (3.1) and presents the reversal of Timon's fortune as well as his reaction to it culminates not in the mock banquet but in Timon's departure from Athens and his curse on the city (4.1 [but actually 3.7]). The guests' confusion in the preceding scene permits the misanthrope sufficient time to make his way outside the city walls, at least in the shortened time consciousness of drama; no delay of his flight should be assumed if the gesture is to be Timonesque. After Timon's one-sentence announcement at the end of the mock banquet, one expects that he will execute his intention swiftly. His address to the walls, demanding that they disappear into the ground, is a fitting misanthropic farewell to the city he has just cursed, and his expressive gesture of stripping himself naked to signify his deliverance from the wolves within the walls marks the climactic continuation of his rejection of his friends. His final prayer to the gods announces what will motivate him in the following act: "And grant, as Timon grows, his hate may grow / To the whole race of mankind, high and low! / Amen" (4.1.[3.7.]39–41).

The next scene, a mirror scene that must be thought to occur immediately upon Timon's departure from Athens, should also be assigned to the third act. It connects directly with what goes before, and no time interval is indicated. The house of Timon has fallen, and the servants' laments highlight the pathos of the event. From a structural point of view, the steward's concluding announcement that he will follow Timon to his refuge indicates the direction the action will take in the fourth act. His wish to alleviate his master's misery by gold foreshadows a theme that will be important for the action to come. Again, a gloomy generalization about the effect of fortune is part of the act's last speech, that of the steward:

> For bounty, that makes gods, do still mar men.
> My dearest lord, bless'd to be most accurs'd,

Rich only to be wretched—thy great fortunes
Are made thy chief afflictions.

(4.2.[3.8.]41–44)

As we look back at the third act in the form here proposed, we see it as the critical phase in the tragedy. The hero is plunged from happiness to misery; from a philanthropist, he is turned into a misanthrope, from a pillar of Athens, into a wreck. His fall is paralleled with that of Alcibiades; his self-chosen exile, with the general's banishment. There is a double climax, a double *peripeteia*; but the focus is properly on Timon, the reversal of Alcibiades' fortunes being dealt with briefly. This act presents the greatest dramatic turbulence, the crisis of Timon's life that subjects him to a total change of his initial situation—features Nevo calls characteristic of the hero's progress during this phase. The reversal is nowhere else so spectacularly dramatized. Timon appears for the first time alone on the stage, outside the city in which he has lived surrounded by servants and friends. He rids himself, as it were, of his former self along with his clothes.

Radical and complete as Timon's change is, it is not unduly abrupt in dramatic terms. A turn of fortune is foreshadowed from the beginning of the play, and the *processus turbarum*, the sequence of agitations that brings it, is handled skillfully. The full explosion of Timon's passion is delayed by his being taken off the stage. We get only glimpses of him, only touches of his indignation, as he is pressured by the creditors. The mock banquet, with Timon's first misanthropic tirade, is delayed by Alcibiades' banishment, which thematically prepares for Timon's departure. We may, of course, find Timon too precipitous, too stunned by a development we have seen brewing; but we should not fault the dramatic design that presents purposely a turn from absolute benevolence to total hatred, from all to nothing. This design has allowed us to see and anticipate the reversal. There is a human abruptness here but no structural weakness, no dramatic lapse, no mishandling of the grand design.

Beginning the fourth act after the lament of the servants, as I propose, permits emphasis to fall on a crucial lapse of time. Timon has established himself in a cave in the woods, and the news of his voluntary exile has reached Athens at least by the time Apemantus arrives, spurred by envy at the competition in cynicism and pessimism given him by the misanthrope. Also, some time must be allowed for the discontented Alcibiades, whose exile was still news at Timon's mock banquet (3.6.51–56), to gather troops before he enters as the first of Timon's visitors. From the moment Timon appears in the woods until the action returns again to Athens, a series of episodes rolls off (they could also be conceived as separate scenes) that are continuous in the flow of time. They end with what in our texts is the first scene of the fifth act, in which the poet and the painter, announced as in sight earlier, and finally even the senators flock to Timon's new dwelling. I shall assign these two episodes, which could also be designated as separate scenes, to the fourth act and consider them, for simplicity's sake, the second scene. From the first to the last, these visits to Timon's cave are cohesive and have a way of commenting on one another; there should certainly be no act division between them.

According to the Renaissance formula, "the fourth act exhibits the desperate state of the matter begun in the *epitasis*, and in the end is brought forth the occasion of the *catastrophe*."[16] This the fourth act of *Timon* as here constituted does. Many critics, however, have felt that the theatrical interest lags in this act. This is a remark not infrequently made about fourth acts, the phase in which Shakespeare's structural conception insists on a certain emphasis and a repetition of ideas and motifs; but it is true that the fourth act of *Timon* lacks the spectacular incidents common in other tragedies, such as, for instance, Othello's epileptic breakdown or the mad Lear's heartrending meeting with the blind Gloucester. However, if we grant that the act must serve the dramatization of Timon's misanthropy as a tragic phenomenon, I do not think that we can find it ill-designed or weak. Timon's adversary is human nature, an adversary that is in all who come to him and even in himself. There can be no antagonist in the usual sense, just as there can be no foil to detract from Timon's pessimism, and his misanthropy has to erupt primarily in words, in harangues, insults, and curses. What the fourth act lacks in dramatic conflict, it makes up through projection and inclusiveness: it takes in not only the characters who are drawn to his abode but also Athens and all humanity and even the forces of nature and the universe. The invectives grow out of the situations, radiate rhetorical brilliance, and breathe an enormous power. Shakespeare's expert workmanship and imaginative fecundity display themselves in ingenious variations on a single theme.

The sequence of arrivals at Timon's cave creates the impression of being accidental; but this is not from a lack of design. What appears casual is a calculated plan made unobtrusive, a plan that breathes awareness of the unexpected, of fortune's whims. The first to arrive is not the steward, as might be expected from his announcement that he would follow his master, but Alcibiades, accompanied by the courtesans Phrynia and Timandra. Alcibiades has not been mentioned since the mock banquet, and it is dramatically appropriate that he should reappear before he fades from the audience's mind. A trumpet announces his entry on the stage, drums and fife provide the martial background —the musical accompaniment here and elsewhere is part of the structural pattern. By the army's march over the stage together with the concubines, Timon is given the opportunity to denounce Alcibiades, war, and lechery, and to prophesy the fall of Athens and the destruction of man. Ironically, although Alcibiades offers Timon money from his meager war chest, it is the general who leaves with his finances improved from the gold Timon has found. Once again what is offered to Timon breeds increase by making him give, but now he gives deliberately for mankind's bane.

After Alcibiades leaves and Timon resumes his quest for the one poor root by which to feed himself, Apemantus, the apostle of the simple life, appears on the scene. The valuing the two undertake of each other contrasts with the valuing of the world that Timon accepted during the days of his glory. There is a double-edged satire in the episode as each scores some hits against the other. But we are made to feel the strength and depth of Timon's pessimism by his decreasing interest in winning the victory. His declaration that he will prepare his grave shows that his sickness of the world is a sickness unto death. Structurally, this announcement points forward to Timon's devising of his epitaph and his "oracle" for Athens during the appearance of his last visitors.

The next to appear are the bandits. Although Apemantus describes the poet and the painter as in sight several minutes before he leaves (4.3.[4.1.]353), the two artists actually do not arrive until the bandits as well as the steward have come and gone. Critics generally see in this delay proof that Shakespeare changed his mind and failed to erase the traces of his earlier intention; this was one of the alleged discrepancies of the text the disintegrators used to demonstrate that two hands were discernible in the play, and it is now, as are some others of these, held to show that Shakespeare failed to revise the play. But a sympathetic reading indicates that Shakespeare's arrangement as it stands has definite dramatic advantages.

It should be noted that the appearance of poet and painter provides Apemantus with a splendid illustration of what Athens is like:

Apem. . . . The commonwealth of Athens is become a forest of beasts.

Tim. How has the ass broke the wall, that thou are out of the city?

Apem. Yonder comes a poet and a painter. The plague of
company light upon thee!

(4.3.[4.1.]349–54)

If the two sycophants remain backstage and do not exit until
after Apemantus prophesies, appropos Timon's mentioning
his gold, "Thou wilt be throng'd to" (397), they illustrate
that prediction too. The arrival of the bandits swells the number
of visitors that have come and are announced: Alcibiades, his
concubines, and his army; Apemantus; the bandits; the steward;
and the poet and painter—a second confluence of visitors to
Timon is to occur! There will be an additional, unexpected group:
the senators. That the later entry of poet and painter 140 lines
after Apemantus sights them is a return rather than a first
arrival appears indicated by the painter's remark "As I took note
of the place, it cannot be far where he abides" (5.1.[4.2.]1). The
painter then explains that Alcibiades, the concubines, some "poor
straggling soldiers" (the bandits), and the steward received gold
from Timon; evidently the two artists were not aware of Timon's
new riches at their first entry, which gave them no motivation to
press the visit.

This change in the predicted sequence of visits makes the
bandits' appearance, a normal enough occurrence otherwise,
into something of an unexpected, out-of-sequence event.
Their visit provides the occasion for one of Timon's most
scathing speeches, that on universal thievery. Its awesome-
ness is attested by the reaction of one of the degenerates:
"I'll believe him as an enemy, and give over my trade"
(4.3.[4.1.]457–58). Open criminality, we might say, is more
curable than villainous sophistication were it not that the
satirical key of the scene undercuts the moral. If the first
bandit has his way, amelioration of his softer brother-in-
arms will not take place until a later, indefinite time: "Let
us first see peace in Athens. There is no time so miserable but
a man may be true" (459–60).

Next to arrive is the steward. In interpreting this episode,
I am obliged to question the usual, rather sentimental view
that sees it as the one point where Timon shows a softer
strain. Does he not, we are urged, show a touch of regret
when he finds a man "so true" and proclaims him the "one
honest man" (4.3.[4.1.]494–501)? Does he not say that the
steward's loyalty "almost turns my dangerous nature mild"
(496)? And does he not say, "How fain would I have hated
all mankind, / And thou redeem'st thyself" (503–4)? Is not
Timon's whole misanthropy proved unfounded in the face of
such honesty and decency? There is an alternative, to me
more convincing, of this reading, and this is to consider the
episode from the point of view of the savage game the misan-

thrope plays with mankind, including the steward. As such it becomes a clever exposé of the pitfalls that lurk in the ideas of honor and honesty. This satirical theme is initiated early in the play by Apemantus's jest of being on his way "to knock out an honest Athenian's brains" (1.1.192)—a vain pursuit for lack of an eligible individual—it continues with Sempronius's mock indignation about the insult to his "honor," is debated between Alcibiades and the senators, varied in a scherzo mood in the bandit's wordly wisdom about the opportune time to be "true," which precedes the steward's entry, and shades off into burlesque after his departure when Timon has his fun with the poet and painter, the "two honest men." Even while approaching Timon, Flavius harps on "honour" and "honest": Timon's fall has brought about an "alteration of honour" (465); Flavius will therefore present his "honest" grief to his master (473). He introduces himself then as "an honest poor servant of yours" (479). When he protests that no poor steward ever bore "truer grief" (484), one remembers the bandit's jest about the time to be true; the steward is aware, over-aware I would say, that this is the time. Like others in the play, he is self-conscious about honor, although he has not yet accepted the commercialized version of honor used by Timon's friends. In any case, Timon is much more concerned with the corruptible honesty of the world than with the loyalty of his servant. He parodies Flavius in harping on "honest." When he proclaims him the "one honest man," he uses the jest he remembers from Apemantus. His irony shows in calling the steward "more honest now than wise" (506). To this "singly honest man" (527), he says, the gods have sent treasure out of his own misery. One remembers that he has called this very treasure the perverter and degrader of mankind. Timon evidently seeks to make gold effect its "true nature" with Flavius, that is, confound and destroy him, just as he does with Alcibiades, the prostitutes, and the thieves. It is not, I think, of paramount importance whether we believe that this strategy actually will work with Flavius or not.

The poet-and-painter episode, which follows, continues the satirical exploration of mundane honesty—another reason that it should not be separated by an act division from the steward's visit. If the steward's self-consciousness and acceptance of gold raise the suspicion that his sense of honesty is vulnerable to perversion, the poet's vulgar exchange of confidences with the painter exposes flagrantly the "courtly and fashionable" honesty of Athens that puts appearance above substance. The two villains find promising preferable to performing; they have come because "it will *show* honestly in us" (5.1.[4.2.]14). Timon's mounting sarcasm inundates the duplicate hypocrites with repetitions of "honest" (55, 67, 70, 75, 76, 79, 85). He invites them to kill themselves; instead of the gold they came to seek, he pelts them with dirt and stones.

The next episode, the visit of the senators, is contiguous; one more time, the misanthrope is faced with the world and its pretensions to honesty and honor. It is almost as if the senators came in order to prove the painter's line that "promising is the very air o' th' time" (5.1.[4.2.]22–23). Their "sorrowed render" is accompanied by the offer of new "dignities" for Timon: the Athenians will provide a "recompense more fruitful / Than their offence can weigh down by the dram," and they will give Timon "heaps and sums of love" that "blot out what wrongs were theirs, and write in thee the figures of their love" (5.1.[4.2.]149–53). One would trust these protests more if they were not imbued with commercial metaphors that betray a calculating egotism.

Timon's sarcastic comment "You witch me in it" (154) indicates that he sees through the hypocrisy even before he learns the reason for the plea: his restoration to Athens is needed because of the threat of Alcibiades. Stingingly he recommends his solicitors "to the protection of the prosperous gods, / As thieves to keepers" (182–83). He becomes increasingly distracted, concerned with dying rather than living; but the senators' persistence arouses him to one more invective, the offer to the Athenians to hang themselves on his tree. Shakespeare thus kept the most effective vituperative gesture of his sources, the one that was most widely known because it was in Plutarch, for this climactic moment, adapting it neatly to the self-destructive mania of his hero: the hanging tree will have to be felled soon for Timon's "own use" (205)—one thinks of his coffin.

Timon's last speech evokes the nadir of the wheel of Fortune at which, according to the world's judgment, he has arrived. The image of the "salt flood, / Who once a day with his embossed froth / The turbulent surge shall cover" (215–17) recalls the up-and-down movement in the poet's opening allegory of Fortune; but the suggestion of the strong pulsation of the tide also speaks of the harshness of a will that escapes from humanity to an outer edge to which few may venture. Timon has ceased to reign.

If we look back at the fourth act as here delineated, we see how it fulfills the demands both of the structural formula and of the progressive tragic development of the hero. The formula required the protraction and intensification of passion into a *summa epitasis* or *catastasis*, which displays "the full vigor and crisis of the play."[17] The departure of the frustrated senators and Timon's suicidal frame of mind certainly constitute such a crisis.

As Nevo has shown, Shakespeare gave the passionate selves of his heroes in the fourth act particular emphasis and perspective through irony; here "the subsuming category of responses is irony."[18] Timon's passion is strongly emphasized by ironic situations and behavior patterns, all of them pointing up the ironies of fortune. The whole act is predicated on the overwhelming irony that the bankrupt Timon becomes as much a magnet of attraction as he was in prosperity. The procession to his new domicile has the appearance of a tribute to his mesmerizing invective. Of course, we know that the real reasons of the visitors are of a different kind, and are not unlike those that drew crowds to Timon's hospitable house: the visitors hope for enrichment, or, at least, they combine their concern for him with self-interest. Alcibiades appears to be an exception: he probably comes upon Timon by accident. But he sees quickly his value as a potential ally. Apemantus seeks Timon out in anger about his amateur competition in cynicism. The bandits and the poet and painter are simply after his gold. The steward, it is true, comes to succor his master; but, as I have suggested, a self-centered concern with the mere image of honor also motivates him. The senators, as much as they pretend to love and honor Timon, are driven by their instinct for survival. That they, who first abandoned Timon in his need and precipitated his fall, should have to turn to him in their distress and be rejected is the climactic point of the ironic movement. There are smaller ironies within the larger one: Timon, who seeks roots, finds gold; those who come to offer him gold go away enriched; those who seek gold from him get stones and dirt. And there are comic incidents that set off the passion of Timon, distance us somewhat from it (although I do not think that they diminish it): the sparring match between Apemantus and Timon and the clownish thieves' bewilderment at Timon's harangue. Throughout, he sustains his passion with a baroque power and energy and bends his will adamantly to the destruction of mankind and himself. Even his abdication from Fortune's wheel is a defiant voluntary act, not a submission.

According to the Renaissance formula, the ending of the *epitasis* must bring forth the occasion of the *catastrophe*; and this conclusion of the fourth act of *Timon* does so clearly. After Timon's rejection of the senators, the action requires a bifurcation and a double solution, one for Timon, another for Alcibiades and the senators. The first is signaled by Timon's announcement of his coming death, proof that his perturbations are heightened to the "desperate state" expected at this juncture; the tragic catastrophe is thus anticipated. But Shakespeare seems also to have had the version of the dramatic structure in mind that applied to comedy; from it, after all, the structure for tragedy was derived and modified. It stipulated that in the fourth act "there should begin a way of giving a remedy to the troubles."[19] Timon conceives this remedy for himself in his own transvaluating manner: "My long sickness / Of health and living now begins to mend, / And nothing brings me all things" (185–87). For the senators, Timon sarcastically offers several solutions: to hang themselves together with all other Athenians on his tree, to let Alcibiades harass them and harass him in return, and to be "mended" with the rest of the degenerate world by infection and the plague. The question is, just how will the senators extract themselves from their predicament? The ending of the fourth act thus creates the proper suspense for the *catastrophe*, which, according to the formula, must bring the "outcome of the desperate plans."[20] A senator appropriately says at the end of the act, "Let us return, / And strain what other means is left unto us / In our dear peril" (225–27).

We cannot here deal fully with the structural function of the fifth act as the *catastrophe* because it depends in large manner on the role of Alcibiades, yet to be discussed. The act, as we noted, is too short, and it moves in a staccato fashion until the last and very effective scene. The first short scene (the second in the customary divisions), in which the senators return to Athens after their abortive mission to Timon, is abruptly followed by the short speech of the soldier on finding Timon's grave and epitaph. An intermediate scene may have been lost, and there may also have been some abridgment or rewriting of the soldier's speech, since it is slightly confusing. We cannot be sure whether his lines "Timon is dead, who hath outstretched his span: / Some beast read this; there does not live a man" (5.3.[5.2.]3–4) are the soldier's personal comment or an inscription on Timon's tomb, followed by an epitaph in a language he cannot read. However, I do not think that the idea of taking the epitaph in wax so that Alcibiades can decipher it must be held unworthy of Shakespeare. It is true that it is a rather palpable device for having Alcibiades read the epitaph at the end and comment on it, but it is not so different from implausible expedients, such as letters that turn up conveniently, with which Shakespeare effects the endings of other plays. And having Timon's death reported through a messenger's speech fits with the slightly classical aura of the tragedy.

Certainly, everything that concerns Timon in the ending is handled skillfully. It is appropriate for the misanthrope who has rejected the world to die away from it. His death, to use Charney's phrase, is left "poetically obscure."[21] After Timon's willful and desperate search for self-destruction, it must be due to suicide of some sort, but the sting of the deed is lessened by its occurring offstage and by not being described. If the hero does not appear any longer in the fifth act (as defined here), he is evoked as a potent memory, a powerful legend, and a force to be reckoned with in settling the fate of Athens. The focus, however, is on the manner in which Alicibiades shapes this legend.

4

The Rise of Alcibiades

Our captain hath in every figure skill

Alcibiades is a puzzling character; the question is whether he is so owing to design or to the unsatisfactory state of the text. Critics frequently think him not fully developed. As H. J. Oliver says, "It would be easy to compile an anthology of contradictory remarks about Alcibiades, and their very number is no doubt some indication that Shakespeare has not made his intention perfectly clear."[1] But we must not take contradictory critical responses to a Shakespearean character as indications that the character is unsatisfactory. Most major and many minor characters are hotly disputed, and puzzlement about a character's actions and motivations may indicate complexity, as is true for Hamlet.

For the second most important character of the play, Alcibiades has a surprisingly low share of words (6.614 percent), which puts him behind Apemantus (9.877 percent) and even the steward (8.553 percent). If a longer version of the play existed at one time, as I suspect, he may have had more than the few lines he speaks in the first two acts and been even more prominent in the ending than he is now. But I do not think that this would have changed the impression of Alcibiades' verbal reticence. He is a man not only of few words but also of short speeches who makes longer speeches only at turning points of his career: the thirteen-line soliloquy when he is exiled, the thirteen-line address to the senators before the gates of Athens, and the fifteen lines that conclude the play. All these speeches initiate significant action, and even his brief remarks are deliberately and pregnantly phrased. He recalls another man of power, Bolingbroke in *Richard II*, who is verbally reticent and not given to explanations of himself or his actions. In both cases, but more so with Alcibiades, the importance of the man and what he stands for is underlined by nonverbal dramatic means, by significant positioning in scenes, and by military uniform, armor, and martial sounds.

If, in spite of his sufficient prominence, Shakespeare's Alcibiades remains something of a puzzle, I shall argue that this is by design, a design consistent with Plutarch's portrayal of the man. Since Shakespeare took few factual details from "The Life of Alcibiades," critics sometimes claim that he was not influenced by it; Geoffrey Bullough, for instance, says that Shakespeare's focus on Timon made it impossible for him to develop Alcibiades into the "subtle, adaptable and various man of Plutarch." Instead, Bullough says, Shakespeare aimed at making Alibiades into Timon's foil, a reasonable man who unlike the misanthrope knows how to cope with the world; the play's lack of completion is responsible for this plan not being fully realized.[2] If Bullough were right, Shakespeare would have seen Alcibiades quite differently from Plutarch and from the Renaissance tradition based on Plutarch because the total effect of this portrait was more negative than positive. Plutarch saw Alcibiades sharing the guilt for the Athenian debacle with the oligarchy, the people, and the political circumstances. Although he said much in praise of the general, on balance he judged him to have been a misfortune for Athens. It is symptomatic that he mentioned Timon's interest in Alcibiades as one that someday would do great mischief to the Athenians[3]—a saying that forms the nucleus of Timon's tirades against Alcibiades in the fourth act. The young general, said Plutarch, was handsome, strong, brave, gifted, well-educated, and experienced in martial affairs. Although halting of speech, he was eloquent: he often paused to consider what he would say and brought it forth wittily and with good delivery. He was endowed with ambition and a desire for honor. However, he inclined to dissoluteness, effeminacy of dress, and lavish expenditures. Most of all, he was greatly adaptable—Plutarch compared his changeability to that of the chameleon. His failure to keep promises showed his lack of firm principles.

Plutarch anticipated somewhat the later conception of Alcibiades as a climber on Fortune's wheel, who became the goddess's victim. Alcibiades' successes constantly drew envy. When he returned from exile, the greatest men of the city remained envious; the suspicion that he might make himself king clung to him; even those who welcomed his return were torn between joy and grief. Whatever feeling of triumph he experienced was undercut by doubt and fear. Outwardly, however, he appeared serene; his speech to the people cleverly put the blame for his tribulations not on the Athenians but on "cursed fortune and some spiteful god that envied his glory and prosperity."[4] Boccaccio put this fortune theme into the *de casibus* formula; in the same tradition, Lydgate saw Alcibiades defeated by ambition and "Fortunys fals mutabilitie."[5]

Renaissance political theorists were more severe with Alcibiades. He was the main culprit of the Athenian defeat by Sparta for Louis Leroy in his commentary on Aristotle's *Politics* (translated into English in 1598) and for Jean Bodin in *The Six Books of a Commonweal* (translated in 1606). According to Bodin, Alcibiades brought about political instability by changing the government into a democracy, which Bodin conceived in Aristotelian terms as the rule of the populace.[6] Incidentally, somewhere in the background literature Shakespeare would have gathered the idea that Alcibiades had trouble with the Athenian "senate"—Leroy and Lydgate used this romanizing term for the oligarchy, a term that should not surprise us in *Timon*.

Aldibiades certainly did not have a good press in Shakespeare's England. A quite negative satirical portrayal of his character was that by Thomas Lodge in *Wit's Misery and the World's Madness* (1596). Shakespeare is likely to have known the book; it carries the famous reference to the Ur-Hamlet. According to Lodge's curious genealogy, Alcibiades was a descendant of one of Satan's seven ministers, that is, the deadly sins, specifically the son of Leviathan (Pride). Lodge saw the degradation of his own time evidenced by London's being replete with vainglorious, boastful, and quarrelsome rakes. These, he said, play gallant courtiers near St. Paul, pride themselves on ancestors, stratagems, and policies, and "sail by the wind of his fortune, become chameleons like Alcibiades, feeding on the vanity of his tongue with the foolish credulity of their ears."[7] Lodge's characterization of Alcibiades has some resemblance to that of Alcibiades' friend in Shakespeare's play, at least if we take the senators' word for his quarrelsomeness and riotous living (3.5.68–75). This, of course, is disputable evidence, coming as it does from suspect witnesses; but in any case the senators make good use of the ill reputation of Alcibiades' followers. It is worth noting that elsewhere, in *Catharos: Diogenes in his Singularity* (1591), Lodge attacked usury and wished for "some wise wag like Alcibiades to burn usurers' bonds, bills, and contracts in the market place, which if they were set on fire, the bonfire would be so big, as I fear me would consume the whole city."[8] It seems likely that Shakespeare got the idea of making Alcibiades a fighter against usury, and an unexpected one at that, from Lodge. Plutarch has nothing of the sort.

It would surely have been difficult for Shakespeare to alter the character of Alcibiades essentially from this firmly established unfavorable picture and make him into a morally positive figure to set off Timon's negativism. Any significant cosmetic surgery would have run counter to audience expectation, and the play gives no evidence that Shakespeare undertook it or intended to undertake it. The few lines Alcibiades speaks in the first two acts convey the impression that he must be taken as an important man of questionable character; his intelligence and his courage are not in doubt, but his moral fiber is. The trumpet that announces him and the uniforms and arms he and his followers wear demonstrate his military potential. Yet the one sentence he utters on this occasion has an almost saccharine sweetness: "Sir, you have sav'd my longing, and I feed / Most hungerly on your sight" (251–52).[9] Oliver notes that the expression "to save one's longing" is recorded as meaning to anticipate and so to prevent a woman's longing. Perhaps Shakespeare was aware of Alcibiades' reputed homosexual tendency. If so, he thought of him as bisexual since a page is later shown to carry letters from a courtesan to him as well as to Timon (2.2.86). Unpleasantly, Alcibiades' phrase of feeding hungrily on Timon's sight continues the cannibalistic food imagery with which Apemantus has just refused Timon's invitation to dine with him: "No; I eat not lords" (1.1.204). Further, Apemantus's comment on the mutual greetings of Alcibiades, Timon, and their retinue has a way of associating Alcibiades with Timon's sycophantic friends: "That there should be small love amongst these sweet knaves, / And all this courtesy!" (248–49).

During the banquet, when flattery envelops Timon most odiously, Alcibiades says very little. To Timon's coarse remark "You had rather be at a breakfast of enemies than a dinner of friends" he answers compliantly: "So they were bleeding new, my lord, there's no meat like 'em; I could wish my best friend at such a feast" (1.2.75–79). This argues a streak of cruelty in Alcibiades; unpleasantly, the image continues the meat-blood association by which Apemantus has just characterized Timon's friends as his cannibalistic exploiters: "O you gods! What a number of men eats Timon, and he sees 'em not! It grieves me to see so many dip their meat in one man's blood; and all the madness is, he cheers them up too" (39–42). The same cannibalistic strain sounds again in Apemantus's derisive comment on Alcibiades' boast about feeding on his enemies: "Would all those flatterers were thine enemies then, that then thou mightst kill 'em—and bid me to 'em" (80–81). Apemantus's remark seems to indicate that he does not put Alcibiades among Timon's flatterers, and it is true that, deferential and obliging as the general is, he is not a blatant sycophant. Timon seems to look upon him as special friend since he singles him out as "my Alcibiades" when he decides to go hunting (2.2.18). Yet the relationship is not shown as being a close friendship. If it were, it would interfere with the impression of Timon's being isolated even in prosperity.

Alcibiades accepts Timon's gifts and answers the pleasantries with which they are proffered without in return fawning over Timon as do the others. At a later point during the banquet, Timon turns again to Alcibiades, accompanying a gift for him with another allusion to his profession: "Thou art a soldier, therefore seldom rich; / It comes in charity to thee: for all thy living / Is 'mongst the dead, and all the lands thou hast / Lie in a pitch's field" (221–24). Alcibiades' reply, "Ay, defil'd land, my lord," is at least witty synonymy, enough to set him off from the others without making him a moral exemplar. The focus is on his soldiership, which becomes important later. Although quiet, he is quick at repartee and mentally agile. These impressions one gets of the earlier Alcibiades make the subsequent characterization of him as "an ag'd interpreter, though young in days" (5.3.6) believable enough.

Little as the character of Alcibiades is developed in the first two acts, it is sufficient to create expectations. The test of his intellectual and moral caliber comes in his debate with the senators, a debate that vies with that among the Trojan princes in *Troilus and Cressida* (2.2) for the distinction of being the strangest discussion of justice and honor in Shakespeare's plays. In both cases, the issues debated are much less important than the attitudes displayed, and the real reason for the contention lies in these attitudes. In *Timon*, the insubstantiality of the arguments is increased by the triteness of the rhyming couplets bandied about.

The issue is *per se* problematic; it involves a matter of honor on which Shakepeare's contemporaries held conflicting opinions: Alcibiades' friend has killed a man in a duel and, the senator says, must die. The incident and the judgment were common in Shakespeare's day, but so was the mercy for which Alcibiades pleads. Custom and morality pointed in different directions on the permissibility of dueling.[10] It was a fact of life (and of death) for the aristocracy, and it increased under James; so did the anti-dueling literature. Shakespeare does not provide enough data to judge this particular case, a judgment that would be problematic even then; the focus is not on the validity of the arguments, but on the ambiguity of Alcibiades' character and the arbitrariness and villainy of the senators. We have no way of knowing whether Alcibiades' friend is really the man of moderation he claims him to be:

> And with such sober and unnoted passion
> He did behove ["manage"] his anger, ere 'twas spent,
> As if he had but prov'd an argument.
>
> (3.5.21–23)

Alcibiades may forge here "too strict a paradox" as the senators say; their description of the duelist as a "sworn riotor" would ring familiarly in the ears of Shakespeare's audience, who had firsthand experience with quarrelsome, debauched soldiers, kept from employment by the long peace. But the senators make their position, whatever its justice, sound specious by the string of conventional paradoxes of a Stoic kind they utter. And they contradict their recipe by their action: instead of wearing insults like their "raiment, carelessly," they banish Alcibiades on the slightest provocation. The general has a point when he protests that in view of his deserts he merits greater consideration.

Whatever the validity of his position, Alcibiades is an excellent debater who recognizes the value of the trumps he holds. He hints at the weakness of the senators, their greed, which he dubs love of "security"; and he knows how to use the commercial metaphors of which they are fond: he will "pawn" his victory and honor to them (81–83). His angry reaction to his banishment shows that he also knows how to attack the senators where they are most vulnerable: "Banish your dotage, banish usury, / That makes the senate ugly!" (99–100). But his espousal of the usury issue at this point smells of opportunism: there is no indication that he has as yet learned of Timon's plight, and he has not said anything about usury until now, when attacking it serves his personal purpose against the unpopular senate.

When alone, Alcibiades shows how he will transform defeat into victory:

> Banishment!
> It comes not ill. I hate not to be banish'd;
> It is a cause worthy my spleen and fury,
> That I may strike at Athens. I'll cheer up
> My discontented troops, and lay for hearts.
> 'Tis honour with most lands to be at odds;
> Soldiers should brook as little wrongs as gods.
>
> (3.5.112–18)

The light of irony is on the concept of honor here. It is hardly honorable to be at odds "with most lands," and it is certainly not divine to take revenge. Alcibiades' political action aims no more at the welfare of the state than does the senators';

he betrays no shred of patriotism, no regret at having to wage war against Athens, and his likening of soldiers to gods adds a touch of arrogance. By contrast, the misanthropic Timon sounds almost patriotic when he curses Alcibiades because "by killing of villains / Thou wast born to conquer my country" (4.3.107–8).

Alcibiades' shrewd Machiavellism, indicated by his intention to "lay for hearts," proves clearly that, unlike Timon, he knows the realities of the power situation: he must make himself valued again by a display of power, and therefore, as a soldier will say later, the fall of Athens is the mark of his ambition (5.3.10). His military progress is obvious at his next entry when he marches on the stage to the sound of drum and fife. But this is not a moral ascendance. Lechery as well as war holds the fashion with him; he is accompanied by a "brace of harlots" (4.3.81), giving Timon the opportunity of castigating the two most common vices of mankind.

This, the last meeting of Alcibiades and Timon bears looking at closely, since commentators have seen an inconsistency in Alcibiades' at first seeming to know little or nothing of Timon's treatment, declaring that he is "unlearn'd and strange" in the misanthrope's fortunes (57), then admitting "I have heard in some sort of thy miseries" (78), and finally waxing eloquent about these miseries:

> I have heard and griev'd
> How cursed Athens, mindless of thy worth,
> Forgetting thy great deeds, when neighbour states,
> But for thy sword and fortune, trod upon them—
>
> (93-96)

The gradualism in this revelation of knowledge surely indicates that Shakespeare wanted it to be understood as Alcibiades' deliberate strategy rather than that he failed to revise uncertainties in his design. Alcibiades knows more of Timon's situation than he lets on at first; he would prefer learning of Timon's grievances from the misanthrope himself in order to make his offer of aid and redress more spontaneous. It is also to Alcibiades' purpose to recall at this point the Athenians' ingratitude for Timon's military deserts. Timon earlier professed to have done the state some service (2.2.201–2); when Alcibiades now adds that he did so with his "sword and fortune," we are impressed not only by the Athenians' ingratitude but also by the subtlety of Alcibiades' appeal to Timon as a comrade-in-arms. The general is obviously not deterred by Timon's insults and his refusal to accept the gold Alcibiades proffers him; as we learn later, he sends letters to Timon to join in the campaign against Athens, "in part for his [Timon's] sake mov'd" (5.2.12)

—we know, of course that thoughts of Timon played no role in Alcibiades' decision. Alcibiades' strategy of gradual revelation points up his diplomatic prudence, which contrasts with Timon's vehement but honest misanthropy.

Shakespeare's characterization of Alcibiades before he becomes master of Athens in the fifth act is thus in the Plutarchian pattern. Alcibiades is indeed subtle, adaptable, and various. He is ingratiating to the point of effeminacy, but his soldiership is never in question. His lax morals are evident when we see him accompanied by prostitutes. He is ambitious, but he does not consume himself with passion; and he is greatly flexible in the pursuit of his goals, as when he does not press his appeal for Timon's help. He is not a man to give way to boundless anger like Timon—it is as if he were characterizing himself when he describes his comrade who killed an opponent as a man who knows how to control and manage his anger. Shakespeare may have been induced to emphasize the temperamental contrast between Alcibiades and Timon because of a notable distinction Plutarch made in this respect between Alcibiades and Coriolanus: the latter was a man who, "following his choleric mood, would be pleased with nothing," whereas Alcibiades, when he saw they [his countrymen] repented them of the injury they had done him, came to himself and did withdraw his army."[11] This is quite Alcibiades' procedure at the end of Shakespeare's play.

When analyzing the ending of the play, the critic is hampered by the unsatisfactory state of the text, which, as I have argued, contains some lacunae here. I doubt that whatever may be missing could have cleared up the ambiguities of Alcibiades' character and turned the portrait from dubious to positive. Nothing warrants such change. In fact, the original text, rather than making Alcibiades more likable and a viable alternative to Timon, as Bullough thinks, may well have brought the negative aspects of his character into sharper focus. If I may indulge in a speculation about what is missing, a scene of desperate debate in Athens before Alcibiades' arrival at the gates and a crowd scene after his demand for surrender suggest themselves to me. Both or either of these scenes would have offered an opportunity for the one character to reappear whom I miss in the fifth act, the character who would be a keen critic of Alcibiades' words and actions: Apemantus. Shakespeare's other satirical and acerbic commentators, Thersites, Lucio, Parolles, and Menenius, reappear in the fifth acts of their plays for significant comments; the fool in *Lear*, it is true, does not, but his presence would hardly be compatible with the starkly tragic finale. Although Shadwell's expansion of

Shakespeare's *Timon* cannot generally be commended, I think his feeling was right that Apemantus should have a part in the ending. Shadwell gave Apemantus several speeches, which, though they do not spare the Athenians, primarily chastise Alcibiades for his private revenge, base passion, false sense of honor, dishonesty, folly, and madness. This is neoclassical moralizing; Shakespeare could have done better with a few of Apemantus's characteristic mutterings.

The final scene is, I think, complete; it is, at any rate, effective. True, it does not vie in spectacle with some of Shakespeare's greatest finales, such as those of *Hamlet* and *Lear*. There is no death, only the report of one, and we have heard it before; instead, there is a reconciliation, one that resembles not so much those of the tragedies as of the problem plays. There is a certain open-endedness here, a lack of total conviction characteristic of the endings of *All's Well That Ends Well*, *Measure for Measure*, and particularly *Troilus and Cressida*. But we have come to look upon open-endedness as rather a virtue, and in *Timon* it has intriguingly ironic implications.

Alcibiades' military power is underlined musically, first by trumpets, then by drums. Several trumpets announce his arrival before the walls of Athens in contrast to the one trumpet at the beginning of the play; it was Timon then who had the stronger musical emphasis. We are conscious of the turn of Fortune's wheel; so are the senators. Alcibiades rises to eloquent accusation; his conceit that contrasts the ease and nonchalanace of the senators' use of their time with the breathlessness of his own shows him a master of judicial oratory (5.4.3–13). However, the epithets of "lascivious town" and "licentious measure" he has for Athens sound ironic in the mouth of a patron of camp followers. One of the senators, in answer, speaks of Alcibiades' earlier grief, before he became mighty and they had cause to fear him, as a "mere conceit" (14), that is, an idea not yet transformed into action. But Alcibiades' grief is a conceit in this sense even now, better in words than in fact; we remember that he felt his exile did not come "ill." We may note that "conceit" was assuming in Shakespeare's time its later meaning of deception. Alcibiades' oratory has a special artifice that draws its sincerity into doubt.

Artifice becomes artificiality in the two senators' answer. One should hesitate to call set speeches in Shakespeare rehearsed because they are by definition factitious; but here they are so deliberately and carefully phrased and carried forward in the form of a duet as to give the impression of a deliberate and contrived pattern that wraps unpleasant

truths in delicate ambiguities. The second senator's contention that Athens has shown its good faith by wooing not
only Alcibiades but also Timon "by humble message and by
promis'd means" (20) conveniently omits to mention that the
senators solicited Timon for help against the "boar" Alcibiades. It is quite true that in Athens "all have not offended,"
but to Timon the senators more justly admitted earlier a
"forgetfulness too general gross." The senators' plea not to
raze the innocent walls of Athens is apt to make one recall
Timon's impressive condemnation of these walls for pro-
tecting the Athenian wolves. Quite suspect is the senators'
poetic explanation of the demise of Alcibiades's enemies
"Shame, that they wanted cunning in excess,/ Hath broke
their hearts" (28–29)—believe who will this cause of death.
Whatever has happened to the guilty senators, cunning is
still alive in Athens.

And so is commercial-mindedness. Alcibiades is reminded
that efforts were made "to give thy rages balm, / To wipe
out our ingratitude, with loves / Above their quantity"
(16–18)—moral accountancy at work again! The "decima-
tion and a tithed death" (31) that the senators see as a consequence of Alcibiades' military conquest are estimations of
expert tax collectors. It is true that "crimes, like lands, / Are
not inherited" (37–38); but this phrase recalls how Timon
lost his land, and it evokes Timon's saying of the senators
that they have "their ingratitude in them hereditary." Such
ironic echoes combine with calculating phrases and half-
truths to suggest less than total senatorial repentance. The
appeal of the senators to Alcibiades, like their earlier one to
Timon, is by "promised means" and "special dignities"; one
remembers the "heaps and sums of love and wealth" they
dangled before the misanthrope's eyes. Promising will still
be more fashionable than performance in Athens.

Alcibiades is notably silent during the rhetorical pyrotechnics. Then he answers nobly and settles with the senate
on generous terms. Only his and Timon's enemies, to be selected
by the senators themselves, will be punished. Thus Alcibiades
again associates his name with Timon's; although the misanthrope refused to become his ally, Alcibiades succeeds in making
Timon's cause his own. Apparently, he is aware that he may need
whatever material and moral help he can get; his demand to the
senators "Descend, and keep your words" (64) indicates his
wariness. To those in Shakespeare's audience who remembered
the historical Alcibiades' record in promise-breaking, this
admonition must have had a certain irony. At any rate, we are
again reminded that in Athens promises can be broken and often
are.

Considering the senators' evasions and half-truths,

Alcibiades seems too accommodating, too forgiving here, quite like the historical Alcibiades on his last return to Athens. Even if one does not know of the latter's continued trouble with the Athenians and theirs with him, one is likely to have doubts about the duration of mutual amity. "Be Alcibiades your plague, you his" still rings more loudly in one's ears than the strains of concord that fail to muffle the subtle dissonances. In this play of relatively few strong stage movements, it is significant that the senators' descent from above (the playhouse balcony presumably) is the second such descent; the first was that of the usurer Lucullus, who refused to aid Timon. If the second descent recalls the first, it contributes to evoking the dangerous corruption of Athens.

In agreement with his role as the final, even though precarious and questionable, order figure of the play, Alcibiades reads Timon's epitaph and adds a flowery tribute of his own.[12] There could be no greater contrast in tone and style than that between the rugged fourteeners of Timon's epitaph with its insulting gesture ("A plague consume you wicked caitiffs left") and Alcibiades' soothing, polished lines composed in what we have come to call the metaphysical style:

> Though thou abhorr'dst in us our human griefs,
> Scorn'dst our brains' flow and those our droplets which
> From niggard nature fall, yet rich conceit
> Taught thee to make vast Neptune weep for aye,
> On thy low grave, on faults forgiven
>
> (5.4.[5.3.]75–79)

These lines vie with the senators' defense in ambiguities. Who, after all, wept for Timon the misanthrope? Flavius, of course, did, but his tears are presumably stilled now. And whose are the "faults forgiven"? They are hardly Timon's, since it was supposedly his conceit to make Neptune weep by erecting his grave at the seaside. Timon never forgave the Athenians, and they, guilty of ingratitude, would forget their own faults if they forgave Timon. The "conceit," a term associated with Alcibiades, is really his; and its polish should not blind us to the politically advantageous image it creates for him. The extravagant figure makes Alcibiades the universal forgiver and the inheritor of Timon's legend—quite contrary to the dead man's wishes. If this is a "rich conceit," its riches are for the survivors. After Alcibiades' spiderweb-thin eulogy of Timon, his concluding phrase has a quality of perfuntoriness, even of embarrassment: "Dead/ Is noble Timon, of whose memory / Hereafter more."

The ambiguities, ironies, and paradoxes are carried through to the end of the play; in fact, they find here a culmination until the very last line brings a note of certainty, a precise and clear command that evokes the reality of Alcibiades' present power:

> Bring me into your city,
> And I will use the olive with my sword,
> Make war breed peace, make peace stint war, make each
> Prescribe to other, as each other's leech.
> Let our drums strike.

For many modern commentators, Alcibiades' paradoxes seem to be promising the olives of an endless age. One critic finds him fusing humanistic virtues with chivalric military values to regenerate Athens.[13] For another, "it is as if Shakespeare is now prepared to see goodness in the dominion of a strong man who will exercise his power with benevolence."[14] If nothing else, the "leech" metaphor, coming as it does at the end of the long line of unpleasant animal and food images in the play, ought to make us pause; the blood-sucking worms are imagined to be feeding on each other, a reciprocal relationship that evokes Timon's wish that Alcibiades become the plague of the Athenians, and they his. Even if we stay merely with the medical side of the metaphor, there is no reason to assume that the prescription presages health. Draw who will comfort from the idea that in a body politic peace must follow war, and war peace, just as in a healthy human body there must be a tension and balance of humors.[15] Certainly not all Shakespeare's contemporaries drew such comfort. Of course, the dangers of peace, that is, idleness, luxury, and corruption, were often held up as warnings, and Hamlet's diagnosis of Fortinbras's martial enterprise (a rather questionable adventure it seems) is in this tradition: "This is th' imposthume of much wealth and peace / That inward breaks" (4.4.27–28). On the other hand, there were attacks on the old commonplace of war as a healer, Montaigne's among them.[16] Sir William Cornwallis too looked skeptically at war as the "medicine for commonwealths, sick of too much ease and tranquility."[17] Even Barnabe Rich, the old soldier who never ceased to warn of the fatness of these pursy times, took a dim view of those that sought to advance their fortunes by war or the threat of war: "I must confess that these war lovers are like physicians that could wish the city to be full of diseases, whereby they might be employed for their own gain."[18] Certainly the quality of the military physician who was to heal the state mattered for Rich. And as to Shakespeare's attitude, we may remember that Macbeth felt himself a purger of the body politic—hardly a commendation for the commonplace. Also, Coriolanus's attempt to steel the sinews of Rome is not sympathetically portrayed. He all-too-joyfully hopes that the Volscian invasion will provide means "to vent / Our musty superfluity" (1.1.225–26). Antony finds Pompey's sedition, nourished by the indolence of peace, a bad remedy: "And quietness, grown sick of rest, would purge / By any desperate change" (1.3.53–54). How fitting a comment on all this is Timon's "trust not the physician; / His antidotes are poison, and he slays / More than you rob" (4.3. 434–36).

The sequential evocation of war and peace, peace and war at the end of *Timon* evokes the cyclical idea of history and with it the rhythm of fortune. Renaissance emblematists knew of a wheel of fortune that put nations into a circular motion in which peace produced wealth, wealth pride, pride war, war poverty, poverty humility, humility peace, peace wealth, and so on.[19] The emblematists thought this wheel a warning, and its rhythm of fortune was viewed pessimistically by the moralists, as for instance by Richard Barckley:

> . . . A long continued peace engendreth luxuriousness and intemperance, whereof ensueth . . . an infinite number of diseases, both of body and mind, that besides many torments that hasten men to their end, it encreaseth riches, which bringeth forth covetousness, pride, vain-glory, and ambition which ensueth uncharitable contention by law and effusion of innocent blood by Civil Wars, to the utter ruin and destruction oftentimes of many goodly kingdoms and commonwealths.[20]

Alcibiades and Athens are together on one wheel now, and it will turn as it must.

By making Alcibiades into a character who fails to inspire assurance and by not providing a conclusive ending for the play, Shakespeare refrained from lightening the pessimism. He evidently did not wish to have Timon's faultiness set off by a contrasting example of goodness. Consequently, the foil relationship between the two characters is very subtle, and it tends to make us think somewhat better of Timon than of Alcibiades. Both are faced with ingratitude, but only Timon is really its victim. Both react angrily on the basis of a grudge that they generalize into a quarrel with Athens, but Alcibiades' anger remains colored by personal goals whereas Timon abandons all considerations of himself. In dealing with Athens, Alcibiades may be said merely to apply principles of ordinary *Realpolitik*, but these have never made good moral prescriptions. Moreover, Alcibiades' credentials as champion of good against evil are weakened by his lax morality and excessive flexibility.

Alcibiades' triumph of fortune in the end resounds with ironies. By the standards of the world, he is a success, the agent of history, and Timon a failure; but it is Timon who creates as misanthrope the more consistent and spectacular image. Minion of Fortune that Alcibiades is, he remains subject to her changes, whereas Timon takes himself out of the range of her false mutability. Although Alcibiades makes himself revalued by the Athenians and keeps the state going when Timon burns himself out in hatred, Timon's is the more enduring legend.

5

Timon the Misanthrope

The extremity of both ends

Timon is one of the strangest and most baffling of Shakespeare's tragic heroes. It is true that there is a simple view of his character. It is not altogether wrong, I think; like almost everybody else who has written about the play, I could not help taking it occasionally. But without considerable modification, it is too simple and does not do justice to what the play presents.

This simple view is that of Timon as an extremist. One can put it quite unsympathetically, as does David Cook: "Our untrammeled reaction is surely to feel that at first he is a well-meaning fool and that later his misanthropy, however provoked, is perverse."[1] Or, one can put it benevolently, as did Leigh Hunt, who saw Edmund Kean's romantic portrayal of the role and pointed the moral: "Human nature will allow of no excess, and . . . if we set out in the world with animal spirits which lead us to think too highly of it, we shall be disappointed."[2] Like all Shakespeare's tragic heroes, Timon is a man of emotional excesses; he never gives an indication that he might be able to live on the simple plane on which most men are content to stay or to which they have adjusted. His propensity to strong reactions shows itself in prosperity when, with tears in his eyes, he wishes he could deal kingdoms to his friends; it reaches a fortissimo in the torrents of denunciation and malediction he pours on the Athenians and the human race. The limitless giver and benefactor becomes a nihilist and boundless hater. What seems more pertinent than to quote, as many critics do, Apemantus's stab at Timon in the memorable dispute the two have in the woods: "The middle of humanity thou never knewest, but the extremity of both ends" (4.3.301–2)?

Yet, if one reflects on the speaker of these lines and his position in the spectrum of humanity, they appear less clearly a key to the character of Timon, let alone to the meaning of the play. Apemantus, who posits himself at the fringe of humanity, is a strange advocate of the golden mean, and the "middle of humanity" is no *a priori* concept; it depends on what the definer, by his expectation and his experience, has come to believe man is like. It is no virtue at all when the common denominator is very common. Where really is the middle in Athenian humanity when the average is one of depravity?

We need also put in perspective the view of Timon as not one character but as two extreme portraits, the one in swanwhite, the other in raven-black. It is true that Timon makes an abrupt *volte-face*, but it should be said that antithetically baroque contrasts between a tragic hero's earlier and later behavior are indigenous to Shakespeare's tragic art. The calm and composed general Othello becomes a blind slave of jealousy. The valiant and victorious Macbeth proves a bloody murderer. The pillar of the world Antony is, to take the Roman view, a strumpet's fool. All Shakespeare's tragic heroes, in a sense, are discontinuous characters since their behavior patterns change as they react to deeds of shame or horror in their worlds. They all become "new" persons, although sometimes, like Hamlet, they have changed anterior to the play itself. Timon's disruption of personality is distinguished from that of the others mainly by the fact that the two sides of his character or, if one prefers, his two characters are given almost equal emphasis.

Renaissance psychology had no problems in explaining sudden and astonishing metamorphoses of the kind undergone by Shakespeare's tragic heroes including Timon: it attributed them to changes of humor. In terms of humor physiology and psychology, Timon is transformed from the sanguine complexion with its high spirits, *joie de vivre*, and hearty hospitality into a frenzy of choler, which, like other extreme humoral states, can be described as melancholy, the "melancholy adust" that comes from the burning of the original humor.[3] In his encounter with Apemantus, Timon himself speaks of his "choler" (4.3.369); and both Apemantus and the bandit see the misanthropic Timon as melancholy, the former diagnosing his illness as due to a "change of future" (4.3.206), the latter as stemming from want of gold and the desertion of his friends (404). If they guess wrongly as to the causes, this does not vitiate their diagnosis of the illness, the symptoms of which were thought to be well known. Physiologically, Timon's change is thus parallel to Richard II's or Hamlet's, a disruption owing to psychic shock and to the development of a life-harming melancholy. The resemblance of Timon's misanthropy to the behavior of Elizabethan and Jacobean malcontents on the stage gave Shakespeare's audience an access to his transformation and character that the ordinary modern reader no longer has.

The twentieth-century reader or theatergoer, however, will hardly be as worried about the discontinuity of Timon's character as some critics of the past have been. Contemporary fiction and drama have accustomed us to disrupted characters who refuse to stay in character and who reject their past as if it had never existed. All we ask in such psychic revolutions is that their causes are strong enough; and we may even drop this stipulation if either of the two or both behavior patterns of the character strike us in some way as demented, or if the behavior of those around him is demented enough to make his reaction, strange as it may be by itself, appear normal by contrast. Modern literature frequently presents us with variations of such situations that are sometimes so complex as to make us wonder just where the emphasis is. We have become much more aware of the shifting lines between normality and madness and of difficulties in defining these terms. Those that have been called mad have sometimes proved the sanest of their time. "What's madness but nobility of soul at odds with circumstance?", asks Theodore Roethke.

Considerations and questions of this kind are, in fact, posed by the play. Who is mad is a matter of perspective. Timon, speaking with the voice of the world, calls Apemantus mad ("*furor*," 1.2.28). For Apemantus, the earlier Timon is a madman, the later a fool (4.3.223)—a judgment that modern critics have a way of turning around. Timon's guests at the mock banquet, Alcibiades in his encounter with Timon in the wood, and the senators who are mocked by him in their quest for aid all think that he has lost his wits (3.6.114; 4.3.89–90; 5.1.223–24). And, in a sense, Timon, with his futile gestures and inveterate hatred, can be called mad. But then, those who call him so speak with the voice of the world that we have come to distrust, and Timon's grand defiance of this world also has a quixotic sanity. If Timon is mad, his world is madder.

I am running ahead of my story; we must concern ourselves further with Timon the philanthropist. We should not do so, however, without a sense of what he will become; Shakespeare's audience would have been very much aware of his proverbial misanthropy even while he intones his grand hymn to friendship and philanthropy. Shakespeare faced here a dramatic problem: Timon's conversion to misanthropic hate, according to general human standards, is a deterioration; but tragedy also demands an upward movement in the hero; it requires that he learn something, become in some sense greater than he was.

The need for ascertainable growth in Timon would alone have compelled Shakespeare to make the pre-misanthropic Timon into a character less admirable than the personification of generosity enshrined by Wilson Knight. But if Timon is no saint, he is by no means merely an extravagant spender, such as eighteenth-century critics described him when they moralized the play into an exemplum. Johnson's moral that the play is "a very powerful warning against ostentatious liberality"[4] puts the accent quite wrongly and does not do justice to the complexity of Shakespeare's hero. Shakespeare poised him delicately and made him neither a quite sympathetic, if imprudent, idealist nor a glaring prodigal. Timon is an intricate blend of nobility, egotism, and foolishness.

Shakespeare evidently conceived him as rather young. Timon betrays a young man's attitude toward age when he explains the senators' refusal to come to his aid: "These old fellows / Have their ingratitude in them hereditary" (2.2.218–19). When later the poet thinks of appealing once more for his patronage, he speaks of a work dedicated to a young man: "It must be a personating of himself; a satire against the softness of prosperity, with a discovery of the infinite flatteries that follow youth and opulency" (5.1.33–35). It is significant that the only other character specially designated as young is Timon's bosom friend Alcibiades. He too finds the senators too aged to remember his merits (3.5.93–95). One gains thus the impression of an old Athens that—to use Timon's characterization of the senators—lacks kindly warmth and that grows, like nature, toward the earth, turning against the two prominent young men in order to ruin one financially and drive the other from the city. The aura of youth, however, remains only with the "noble and young" general (5.3.8; 5.4.13). The misanthrope is "full of decay and failing" (4.3.463), and compares himself to an oak stripped of leaves in winter (4.3.266). Oddly Shakespeare seems to have thought of his hero as aging during the play, which cannot be imagined as lasting more than a few weeks or, at most, months. We have a difficulty here, if indeed it is a difficulty, analogous to that with Hamlet, who ages from a youthful wooer of Ophelia into the thirty-year-old man of the graveyard scene.

The explanation in both cases is presumably that Shakespeare, indifferent to mathematical calculation, sought to create the impression of the hero's aging because of his tragic experience. In Timon's case, this process accentuates the contrast between the hero's growing toward death and the specious rejuvenation of Athens on a globe that is doomed to wear away, as the painter says in the beginning of the play.

At the outset, Timon emanates a youthful nobility. We are not immediately aware of his shortcomings when he appears on the scene. His first deed is unequivocally noble: he frees Ventidius from debtor's prison. Ventidius is a man in need, and Timon helps. But his second good deed, the endowing of his servant for marrying the old Athenian's daughter, generous as it is by itself, is yet fraught with ambiguities of rationale and effect. Timon says of his servant, "To build his fortune I will strain a little, / For 'tis a bond in men" (1.1.146–47). Insofar as he thinks of a bond of loyalty between himself and the servant, this is fine; but since money is the nexus for it, he betrays a habit of thought that is akin to his false friends' mentality. These will later clamor about "broken bonds" without any regard for human relationships. The father of the bride is quite willing to subordinate his daughter's happiness to his financial goals: rather than have her marry the indigent servant, he swears absurdly, he will choose his "heir from forth the beggars of the world, / And dispossess her all" (1.1.141–42). Timon should not endorse the old man's attitude, that of greedy Athens, which buys and ties human relationships through money. But at least he does so with no gain for himself and with the best of motives—well, uneducated motives.

Elsewhere, when Timon scatters his gifts among his sycophantic friends, our primary impression of his nobility is superseded by one of his blindness and foolishness. His economic imprudence is here accompanied by psychological and moral failings. That he is careless in the administration of his estate we are apt to hold least against him, although it probably struck Shakespeare's contemporaries as a violation of his obligation and trust as a landholder. But that he gives to flatterers and sycophants is a serious human failing. By allowing and encouraging the tribute of his friends and assenting to the honor they bestow upon him for his material giving, he accepts in effect their system of valuing. This is obvious even in the way he hands out his rewards and signs of affection. In order to urge a horse admired by one of his guests on him, he says that "no man / Can justly praise but what he does affect" (1.2.212–13) —that things can be admired disinterestedly does not seem to occur to him. Even if we take the remark as a socially determined way of being gracious in generosity, it uncomfortably reflects the acquisitive principles of Athenian society. Yet, it must also be said that as much as he mouths these principles, he has not adopted the harmful practices with which they are accompanied, particularly the acquisition of possessions at another's expense. He does not realize that his old-fashioned belief that giving is sweeter than receiving clashes with the greed and worship of fortune around him.

The ideas of the philanthropic Timon are a hodgepodge of idealism and the commonplaces of his (or rather Shakespeare's) age. He is not even an extreme and reckless lover of mankind and boundless optimist. He shows once that he is aware, at least in a commonplace way, that evil exists in Athens and the world. In one of his first utterances, as he is offered the portrait by the painter, he says:

> The painting is almost the natural man:
> For since dishonour traffics with man's nature,
> He is but out-side; these pencill'd figures are
> Even such as they give out.

> (1.1.160–63)

Timon's remark on the unpleasant truth beneath human appearances is casual, uttered without realizing its potential terror, just like the painter's remark on the world that wears itself down as it grows; yet it is powerfully ironic. The kinetic metaphor "traffic" establishes an association with the venality of Athens; only a few lines later the word occurs with triple emphasis as Apemantus wishes that traffic, the merchant's god, will confound the merchant (236). Since the portrait surely depicts Timon, there is a particular irony in Timon's comment: if the portrait is by its nature innocent, dishonor in the form of commercial corruption has subtly affected the sitter.

Timon evidently believes that the "natural man" evoked by the idealization of art symbolizes the inhabitant of the golden world unspoiled by the traffic of the modern age.[5] Traditional Christianity with its deeper pessimism has always denied this claim of man's essential goodness. It should be noted that even for Timon actual man is not unconditionally good; his remark betrays a passing dark thought since it suggests that acquired evil may be in the men around him. A lesser dramatist than Shakespeare might not have dared to give such a notion to a figure of benevolence like Timon; in fact, in Shadwell's adaptation, it is given to Apemantus, for whom, however, it is too charitable. With his remark on the existence of evil in the world, contradicted as it is by his acting as if he were in a paradise of innocence and goodness, Timon shows himself just a little less grandly idealistic, a little more human in the sense of being prone to error in spite of better knowledge than he would otherwise be. Consequently, his awakening to the real evil that surrounds him does represent mental growth. Whatever one may think of Timon the misanthrope, he is not a gullible spender and repeater of commonplaces; his hatred is formed and informed by bitter experience.

The pre-misanthropic Timon is too individualistic and too human to resemble the stereotype of the prodigal except in a few superficial features. He is certainly quite different from the morality figure of Prodigality in *The Contention Between Liberality and Prodigality* (1602) or the Theophrastian character of the Unthrift in Joseph Hall's *Characters of Virtues and Vices* (1608), both of which are crude and profligate. Timon's prodigality is not self-degrading, and it is debatable where his generosity ends and his prodigality begins. The prodigality, to a large degree, is an outgrowth of his warm and sensuous nature; but this nature, unfortunately, is not subject to the control of reason. In this respect, Timon's first banquet of friendship is highly revealing. As a celebration of friendship, it evokes the shadow of the Platonic banquets celebrated in the Renaissance; but even without Apemantus's cutting remarks, we would know how very much this celebration lacks substance. In fact, the banquet resembles the opposite of Platonic ones, the banquets of sense with their dangerous allurement to the appetites, such as emblems and moral poems characterized them.[6]

This concept is given iconographic emphasis by the masque that is Timon's "own device" (1.2.146). Cupid, the presenter, labels the show as intended to gratify the senses:

The five best senses acknowledge thee their patron, and come
    freely to gratulate thy plenteous bosom.
There, taste, touch, all, pleas'd from thy table rise;
They only now come but to feast thine eyes. (119–23)

Perhaps this acknowledgment should be imagined as a dumb show in which Cupid leads the senses, with the sense of sight, the noblest, first, and with the other four bowing to it. Even in the most generous interpretation, what is fed by the masque is not the philosophic mind but the eye; likewise the banquet itself gratifies merely the senses. Moreover, the entry of the Amazons for the masque brings a dissonance, heightened by Apemantus's obscenity. What Timon presumably intends with the device of Cupid and the Amazons is to present the reconciliation of opposites; what he produces is ominously discordant: when blind love leads warlike femininity, disaster is likely to result. The masque demonstrates Timon's sensual extravagance, an ingredient in the societal disorder satirized by Apemantus. At the same time, the banquet and masque, as much as they show Timon's shortcomings, betray also his simple, childlike desire for a good and harmonious life—an urge aesthetically and morally far more pleasing than the realistic calculations of his ironhearted friends who live in the age of gold.

Timon's notion of friendship too combines idealism and foolishness. His eloquently wrongheaded hymn to friendship is worth quoting here at some length:

> O no doubt, my good friends, but the gods themselves have provided that I shall have much help from you: how had you been my friends else? Why have you that charitable title from thousands, did not you chiefly belong to my heart? . . . O you gods, think I, what need we have any friends, if we should ne'er have need of 'em? They were the most needless creatures living should we ne'er have use for 'em, and would most resemble sweet instruments hung up in cases, that keeps their sounds to themselves. Why, I have often wish'd myself poorer that I might come nearer to you. We are born to do benefits; and what better or properer can we call our own than the riches of our friends? (1.2.86–101)

The idea of basing friendship on need (an idea that Timon does not actually practice) runs counter to classical and Renaissance conceptions of friendship. Cicero's *De amicitia*, the Renaissance primer on friendship, decried utility in selecting friends and declared that friendship is not cultivated because of need (14.51). It is true that Timon aspires to a harmony of friendship such as the moralists thought it necessary for the *concordia* of society.[7] Yet, as Plutarch pointed out in his essay "On Having Many Friends," harmony can be achieved only by the similarity of the instruments, and their congruence demands careful selection and testing. Plutarch warned here and in "How to Tell a Flatterer from a Friend" against choosing hypocrites and parasites. If I may be anachronistic, Timon would have done well to read these essays (if it is true that reading forms character). Shakespeare presumably did read them; at any rate, he and his audience were familiar with the basic principles of friendship as understood by his age. Shakespeare's image makes an additional ironic point when Timon likens his friends to cased instruments: these particular specimens do keep their true sound to themselves.

Timon is, however, on better theoretical grounds when he insists on the equality of friends. In *De amicitia* (19.69), Cicero stipulated that friendship must be based on an acceptance of essential equality, even if one friend is superior to the other in rank or status. When Timon's guests arrive for the banquet and compliment each other on the order of precedence, he decries all etiquette:

> Nay, my lords, ceremony was but devis'd at first
> To set a gloss on faint deeds, hollow welcomes,
> Recanting goodness, sorry ere 'tis shown,
> But where there is true friendship, there needs none.
>
> (1.2.15–18)

It is possible that even this mild egalitarianism was too much for the conservatives in Shakespeare's audience, who saw in the violation of degree the breakdown of all order and a trend toward the "democracy" they distrusted. They might have looked upon Timon as one of those who babbled like Jean Bodin's Utopian leveler:

> If then society between man and man cannot be maintained without friendship, and that the nurse of friendship is equality, seeing there is no equality but in popular state, of necessity that form of commonwealth must be best in the which a natural liberty and justice is equally distributed to all men without fear of tyranny, cruelty, or exaction, and the sweetness of the sociable life seems to draw all men to the felicity which nature has taught us.

Not so, said Bodin, and pointed at the disorders in the Athenian state when it practiced democracy. Experience disproved the levelers: "the equality they seek doth ruin the grounds of love and amity, the which can hardly subsist among them that are equal."[8]

But Timon's dream, after all, does not go quite so far, and his decrying of mere ceremonial politeness echoes the ring of sincerity of Henry V's soliloquy on "idle ceremony." In any case, *Timon* does not provide an apology for, or defense of, degree—the specious courtesy of Timon's friends is not a remnant of an old-fashioned sense of hierarchy and order but rather betrays their uneasiness about the order of precedence in the shifting world of values to which they pay tribute. It masks competition and strife. By contrast, ill-conceived and wrongheaded as some of Timon's ideas of friendship are and imprudent as he is in the choice of his friends, his emotional tribute to the ideal of friendship recalls the old dream of the brotherhood of man, of a Utopia in which, as in More's, men have everything in common. It is an imaginative dream that raises Timon far above his realistic friends and, with all his faults, gives him a certain splendor. If Timon's strength and attraction lie in his emotional commitment rather than in the depth of his thought, as much could be said about other tragic heroes of Shakespeare, notably Othello, Antony, and Coriolanus.

It is Antony most of all whom Timon resembles. He has the Roman general's penchant for charismatic utterances. Timon's sentence "Methinks I could deal kingdoms to my friends, / And ne'er be weary" (1.2.219–20) could easily have been spoken by Antony. We have the paradoxical feeling in hearing Timon utter these lines that we have so often with him. True, it is economically foolish for a private man to assume such royal posture, and he is touched with hubris. Yet, the gesture is grand; and if it proves his recklessness, he is at least nobly reckless. Like Antony, Timon is a big magnetic man who courts disaster. His portrait, as executed by the painter, projects grace and a compelling power:

> How this grace
> Speaks his own standing! What a mental power
> This eye shoots forth! How big imagination
> Moves in this lip!
>
> (1.1.30–33)

The description fits a Titian or a Rubens better than the usual mediocre product of the Renaissance English portrait painters, and the commendation the poet gives the painting sounds indeed like a paraphrase of Titian's motto "Natura potentior ars": it "tutors nature" and is "livelier than life" (37–38). Whatever the actual portrait is like, its function is in part to reflect Timon's projection of himself into a world that, by his imagination, becomes an expression of his will.

Even the senator who is the first to reclaim the money he has lent to Timon and who expects him to succumb pays an implicit tribute to his charisma when he coins the memorable phrase that Timon "flashes now a phoenix":

> I do fear,
> When every feather sticks in his own wing,
> Lord Timon will be left a naked gull,
> Which flashes now a phoenix.
>
> (2.1.29–32)

Though the intention is derogatory, the phoenix image conveys some notion of glamor and rarity; it suggests the mysterious fire flashing from the legendary bird's eyes, and it corroborates the description of the "mental power" that "shoots forth" from the eyes of Timon's portrait.

This image has still other associations. Its basic pattern is actually the Aesopian fable of the borrowed feathers of the crow. Shakespeare had no reason to like this fable since in 1592 Robert Greene had used it against him, calling him "an upstart crow beautified with our feathers."[9] Its moral application was to expose pride, and in the *de casibus* tradition, Fortuna was often described as pulling the feathers of her former favorite.[10] It must have been used quite commonly for financial failure due to extravagance; Gerald de Malynes wrote in 1601 that in these times of economic upheavals some men who had the appearance of substance were "like Aesop's jay, clad in the feathers of other birds, which being discovered and stripped of all for a reward are thoroughly sored and turned from their scarlet gowns into black threadbare cloaks."[11] But Timon is no ugly crow or garish jay. He characterizes himself as a more attractive bird when he says that he is "not of that feather to shake off / My friend when he must need me" (1.1.103–4)—the contrast between him and his friends who do not lend money upon "bare" friendship is glaring. Timon at least has a potential, a capacity for true friendship; and in this context, the phoenix image applied to him may have reminded some in Shakespeare's audience of the proverb that "a faithful friend is like a phoenix."[12]

Possibly, the image may also have suggested to some in this audience the medieval Christian symbol of the phoenix as Christ; the immortal bird's rebirth from its ashes was thought to be symbolic of the Resurrection. If so, I do not think that they would have considered Timon to be another Christ. The play gives no warrant for this; critics who have elevated Timon to Christ status have fallen prey to the paradoxical lure of his personality and misunderstood Shakespeare's dramatic strategy.[13] It is true that Timon is placed in situations that resemble Christ's: when Apemantus at the first banquet characterizes Timon's guests as Judases and when, at the second, Timon chases his calculating friends from the hall somewhat as Christ ejected the moneylenders from the temple. But surely a wealthy man who is infected by the materialism of his time, eats up the flatteries of his friends, and closes his eyes to the evil around him is an odd candidate for the role of Christ. Besides, Timon has some quite ordinary human foibles and prejudices. He shows a young man's attitude toward old age when he attributes the senators' ingratitude to their ossification. Rather than displaying a Christ-like patience, he becomes sometimes irritated about minor matters. He is annoyed with Apemantus for refusing his invitation and, on first learning of his financial stress, accuses the steward of having falsified his accounts. If nothing else, Timon's latent propensity to hatred, which breaks out later, should eliminate him as a Christ surrogate.

If we look closer at the Christ parallels, they show up as partial analogues only. This weakness invades even the strongest parallel, Apemantus's sarcastic comment during the first banquet:

> O you gods! What number of men eats Timon, and he sees 'em not! It grieves me to see so many dip their meat in one man's blood; and all the madness is, he cheers them up too. (1.2.39–42)

Undoubtedly Apemantus's is an allusion to the Judas betrayal, an allusion later supported by the stranger's question, "Who can call him his friend / That dips in the same dish?" (3.2. 67–68). Before taking Apemantus's words as sacramental, however, it is wholesome to realize that a second and different biblical analogue runs through the banquet scene: Ecclesiasticus 12–13, with its warning against trusting friends in prosperity and engaging in false charity by entertaining the proud and rich. The Timon-Alcibiades exchange, which hinges on "pitched" and "defiled" (224), would evoke Ecclesiasticus 13:1: "He that touches pitch shall be defiled with it, and he that is familiar with the proud shall be like unto him." Apemantus's words about sharing the same dish with an alleged friend are apt to have evoked also the advice of Ecclesiasticus 13:7 not to befriend the rich and powerful who shame the poor in their meat until they have "supped" them twice or thrice. Thus the image turns cannibalistic, and cannibalistic images were customarily applied to usurers in Shakespeare's time.[14] Like other such images, it is inseparable from animal imagery; to Dr. Johnson it suggested a pack of hounds being rewarded with the blood of animals they have killed in a hunt.[15] As an animal image, it suggests the kind of moral warning of Ecclesiasticus 13:20 that the poor are the meat of the rich as the wild asses are those of the lion.

The function of the analogues to the Christ story is not to enhance Timon's moral quality but to lower that of his friends by emphasizing their disloyalty. If the figure of the phoenix suggests Christ, it is to intimate that what his friends are doing is not merely a stripping bare of a man but also a kind of crucifixion. We are thus teased into considering the events in a somewhat different light. True, Timon is no Christ, but he is still the only one in his circle who is generous and has faith in others. Would not his friends seek to exploit and ruin him just as well if he were more Christ-like, if he were indeed Christ? And would not a man who sought to apply Christian ethics in this society be destroyed as much as is Timon? An even more disturbing question: would not any man who did so be destroyed in any society?

Both as a philanthropist and as a misanthrope, Timon is a man of large and, in their effect on others, futile gestures. His ideas always exceed his means. He wants to give kingdoms to his friends but settles for bankruptcy. His later attempt to invoke cosmic powers for the destruction of mankind is absurd in view of his inability to shock anyone except a bandit, and not even him permanently. But if everything that Timon does is impractical, the same could be said about greater idealists in human history who have revolted against the utilitarian attitude and the self-interest of their societies.

Timon's projection of himself beyond reality creates a measure of the smallness and insignificance of the others. His idealism shows up their materialism, his financial recklessness makes their selfish computations more glaring, his emotional desire for friendship brings out their callous commercialism, and his cosmic expansiveness throws their lack of concern into relief.

Granted Timon's expansive nature and his solipsistic self-projection, his change to misanthropy, though dramatic and spectacular, is not so surprising. As R. Swigg says, with an accent more unsympathetic than mine, "His misanthropy is a logical extension of his philanthropy, and blown up in size."[16] Leigh Hunt put it more positively: his misanthropy is due to "an unexpected and extreme conviction of the hollowness of the human heart."[17] One could call this an eudaimonistic pessimism since it is a reaction to a too optimistic view of life and man. Timon's feeling of joy and elation, of happiness among his friends, gives way when his illusion of their goodness is shattered and they, whom he regally entertained and overwhelmed with gifts, become merciless creditors. His nausea turns into universal hatred. If it is argued that the "ordinary" ingratitude of Timon's friends is not a serious enough cause for such a change, the argument betrays a rather complacent attitude about human wickedness and about violations of basic social mores and codes. Timon is justified in conceiving this ingratitude as symbolic of general human evil rather than as a commercial meanness restricted to one time and place. The Renaissance moralists, for whom ingratitude was one of the greatest human vices, would have felt likewise.[18] And so surely do we. Such an act threatens the whole notion of community and presages atomistic chaos. We must expect a violent reaction to this threat from a man of Timon's temper and idealism; he whose conception of friendship was high, falls deep. Should Timon take ingratitude as less than monstrous, he would abandon whatever residual value lies in his benevolence; he would deny what he and we felt ennobled him and what he imagined ennobled his friends. His total rejection and all-encompassing hatred prove that, as much as his concept of friendship is flawed and he himself beset with contradictions, his earlier inclusive love is yet rooted in his soul deeply enough to lead to a loss of his desire for living.

It is undeniable, I think, that through his hatred Timon grows in intellectual acumen. His pessimistic thoughts are more probing, if fierce and violent, than his optimistic ones; and his gestures, although equally useless in their effect on the Athenians, are more sweeping and impressive. The mock banquet is better designed than the banquet of sense, and it is its ingenious antithesis. Instead of the music of oboes, we hear the harsh sound of the trumpet; instead of sentimentality, there is mockery; instead of Cupid leading the absurd Amazons, Nemesis drives out the parasites. The food does not flatter the senses now: the lukewarm water does not delight the taste; the smoke lacks the beguiling odor of delicate meats; the hardness of stones hurts the sense of touch. Nor are the eyes delighted by a masque; rather, the societal disorder is caricatured by the topsy-turvy flight of the guests. The mock banquet, like the earlier masque, is again Timon's device, but this time he firmly controls its symbolism.

It is natural for us to wish that Timon would achieve some greater self-knowledge, some understanding beyond the recognition of the folly of his giving. Dramatically, this is unthinkable. No self-knowledge in the humanistic sense can occur since it would require of Timon a recognition that he lacked temperance; after this an outbreak of misanthropy would be impossible. Nor does the moral frame established by Shakespeare make us expect Timon to gain such knowledge: temperance presupposes measure and norm, and the play does not provide these; there is no character that is not in some manner corrupted or corruptible. Timon's reactions cannot be viewed as a deviation from definite human standards; the play presents no such standards, and if we supply them, we do so at our peril. Given the world in which Timon lives, his reaction, even if startling in its singularity, is not exactly indecorous or outrageous.

Shakespeare provided Timon with an awakening from ignorance, which is not the same thing as humanistic self-knowledge, but which entails a total self-change. The discoveries Timon makes are intellectually and dramatically impressive enough not to be wafted aside, vexing as they may be for the optimistic believer in humanity. The program for the change comes appropriately at the beginning of the fourth act as demarcated in this study. At the end of the third act, Timon strips himself naked (an outward manifestation of his emancipation) and asks that his hatred grow to include all mankind. From now on, he is totally alienated from society, and he sees nothing in man, even himself, but villany:

> Therefore be abhorr'd
> All feasts, societies, and throngs of men!
> His semblable, yea himself, Timon disdains.
>
> (4.3.[4.1.] 20–22)

Since Timon's alienation includes self-alienation, it implies some recognition of his responsibility or, better, of his complicity in the failure of mankind. This self-view is in conformity with his misanthropy; it is a kind of self-knowledge, although we may shudder at the pessimistic implication it contains.

On the limited subject of the reasons for the corruption of society, Timon sees now very clearly, and his acuity grows as his thoughts circle around it. As Winifred Nowottny has pointed out, a development of thought, even if in staccato fashion, is traceable through his soliloquies.[19] It leads to his forcefully stripping off the old hypocrisies. He visualizes now a world in which all patterns have broken up so irrevocably that further confusion is the only possibility and destruction the only warranted action. He calls for the subversion of all order, the dissolution of loyalty, piety, and human fellowship, the disappearance of family feelings, the disintegration of households, and the perversion of offices:

> Piety and fear,
> Religion to the gods, peace, justice, truth,
> Domestic awe, night-rest and neighbourhood,
> Instruction, manners, mysteries and trades,
> Degrees, observances, customs and laws,
> Decline to your confounding contraries;
> And yet confusion live!
>
> (4.1.[3.7]15–21)

This is the end of one phase of Timon's development. We should not separate it by an act division from what goes before.

Timon's next soliloquy, the first in the wood, takes a somewhat different tack. He now assails the myth of order as a mere smokescreen that hides the subservience to Fortune. Men lack respect for real superiority; their distinctions are not based on merit. "Degree" is due merely to fortune: "Raise me this beggar, and deny't that lord, / The senators shall bear contempt hereditary, / The beggar native honour" (4.3.[4.1.] 9–11). This soliloquy leads up to Timon's finding the gold and with it to his denunciation of the metal as the agent and symbol of the world's disarrangements. Timon is now in the last phase of his misanthropy, which is characterized by the increased vehemence of his rhetoric. His curses breathe an apocalyptic horror; they demand the disintegration of the whole cosmic fabric from the smallest unit, the family, to the largest, the universe.

Admittedly, the development I have sketched is not straight-line. Timon strikes some apocalyptic notes early, and strands of the older theme of the falsity of the myth of order are still woven into his later speeches of annihilation, as, for instance, when Timon insults the Athenians in their own hypocritical idiom and invites them to hang themselves on his tree "in the sequence of degree, / From high to low throughout" (5.1.207–8). But generally there is a growing violence of themes and language. Timon's curses and maledictions surpass in intensity and comprehensiveness even Lear's raging in the storm, their nearest rival. The kinetic and cosmic images of these speeches carry Timon from an anti-human to a superhuman stance; they overwhelm the mind with a style that is livelier than life. To use the convenient term, they are baroque.

The critic who recognized this style in *Timon* (although he did not expressly call it baroque) was Peter Ure, and it made him uncomfortable. Of Timon's misanthropic speeches, Ure said:

> The extraordinary inclusiveness of his condemnation of all human and animal life and of all Nature is a thing for wonder and dismay. We contemplate him with amazement because he goes so far; but after a while the amazement palls, just as the magnified creatures of Dryden's heroic plays—"as far above the ordinary proportions of the stage, as that is beyond the words and action of common life"—at first make us gasp and stretch our eyes, but later begin to languish before our desire that they should do more than parade their excess.[20]

But these speeches do more than parade their over-advertised excess, and amazement and discomfort are not the only reaction we have to them. For one thing, they disturb us sufficiently to make us ask the question of how to cope with them. L. C. Knights, for instance, ponders why "the speeches of disgust and vituperation addressed to mankind at large are extraordinarily powerful, yet at the same time distorted and excessive," and he rightly adds that "the problem is how to take them."[21] Knights's answer to this question, namely, that we must attribute them to Timon's flawed humanity, strikes me as a less significant critical reaction than his realization that there is a problem. An earlier critic, Swinburne, whose ear was more attuned to infuriated raptures, said that "in the great and terrible fourth act of *Timon* we find such tragedy as Juvenal might have written when half deified with the spirit of Aeschylus."[22] And Timon's speeches have made others think of Isaiah.[23] One reason surely that they are so powerful is that they belong to a tradition of unpleasant observations about man to which we would like to close our ears but which we cannot deny to be at least partially true. They are harsh and grating, but the prophet's trumpet has never sounded pleasant to those whom he calls. The Athenians disregard the trumpet and find Timon diseased; somehow we feel that we should not react in the same manner, since Timon's disease has a way of making their self-proclaimed sanity look ill.

We may well wonder about the effect of Timon's curses and prophecies on Shakespeare's audience at a time when the English were turning into a nation of prophets and the literature that dwelled on man's misery and wickedness was increasing in volume and intensity.[24] This question becomes even more intriguing when we consider that the two pessimistic sources of the Timon story, Barckley's *Discourse* and Boaistuau's *Theatrum Mundi* belonged to this tide. Timon was not merely a strange character in them but also a kind of prophet of the human sickness unto death. Boaistuau, in particular, saw the signs of the world's deadly disease everywhere; the wickedness of man as well as the destructiveness of natural forces signaled the coming end. The world was generally assumed to be anthropocentric; if man, the microcosm, decayed and declined, the macrocosm had to do so perforce, and therefore the eschatological writers discerned signs of the decay en masse in both. They generalized that man was idle, drunken, luxurious, riotous, ambitious, proud, greedy, atheistic, and deceitful; he violated the sabbath worship, suffered priests to be deaf and blind to their flocks, let usurers extort money from their fellow men, rebelled against lawful authority, and so forth. Concomitantly, the writers saw numerous signs of natural decay: soaring of the seas, trembling of the earth, eclipses, unnatural births, ugly monsters, and what not. The variously calculated six thousand years of the life of the earth were thought to be running out, and the apocalypse was approaching.[25] As Thomas Draxe wrote in *The General Signs and Forerunners of Christ's Coming Judgment* (1608), the last signal had appeared; this signal, "yet in motion and not perfectly fulfilled but to continue unto the world's end, is the vanity, corruption, and abuse of the creatures, which has continued from Adam's fall and doth and shall increase by degree unto the consummation of all things."[26]

Timon's repeated addresses to nature, which are reminiscent of Lear's raging in the storm and echo his call for the spilling of nature's germens, derive like these their teleological and cosmological significance from the belief in the interconnected decay of man and nature. Timon's speeches abound with a cosmic imagery, which, as we shall see later, belongs to the context of Renaissance cosmological pessimism and apocalyptic prophecy. In the fearful climate in which this pessimism flourished, Timon's curses and apostrophes to nature must have had a topical ring and disturbed the audience in a manner similar to that of the incessant blasts of the apocalyptic preachers. Timon must have looked

to them like an ancient antecedent of the preachers of gloom
and doom in their midst, perhaps a false preacher to some,
a man with an inkling of the truth to others.

There was then a particular relevance to Timon's last
words, his invitation to the Athenians to come to his grave,
that we can no longer altogether capture:

> Thither come,
> And let my grave-stone be your oracle.
> Lips, let four words go by and language end:
> What is amiss, plague and infection mend!
> Graves only be men's works and death their gain;
> Sun, hide thy beams, Timon hath done his reign.
>
> (5.1.217–22)

The word *oracle* provides a reminder that Timon is an
ancient Greek; but the prophecy itself has a pseudo-biblical
rhythm, and its content has a sufficient similarity to what the
Christian predictors in Shakespeare's time were saying to
have struck Shakespeare's audience by its resemblance. The
"four words" that are to go by evoke the four horsemen of
the apocalypse and in general the magic number four associated with apocalyptic prophecies.[27] Plague and infection, as
Timon wishes them on mankind, were taken as signs of the
decay of the world and God's wrath toward mankind, as for
instance by Boaistuau, who thought the element air in the
service of this wrath "so pernicious to human kind when it
putrifieth and corrupteth that the most part of pestilences
and infections take their original and beginning from their
very author [i.e., the air]."[28] The apocalyptic tracts of Shakespeare's time prophesied a darkening of the earth at the Last
Judgment in the manner of Timon's demand that the sun
hide its beams; as Christ had said, "And immediately after
the tribulation of those days shall the sun be darkened and
the moon shall not give her light and the stars be shaken"
(Math. 24:29; cf. Mark 13:24, Luke 21:25). The latter analogy, as has not escaped commentators, could be interpreted
as Timon's casting himself in the role of a pseudo-Christ;
but Christ himself spoke here as a prophet and in the language of prophecy.

We, whose apocalyptic fears are generally confined to the
threats that are created by man, such as pollution and the
hydrogen bomb, and that are therefore, we hope, subject to
man's control, cannot quite feel the topical urgency that
Timon's words had to the Jacobeans. But we too respond in
some manner to the incantatory tone of the curse and the
vision of annihilation. Aware as we are, here and elsewhere,
of Timon's impotence to turn any of his visions into reality,
we still cannot quite free ourselves from the atavistic power
of his curse. It is through the magic of his language that

Timon exerts this power; yet with nihilistic logic he seeks the end of all language, and he stills his own.

In the final analysis, it is the magic of language Shakespeare bestowed on Timon that gives us the feeling that Timon's descent into misanthropy marks a growth of his powers and has the aspect of an ascent. Unable as he is to move the Athenians, he casts a spell over us. His awesome eloquence affirms his human power even in his inhuman phase; we dare not say that it affirms his human greatness.

6

Apemantus and the Others

That numberless upon me stuck

Timon of Athens is in a very eminent way Timon's play. Among Shakespeare's tragic heroes, only Hamlet ranks higher in his relative share of words; but there is no character in *Timon* comparable to the significance of Claudius, no antagonist properly speaking, and even the three most verbal characters after Timon—Apemantus, Flavius, and Alcibiades—merely achieve the verbal level of such secondary characters as Polonius and Horatio.[1] Timon is not only the overpowering voice, he is also even more signally the center of the thought of his play than Hamlet is the center of his. Apemantus, it is true, has a role in initiating major themes, but he serves very largely to introduce the Timonesque view of society before the protagonist turns misanthrope.

Since Timon amplifies and varies the cynical notes struck earlier by Apemantus, the two reinforce each other; and whatever we may think of them as characters, we find it hard to disprove their pessimism. There are no major characters with whom we can sympathize fully and without reserve: no Banquo, no Cordelia, no Virgilia even. Shakespeare's sympathetic characters are often women, and *Timon* has no major feminine role; its women are objects of pleasure, dancers and prostitutes, and the dramatic statements made through them are derogatory and unpleasant. Timon's loyal servants, particularly Flavius, attract some sympathy; but since they have no major part in the action, they have only a limited influence on our moral bearings. Shakespeare evidently was intent on painting a comprehensively dark picture of Athenian society without giving strong dramatic prominence to anyone but Timon. In no other play is there such a collective anonymity of minor characters. We do not know who was responsible for the imposing full page of "The Actors Names" in the First Folio, but it certainly shows this tendency clearly; it lists "certain senators," "certain maskers," "certain thieves," and "diverse other servants and attendants." The Folio lists dramatis personae for four other plays; none of them has anything comparable. In the text itself, when the names of minor characters are given, it is often for situational identification rather than for individualization. For instance, Lucilius is singled out as the one among Timon's servants who wants to marry the greedy Athenian's daughter (1.1.114, 117); after this scene, in which he says next to nothing, he disappears from the play. Ventidius is identified as the friend whom Timon keeps out of debtor's prison, and we are made to keep him in mind by his offering to pay back Timon, so that a later mention of his name as one who has refused to help Timon suffices to recall the gratitude that he owes and to which he fails to live up. But he is not individualized; in the Folio list he is rightly designated as "one of Timon's false friends": he is an outstandingly odious representative of an odious group.

Shakespeare used names in such a referential way generally only to conjure up the existence of armies, and in *Timon* too he evidently wished to create a semblance of large numbers with a small number of actors. We must assume that Timon has many servants, although we learn the names of only four (including the steward); and we must believe that Timon has many false friends, although again only four are identified by names. Adapters and producers of the play have often tried mistakenly to establish more "order" by conflating roles, e.g., that of the steward with one of Timon's other servants or those of the merely numbered lords at the banquets with Timon's named friends. But Shakespeare seems to have aimed at producing the impression of disorder rather than order; Athenian society presents a frighteningly anonymous, almost Kafkaesque, chaos. For instance, in the first scene, we encounter two unnamed lords, Alcibiades with his "twenty horse," and "certain senators" who pass over the stage. Surely on Shakespeare's stage the number of members of groups like the senators, Timon's guests, and the bandits would have been increased beyond the speaking roles assigned according to the availability of actors. As much credibility as possible would have to be given to Timon's complaint that "the mouths, the tongues, the eyes and hearts of men" stuck upon him "numberless" (4.3.263–65) and also to Apemantus's prediction that Timon will be "thronged to" in the forest (397).

In the first three acts, the method of mentioning names resembles that of mentioning sums given and owed by Timon: the actual names, like the actual sums, are significant only for creating a cumulative impression of Timon's large giving and large indebtedness. When the unnamed senator counts up Timon's debts, he refers to Varro and Isidore (2.1.1 ff.). Neither the senator nor these two creditors appear in order to collect from Timon, but the servants of the latter do, and they are joined by Caphis, an unknown creditor's servant, in importuning Timon (2.2.10 ff.). When the usurers' servants beleaguer Timon in his own house, we learn four new names: Titus, Hortensius, Philotus, and Lucius (the latter presumably being the servant of the Lucius whom Timon singled out for special favors and who refused to aid him). Just as the sums mentioned increase, so does the number of creditors.

In the large degree of namelessness and in the frequent use of professional or class designations, *Timon* resembles *Coriolanus* with its first, second, and third senator, first and second soldier, and several numbered but unnamed citizens. In both plays, such non-individualized characters help to create a panorama of a society, and the picture is unpleasant. It is, however, more so in *Timon;* corruption and degradation penetrate here all segments and strata: the worlds of art, commerce, trade, and politics are all deeply corrupted. What need is there to give names? Change a name or a face, the total impression remains the same. No wonder that Brecht liked the play.

The method of denigration by numbering is most apparent and most brilliant in the case of the senators. Although, when added together, they speak more lines than Alcibiades, we never learn a single senator's name, and except for the one senator who starts the avalanche against Timon, they always appear in numbers. No matter whether the same or different actors were used in Shakespeare's time for their various appearances, they must have worn identical robes, which tended to make the audience identify one group with the others. They are a collective anonymity that we come to associate with usury and greed. The senators who seek out Timon in the woods and those who supplicate Alcibiades to pardon Athens cannot help but evoke the previous senatorial meanness, particularly since they still speak in a language larded with commercial metaphors. Only the circumstances have changed; the mental habits remain the same.

However, when it suited Shakespeare's dramatic purpose, he characterized even minor figures sharply. He did so in the three scenes in which Timon's friends and exploiters—Lucullus, Lucius, and Sempronius—come to Timon's aid (3.1–3). These scenes invite comparison with the handling of a similar situation by Thomas Heywood in *A Woman Killed with Kindness* (pt. 1607), when Susan Mountford appeals to three relatives and friends to help her bankrupt brother and is turned down in quick succession. I venture to think that Shakespeare was induced by this scene of Heywood's (3.3) to demonstrate what he could make of such a simple situation; characterization by contiguous triplicity was not usually his method. Some of the commonplace refusals of Heywood's characters seem to be echoed and varied by Shakespeare's. The second stranger's comment "Men must learn now with pity to dispense, / For policy sits above conscience" (3.2.88–89) resembles Old Mountford's "This is no world to pity men"—not a bad line for Heywood. Lucullus's "this is no time to lend money, especially upon bare friendship, without security" (3.1.41–43) has the same tune and might have been written by Heywood except for the "especially" and "bare." But there is no differentiation of the three refusers in Heywood; they stay on one level of platitudes. In *Timon*, however, the lying evasion of Lucius goes a step beyond the crude refusal and open scorn of Lucullus, and it is trumped by the odious self-righteousness of Sempronius.

In addition, Shakespeare provided mirror commentaries subtly varied in inflection, vocabulary, imagery, and prosody. The plain but poetic eloquence of the servant Flaminius shows up the commonplace vulgarity of Lucullus, and both contrast with the more refined moralistic idiom of the two stranger lords. Lucius's distortion of honor is generalized by them into a perversion of religion and a metamorphosis of the world's soul. The servant's concluding comment on the refined villainy of Sempronius is even stronger in its recoil from villainy: "The devil knew not what he did when he made man politic; he crossed himself by 't: and I cannot think but in the end the villainies of man will set him clear" (3.3.29–30). "Politic" man is worse than the devil for this servant who speaks in the idiom of the people and makes us like it. Altogether, the mirror commentaries combine with the episodes on which they comment to create differentiated but cumulative accounts of villainy.

However, only Alcibiades, Apemantus, and Flavius can be said to be really individualized. Flavius is perhaps a borderline case since he is often understood to be merely a type of loyal servant who warns his master and seeks to aid him in distress. It is sometimes claimed that Shakespeare quickly forgot that he had named the steward Flavius since he used the name only once for him (1.2.153) and later, by mistake, for another servant (2.2.189). But this latter error was presumably the compositor's rather than Shakespeare's, and the one mention of his name is certainly sufficient for identification.

Flavius has a surprisingly large share of words; he is only slightly behind Apemantus, who, as a satirist and philosopher, is expected to trade in words, and he is considerably ahead of Alcibiades. This relative verbosity, I think, comes from an individualizing feature of his character that is generally overlooked: a fondness for sonorous phrases and noble commonplaces. It shows itself most in the scene just after Timon's departure from Athens when the steward laments with three other servants the fall of Timon's house and decides, by himself, to follow his master. There is genuine pathos here, but also, on the steward's part, sentimental exaggeration. He wants it to be recorded "by the righteous gods" that he is as poor as the other servants (4.2.4–5). Actually, he still has something left: "The latest of my wealth I'll share amongst you" (23). What he says about a possible future meeting, in which the servants might come together and shake their heads as a "knell unto our master's fortunes" (26), borders on the ludicrous. The steward exaggerates also when he claims that he is distributing to the servants the "latest" of his wealth; he evidently has enough gold left to take some to Timon. I am not suggesting that Flavius is a humbug or deceiver; he is kind and well-meaning, but he likes pathos and sinks into bathos. This is most notable in the long soliloquy, longer by ten lines than any of Alcibiades' speeches, that ends the scene. These lines read almost like eighteenth-century sentimentalism. One must not of course expect Flavius to evaluate Timon impartially; but he gives Timon much too noble a character when he attributes his fall to "goodness," and he talks merely nonsense when he sees in it a simple natural law according to which glory must produce misery.

When the steward finally arrives at Timon's lair (does he have to persuade himself to carry out his intention?), he self-consciously protests his honor, honesty, and truth—a protest that provides the cue for Timon to play a sly game with him. Flavius's endeavor to help Timon and in the process show himself honorable is bathed in situational irony; he is unaware that his wish that his master should have "power and wealth / To requite me, by making rich yourself [Timon]" (4.3.525–26) is already fulfilled. If we were to have faith in his abiding sense of honor, he should not accept the gold given to him with pernicious advice. Timon knows his servant's weakness for sentimental paradoxes and exploits it by saying that the gods have sent treasure out of Timon's misery—it is hardly honorable to build on somebody else's misery. Since Flavius does not protest against the idea, one may well wonder how long even the best of the Athenians will pursue honor beyond his financial interests. It may be symptomatic that he, man of property himself now, reappears at Timon's cave, contrary to the misanthrope's wishes, as a guide to the senatorial delegation.

A moral ambiguity is also evident in the portrait of Apemantus. There is no doubt about his being individualized: he is unforgettable, and his character is built up carefully and gradually. He gives at first the impression of a total, if rough, integrity; he keeps apart from the contagious society around Timon, and he warns him against his flatterers. However, in practice, Apemantus too depends on Timon and uses him, even if not in the crude manner of his friends. The poet need not be believed when he says that Apemantus "drops down / The knee before him, and returns in peace / Most rich in Timon's nod" (1.1.61–64); actually Apemantus is quite insulting to Timon even though what he says is true, and he pays him homage only to the degree of considering him worthy of receiving his warnings, whereas he has nothing but scorn for his friends. But his singling out Timon for attention is not mere altruism; Apemantus likes to be right, and his smug attitude after Timon's fall gives one the feeling that he has been looking forward to seeing his philosophy proved true. If Apemantus does not belong to those whose mouth is stuck on Timon, to adapt Timon's fanciful figure, his eyes and tongue are.

Apemantus, like Timon, was essentially Shakespeare's own creation. The little about him in the sources was useless for Shakespeare's purposes. Plutarch conceived him as the misanthrope's confidant: "This Timon would have Apemantus in his company because he was like to his nature and conditions and also followed him in manner of life."[2] Cicero in *De amicitia* suggested Apemantus was Timon's misanthropic ally: "Nay, even if anyone were of a nature so savage and fierce as to loathe the society of men—such, for example, as tradition tells us a certain Timon of Athens once was—yet even such a man could not refrain from seeking some person before whom he might pour out the venom of his embittered soul."[3] Shakespeare was wise not to follow Plutarch and Cicero in these points: a friendly Apemantus had no place at the side of a prosperous and optimistic Timon, and if Shakespeare had made Apemantus into the receptacle of Timon's misanthropic effusions, he would have committed a mistake similar to Shadwell's and Cumberland's when they provided him, respectively, with a lover and a daughter.

Apemantus is sometimes said to be in the pattern of that other railer against Greek society, Thersites in *Troilus and Cressida*. But the two share little more than a few tricks, and the scurrilous commentary and sarcastic repartee in which they both excel are used for different purposes. Thersites has no moral fervor; he is no cynic but an allowed fool, and if he lives in the gutter, he does not do so because of philosophical principles. More pertinently, Jan Simko has noticed that Apemantus's function resembles the fool's in *Lear* by uttering truths unpleasant to the tragic hero and criticizing his actions.[4]

Apemantus, more than the fool and much more than Thersites, sets himself apart from the society on which he comments. This is evident even in his manner of speech. It is often as if he were addressing no one in particular; his contemptuous muttering gives some of his remarks the quality of asides without their being that in the technical sense of the word—the banquet offers examples. The very rhythm of his speech differs; as Bryan Vickers has noted, many of his lines have a status between prose and verse, tending toward twelve-feet doggerel. He hardly ever speaks more than two lines of blank verse before he falls into doggerel or prose.[5] No other character talks in such a skipping manner— an idiosyncracy surely due to deliberate characterization rather than to the play's lack of finish. The gruff Apemantus, philosopher of low-keyed pessimism, does not think mankind worthy of the passionate idiom that modulates Timon's misanthropy. Often, he caps his dicta with pessimistic morals about human nature, morals that have a proverbial ring but that, at least in Apemantus's sarcastic form, cannot be found in traditional proverb lore. He is in his element at the banquet: "Those healths will make thee and thy state look ill, Timon" (1.2.56–57); "Feasts are too proud to give thanks to the gods" (61); "Men shut their doors against a setting sun" (141); "O that men's ears should be / To counsel deaf, but not to flattery" (250–51).

A general model for Apemantus can be discerned in the picture of the cynic philosopher as the Renaissance conceived him.[6] John Lily had established the dramatic prototype by the Diogenes of his *Alexander and Campaspe* (1584) who talks back to Alexander somewhat as does Apemantus to Timon. Also, as Peter Pauls has noted, the popular Renaissance Diogeniana provided a rich mine of anecdotes about the cynics and sayings by them of which Shakespeare seems to have been aware. One of these sources was Richard

Barckley's *Discourse* with its short Timon biography.[7] The satirists, in particular, found Diogenes a convenient mouthpiece for their discontents with their own time. Thomas Lodge in *Catharos: Diogenes in His Singularity* (1594) had Diogenes criticize usurers, false friends and flatterers, divines, lawyers, and merchants with quite contemporary applications. Arthur Warren in *The Poor Man's Passions and Poverty's Patience* (1605) wondered what "cousin Diogenes" would say in this "frozen-hearted age" were he alive.[8] Diogenes' popularity as a satirist helped give Athens a bad name; owing to the analogy with England, he was also a kind of contemporary critic of morals. Apemantus is a relative of this Diogenes and as such also a relative of Elizabethan-Jacobean satirists.

As a member of the cynic family, he is a "dog-philosopher": "cynic" was held to be derived from Greek *kunikos*, "doglike,"—an etymology that, together with the cynics' life-style, earned them the epithet of "dogs". Diogenes wittily returned the compliment; Apemantus smartly anticipates it in his first words of the play, before the others have the opportunity to call him a dog, as they amply do later:

> *Tim.* Good morrow to thee, gentle Apemantus.
> *Apem.* Till I be gentle, stay thou for thy good morrow,
> When thou art Timon's dog, and these knaves honest.
>
> (1.1.180–82)

"Honest" is one of Apemantus's key words as it was one of Diogenes'. His opener to Timon is a purposive boorishness, which after the elegant flatteries of the jeweler and others goes to demonstrate the plainness of honesty. Apemantus puts his satirical spotlight on the general dishonesty by wanting to "knock out an honest Athenian's brains" (192)—an impossible endeavor because of a lack of candidates with honesty and brains. Like Diogenes, Apemantus is a great exposer of the truth hidden beneath appearances. He demonstrates this skill first with the painter and the poet: the former is but a filthy piece of work and the latter a feigner and flatterer. The merchant is next: traffic is his god. He continues his campaign against dishonesty with a characteristic answer to a question about the time of day: "Time to be honest" (256).

Apemantus's credentials as a cynic are clearest in his insistence, by word and example, on the need to lead a simple, frugal life. For Apemantus, this is but another side of plain honesty. When Timon asks him how he likes a jewel, he answers, "Not so well as plain-dealing, which will not cost a man a doit" (1.1.210–11). He shuns meat and wine for roots and "honest water" (1.2.59–71). During the dance, he contrasts the madness and the glory around him with the "little oil and root" necessary to sustain life (1.2.130–31). Apemantus lives according to nature and reduces his needs in order to escape the corrupting influence of civilization. His self-sufficiency contrasts with the luxury, hypocrisy, and disorder around him. He fittingly exposes the myth of friendship and harmony at Timon's banquet and during the masque, and what he says about the ensuing dance is moral commentary in the best cynic vein. Here again, Diogenes pointed the way in a sentence attributed to him by Diogenes Laertius, according to which he was surprised when hearing music that "the musicians should tune the string of the lyre while having the disposition of their own souls discordant."[9] John Lily gave his Diogenes a very similar comment on a dancing lesson: "The musicians [are] very bad who only study to have their strings in tune, never framing their manners to order" (*Campaspe*, 5.1). This is the seminal idea for Apemantus's great speech that comments on the dance:

> What a sweep of vanity comes this way.
> They dance? They are madwomen.
> Like madness is the glory of this life,
> As this pomp shows to a little oil and root.
> We make ourselves fools, to disport ourselves,
> And spend our flatteries to drink those men
> Upon whose age we void it up again
> With poisonous spite and envy.
> Who lives that's not depraved or depraves?
> Who dies that bears not one spurn to their graves
> Of their friends' gift?
> I should fear that those that dance before me now
> Would one day stamp upon me. 'T'as been done.
> Men shut their doors against a setting sun.
>
> (1.2.128–41)

Denunciations of dancing were common in Shakespeare's time, but this one takes an unmistakably Apemantian turn by effectively undercutting the theme of the masque with its celebration of societal harmony. A masque of Cupid and Amazons was presumably intended to symbolize the reconciliation of love and war, Venus and Mars, and the concluding dance would have reenacted the creation of order and beauty through love; it was through love, after all, that man had learned how to dance and to imitate by his graceful movement the ordered universe, which itself was held together by a cosmic dance. So, at least, optimistic humanism had it. By his sarcastic comment on the dance, Apemantus makes a ceremony glorifying order into a mocking exposure of disorder. One might even say that Apemantus speaks in the tone of the grotesque anti-masque, which in the full Jonsonian form preceded the orderly masque; in this form the antic show ended when the main actors appeared. But Apemantus's commentary demonstrates that Athenian life itself is a kind of disorderly anti-masque. The dance in Timon's hall is not a cosmic-societal celebration but a dance of fortune, a motif used by the emblematists[10]

Apemantus signally lives up to the reputation of the cynics as angry and furious creatures. Medieval and Renaissance writers saw in this anger some of the sparks that ignited the just anger of the prophets: excessive as this wrath was, it betrayed a fervor for moral purity. It is characteristic of the failure of the Athenians and of the liberal Timon to see no alleviating features in Apemantus's churlishness. Timon even lectures Apemantus on his "humor," which does "not become a man," and finds him a contradiction to the maxim *"Ira foror brevis est"* (the Horatian phrase is an amusing anachronism); Apemantus is "very angry," which, of course, means here also "always angry" (1.2.26–29). These lines strike for the first time the theme of wrath, and they point forward to the later irate competition the two have at Timon's cave. It will be Apemantus then who thinks Timon infected by a humor (4.3.204). Timon's characterization of Apemantus and the Horatian tag set the stage for paralleling and comparing two angry men, and Alcibiades' quarrel with the senate adds a third. Timon's wrath will become greater and more ingrained than that of his two foils; it will ironically prove the truth of his own phrase that anger is a short madness since it will be brief and self-consuming.

Apemantus is true to cynic form in his demonstrative asceticism. This preoccupation of the cynics had been looked upon by ancient and medieval writers with a mixture of awe and scorn. The anecdotes about the cynics showed them in an ambiguous light, humble and yet arrogant in their humility. Diogenes Laertius, for instance, quoted Plato as saying, "How much pride you expose to view, Diogenes, by not seeming to be proud."[11] And Apemantus embodies a similar paradox. Early in the play he shows a certain satisfaction about being a cynic, and we are given a progressive revelation of his professional pride. When Apemantus says to Timon, "I'll lock thy heaven from thee" (1.2.249) he indicates his belief that he has the power to administer and to withhold the truth; one realizes that he is looking forward to revealing heaven to Timon later.

Apemantus's self-complacency shows just a little more in his conversation with the fool, an episode built on a double irony: the usurers' servants happily approach Apemantus and the fool because they expect to poke fun at them, but Apemantus turns the tables and has his sport with them.

However, he too is bested—by the fool, of all people. Although this fool is not one of Shakespeare's great ones—but then we are not allowed to enjoy him long—he has something of the paradoxical wit and appealing honesty of wise folly that transcends the wisdom of the philosophers. He knows that the world is full of fools and that foolishness and wit are relative: "As much foolery as I have, so much wit thou lack'st," he says to a servant. This elicits from Apemantus the admiring comment: "That answer might have become Apemantus" (2.2.120–22). Apemantus's is the ultimate compliment, and it betrays self-admiration. That the philosopher who tells the servants that they do not know themselves (68) should have this blind spot in self-knowledge is one of the subtler ironies of the play.

Apemantus's professional vanity shows mightily in his visit to Timon in the wood. Benevolence is not totally absent from Apemantus's motives—he has brought some food for Timon—but competitive envy appears the main reason: he has heard that the misanthrope affects his manners and uses them (4.3.200–201). His "Do not assume my likeness" (220) is an indication of pride in his image. Apemantus enjoys having a monopoly in pessimism and cynicism, much as earlier Timon had enjoyed his monopoly of giving, and he sees it threatened.

In the debate itself, the central dialectic of ideas in the play, Apemantus does score some hits, or else it were not a good match; but there can be little doubt that Timon wins. Apemantus begins well by rubbing in Timon's subjection to flatterers and by asking him to try being a flatterer of Nature now. But Timon gives him his own medicine by accusing Apemantus of flattering misery (236). Then Timon asks Apemantus why he has come, and when the latter denies any altruistic motive by saying that his purpose is merely to vex Timon, the misanthrope calls this pursuit "always a villain's office, or a fool's." Timon then elicits from the cynic the concession that he is pleased with this role—it is evident now, if it was not before, that the poet was quite wrong when he said that Apemantus loves to abhor himself; he should have said that he loves to abhor others and man in general. Timon can easily turn Apemantus's admission of pleasure in his role of gadfly into a confession of knavery: "What, a knave too" (239–40).

Timon has the edge not only by laying effective traps but also by using arguments on human needs, which should be the cynic's forte. Apemantus has the disadvantage of not having seen the gold or he would not argue that Timon has put on "the sour cold habit . . . enforcedly" (241–43). Apemantus seems to be trying to live up to the etymology of his name, *apemantos*, "the one unharmed by fortune"; but his axiom that "willing misery / Outlives incertain pomp, is crown'd before" (44–45) has a touch of competitive vanity and suggests that he would like to wear a martyr's crown—comfortably. By comparison, Timon's contrasting of his own temptation by fortune with Apemantus's protection from it by poverty and hereditary roguery is a good *argumentum ad hominem*, which counts in this context. Also, Timon's question "What hast thou given?" evokes his own past generosity and hints appropriately at egotism in his opponent (272).

Apemantus's best retort comes when Timon vaunts his suffering and insults Apermantus because of his beggary:

Apem.   Art thou proud yet?
Tim. Ay, that I am not thee.
Apem.   I, that I was
No prodigal.
Tim.   I, that I am one now.
Were all the wealth I have shut up in thee,
I'ld give thee leave to hang it. Get thee gone.

(279–82)

Apemantus does convict Timon of pride. But this is a pride inseparable from tragic glamor; Timon is the center of the action as both lover and hater, and Apemantus fails to move him from this point of gravity, fails to make Timon admit to the truth of the "heaven" he once showed and withheld from him. Timon's prodigal recklessness of giving, both in love and hate, dwarfs Apementus's self-centered wariness.

Apemantus does not improve his position by accusing Timon of extremity, the extremity of both ends, because the accusation draws into question whatever moral benefit Apemantus derived from his own position at the fringe of humanity. And another of Apemantus's better points, his showing that Timon's escape into nature is an invasion of a hostile realm, is bested by Timon's proving that Apemantus's view of nature is sentimental in its core: the cynic, who would rather be a beast with beasts, has not considered that there is a mutual enmity among animals—even animals are their own worst enemies, they too have their dishonesties, villainies, and cruelties, and possess in fact a kind of human depravity (325–47). Although Timon believes that animals are kinder to men than men are to themselves, he has no illusions about beasts in their own habitat.

The prize might still go to Apemantus if his quarrel with Timon were conceived as a contest on how to live. By his new mode of life, Timon has in practice accepted the argument that living according to nature's simple plan is preferable to wealth and luxury. But through Apemantus's competitiveness, the contest becomes one about the deeper anger, the more abiding pessimism. In this, Timon wins, not the least by his indifference to Apemantus and by his death-directedness. He does not need man, not even himself. As his thoughts turn to death, he envisages the end of all men so that "beasts / May have the world in empire" (394–95). He speaks these lines abstractly as he looks at the pernicious gold beneath him. Apemantus's words that draw him back to the world are comical in betraying an instinct for self-preservation and enjoyment of cynicism: "Would 'twere so! / But not till I am dead" (395–96).

The shouting match is an appropriate climax of the dynamics of pessimism that has developed between the two haters. Attitudes are here more important than issues. Both men are subject to pride, but that of Apemantus carries a professional handicap and lessens the effectiveness of his cynicism. As a fighter against vanity, Apemantus has acquired his own vanity. He is proud of what he does well, even if this comes close to saying that everything and everybody deserve to perish except himself. Wanting to do what one does well may be a universal human desire, but it is something of an indulgence for one who preaches restraint from all indulgence, a surrender of honesty for one who demands absolute honesty, too human a stance for a man "opposite to humanity" (1.1.272). Apemantus's wish to see the world find its destined end is undercut by his professional need of the world for his livelihood.

We may find it difficult to say what all this proves ideologically. Here as elsewhere Shakespeare was no ethical propagandist. The debate certainly does not proclaim cynicism or, for that matter, any kind of primitivism or asceticism as a panacea for the world's evil. If the debate suggests anything about remedies, it is that whatever is attempted, the human attitude with which these remedies are sought is more important than the measures themselves. If we focus on Apemantus, we may go further and say that unfortunately those who seek to reform the world are human beings whose personal flaws cannot be dissociated from their reforming efforts. We should hesitate to extract from this Shakespeare's ideas about human reform in general; if we did, we would have to say that he had no great faith in saints and human reformers.

As we look back at the dramatic role of Apemantus in the play, we see him raising some disturbing questions about men's conduct of their lives and giving a strong direction to the play's pessimism. In the first two acts, when Timon is in his optimistic dream, Apemantus is the deadly accurate commentator on, and satirist of, Athenian corruption. We would understand the degradation of Timon's friends and parasites without Apemantus, but he highlights it and puts it in ironic perspective. His barbs and churlish sayings prepare the ground for the later, more vehement onslaught of Timon, and they do so by anticipating most of the images and themes in the misanthrope's curses and diatribes. It is no exaggeration to say that Apemantus is the inventor and director of most of the play's characteristic images and word patterns. He either initiates these or gives them a pessimistic focus before they are taken up by others: the steward, the servants, Timon's creditors, Alcibiades, and, most of all, Timon when he turns misanthrope. The turning point occurs when Apemantus is not present, at the mock banquet. Timon now adopts Apemantus's attitude and copies even his speaking style when he comments sarcastically in muttered asides on the baseness of his friends. His prayer, a parallel to Apemantus's ironic grace at the first banquet, asks the gods not to let themselves be injured and disappointed by thankless men. Timon is therefore in a sense Apemantus's pupil, and Apemantus is his master; but the disciple outstrips the teacher in their contest at Timon's cave. Timon has now the greater power of invective, the greater contempt of man.

7

Patterns and Images

These hard fractions

The imagery of *Timon* is difficult to describe and categorize. It has a late-Shakespearean compression, multiple allusiveness, and dazzling mobility. In Timon's misanthropic speeches, when the words tumble almost helterskelter from his mouth, the images fuse into bewildering complexes. Earlier commentators, conditioned to find the play incomplete and defective, found the imagery also confusing and unsatisfactory.[1] However, Maurice Charney has noted in a brief discussion that "the imagery of *Timon* has an inner consistency that reflects the completeness of the play as a work of the imagination." Charney appropriately links his discussion of major image strands with a general characterization of the play's language and style. Unpleasant images denotive of disease and disgust loom large, and they fit into a general "anti-lyrical" style that aims at shock effects. Even though there are rough spots because of the state of the text, the language also has extraordinary felicities; often speeches pack complex meanings into concise phrases or imitate the sharp realism of colloquial speech.[2]

I too purpose to discuss the imagery of *Timon* in the context of Shakespeare's verbal strategy and to argue that it is powerful and right for this play. If the test of effective images is that they provide suggestions that emphasize and illuminate themes, support characterizations, and undergird the plot developments, the images of *Timon* are highly effective. They have a dramatic dynamism; where they are rugged and tortured, they express cacophanies in the characters' thoughts.

There is something prosaic about the imagery; the pictorial fancy is either subdued or, where it lights up, it does so disturbingly. *Timon* is a play of ideas, of pessimistic and brutal ideas; the images help to bring them out. Characteristic of the imagery is its alliance with, and sometimes inseparability from, word patterns, that is, iterations of thematically related words; and I shall therefore deal with word patterns and images together here. "Gold" is the example *par excellence* for their inseparability. The word occurs far more frequently in this play than in any other,[3] and it is imprinted strongly on our imagination, the more so as it becomes a "representational" or stage image when Timon digs up the treasure and hands out gold coins to his callers. Yet it hovers somewhere between a word pattern and an image; Caroline Spurgeon objected to Wilson Knight's calling it a persistent symbol and protested that it is merely a subject around which other images are clustered.[4] But it is surely a powerful symbol, the most powerful of the play. And if by "image" we understand a visually conceived idea, many of the references to gold qualify since they invoke vivid impressions of gold: it is a magnet, a bawd, a slave, a god, a destroyer and a killer. To classify these images under "physics," "servants," "deity," and "criminals" would be ridiculous.

The general direction of the images and speech patterns adapts itself to the dramatic structure and accentuates it. Most of the patterns are established by Apemantus and later appropriated, modified, or energized by Timon. The changeover, which begins at the mock banquet, is completed in Timon's climactic speech outside the walls, the scene that our redrawing of the act division assigns still to the third act as its climax. The Timon who appears in the next act in the woods is a different man who has mastered a new idiom. With this change, the whole style of the play undergoes a "remodeling," as Wolfgang Clemen puts it: "Instead of the consistently quiet manner of speaking only occasionally interrupted by exclamations of uneasiness, we have from the fourth act on a new form of utterance vehement in tone, loose in structure as to syntax and increased in speed."[5]

We may begin with images and patterns particularly associated with Timon. Characteristically, they are kinetic, emphasizing, or magnifying; they convey strength and force. Such are the "flowing" and "flood" metaphors. "Breathe" and "breath" also form a pattern suggestive of the hero's dynamism. Cosmic images join with these later when the misanthrope reaches for the ultimate in hatred. These images carry him beyond ordinary human dimensions and give his rhetoric, in spite of its negativism, a baroque intensity and exuberance.

The images suggestive of "flowing" and "flood," like the others, are relatively lightly struck in the opening scene, only to become much more emphatic later. The first impression we receive of Timon is that of his magnetic attraction, the "magic" of his bounty (1.1.6.). "This confluence, this great flood of visitors" (42) gathers in emulation of him at the bottom of Fortune's hill. The "flow" and "flood" patterns accompany even more forcefully the movement in the opposite direction when Timon spends and drains his resources: "He pours it out" (275). At the banquet, a lord demands that he "let it flow this way"—a metaphor that occasions Apemantus's remark that Timon's guest "keeps his tides well" (1.2.54–56). The steward moralizes that his master knows "no stop" and fails to "cease his flow of riot" (2.2.1–3), and he reminds Timon of "the ebb of your estate / And your great flow of debts" (2.2.145–46). The servant's "eyes at flow" because of the waste and riot make an ironic contrast with the tears that gush from Timon's as he emotes on friendship (1.2.105).

At the banquet, the images of flowing join with those of breathing, perhaps the strand most expressive of Timon's personality and career. Shakespeare used this pattern for characterization and dramatic emphasis also in *Antony and Cleopatra*, where the Egyptian queen's sexual attraction and power over Antony is vividly portrayed by Enobarbus:

> I saw her once
> Hop forty paces through the public street;
> And, having lost her breath, she spoke, and panted,
> That she did make defect perfection,
> And, breathless, pow'r breathe forth.

(2.2.228–32)

The contrast of this Cleopatra with the quiet and cold Octavia, more "a statue, than a breather" (3.3.21) is emphatic. But nowhere did Shakespeare put the breath image to such large use as in *Timon*, where it lends force and glamor to the lover and hater of men, accompanies his progress through the play, and helps connect the Alcibiades story with the main plot.

The first direct characterization of Timon through this image, when the merchant calls Timon a "most incomparable man, breath'd, as it were, / To an untirable and con-

tinuate goodness" (1.1.10–11), suggests a vigorous application to benevolence as if it were an athletic exercise. But
this effort, the steward warns, must finally fail:

> . . . the world is but a word:
> Were it all yours, to give it in a breath,
> How quickly were it gone!

(2.2.156–58)

And,

> Ah, when the means are gone that buy this praise,
> The breath is gone whereof this praise is made.

(2.2.173–74)

Insubstantial as the effect of Timon's breath is, it vivifies his
whole being and lifts him, a man not of great intellectual
powers, above his entourage. His portrait, as described by
the poet, shows imagination not as a light in his eyes, as
one might expect, but as an emanation of his mouth: "How
big imagination / Moves in this lip!" (1.1.32–33). The projection, at least, is compelling.

In contrast, the breath of Timon's friends is as nauseating
as they themselves; it blows off Timon's cap, Apemantus
intimates later (4.3.214–15), and we feel its unwholesome-
ness when they pledge their treacherous "healths" to him at
the banquet. Apemantus does not chime in because he fears
for his "windpipe's dangerous notes" (1.2.51). The very
banquet thus becomes a kind of ritual in which Timon's life
substance, his freedom to live and to breathe, are threatened. Timon's friends stifle him—the breath imagery is here
characteristically accompanied by images of tying and bind-
ing, such as J.C. Maxwell has pointed out; these images
contrast with Timon's key word "free."[6]

In the middle portions of the play, the kinetic verbal
images are accompanied by vehement stage movements
when the steward and Timon break through the encirclement by the creditors' servants. The first appearance of the
servants makes him plead, "Give me breath" (2.2.38). Besieged in his own house, in which he was "ever free," he
complains bitterly, "They have e'en put my breath from me,
the slaves" (3.4.79,102). He rushes through the barrage of
bills that prevent his unmolested exit. When during this
scene the steward makes his exit "in a cloak, muffled"—the
stage direction is repeated verbally (3.4.41)—we feel also
how much Timon's previously resounding breath has become
muffled.

At the mock banquet, when Timon hits back at his oppres-
sors, the kinetic movement resumes—with a vengeance.
Instead of having wine flow in their direction, he throws
water and stones at them, driving them out "all in motion."

He who let his friends drown themselves in riot shouts now, "Sink, Athens!" (3.6.98–100). Besides whatever else is symbolized by the "smoke and luke-warm water" he throws at his friends and declares to be their "perfection," these materials suggest the hot air, the hypocritical exhalations, the "reeking villainy" that have enveloped him (3.6.85–89).

The mock banquet redirects these and other images as Timon appropriates the Apemantian cynicism and incorporates it into a rhetoric of annihilation. Timon's heated imagination ranges over the whole universe when he invokes the elements and the heavenly bodies as apocalyptic forces. The breath imagery too becomes apocalyptic in Timon's first soliloquy outside Athens: "Breath infect breath, / That their society, as their friendship, may / Be merely poison!" (4.1.30–32). And the image fuses with cosmic curses when the misanthrope bids Alcibiades to become a planetary plague and poison the air with the smoke of guns, the breath of war (4.3.110–12).

The breath imagery also provides a major linkage between the main plot and the subplot. When Timon's freedom to breathe is choked by the encirclement of his house, the senators simultaneously tell Alcibiades, "You breathe in vain" (3.5.60). The general proves quickly that he will not "suffer / The worst that man can breathe" as is the senators' recipe for honorable behavior (31–32). When Alcibiades stands before the walls of Athens, he who had appropriated Timon's grievances before also appropriates the breath imagery we have come to associate with Timon:

> Till now, myself and such
> As slept within the shadow of your power
> Have wander'd with our travers'd arms, and breath'd
> Our sufferance vainly. . . .
> Now breathless wrong
> Shall sit and pant in your great chairs of ease,
> And pursy insolence shall break his wind
> With fear and horrid flight.
>
> (5.4.5–13)

Alcibiades' breath is given emphasis by his drums, and it is these that impress the Athenians, who were never much touched by the breath of Timon.

The most emphatic of all word patterns associated with Timon points up his uncompromising absoluteness. This is the pattern of "all" and "nothing"—words that occur with greater relative frequency in *Timon* than in any other tragedy.[7] The early iterations of "all" emphasize the large flatteries and the universal pursuit of fortune; the later repetitions point up the wholesale abandonment of Timon by his friends. "All conditions, . . . all minds, . . . All sorts of hearts, . . .

all deserts, all kind of natures" seek to propagate their states at the base of Fortune's hill and look admiringly to Fortune's favorite (1.1.53 ff). The poet rightly predicts that "all his dependants" will abandon him and that not one will accompany his declining foot. "All mankind," Timon comes to recognize, shows him an iron heart (3.4.82). He, the great generalizer, now throws his "nothing" of defiance against the world's "all." Although Apemantus at least slightly anticipates Timon's use of this word pattern when he strips the pretenses of Timon's friends down to "nothing" (1.1.190–268), it is Timon who makes it prominent when he prays at the mock banquet:

> The rest of your fees, O gods, the Senators of Athens, together with the common leg of people—what is amiss in them, you gods, make suitable for destruction. For these my present friends, as they are to me nothing, so in nothing bless them, and to nothing are they welcome. (3.6.77–81)

The Timon who leaves Athens will take "nothing" from the city but nakedness (4.1.32). For him "There's nothing level in our cursed natures / But direct villainy" (4.3.19–20). He draws in the end the logical conclusion for himself in an image of disease:

> My long sickness
> Of health and living now begins to mend,
> And nothing brings me all things.
>
> (5.1.185–87)

Timon's paradox has the ring of an old commonplace. That life is a disease and dying a restoration to health is a *topos* that traces back at least as far as Plato's *Phaedo;* the Christian humanists used it for their paradoxical *encomia,* although it appears to have struck some of them as a clever rhetorical trick rather than an effective consolation.[8] But Timon shows no interest in a consolation at all. The "all things" he says death brings entail no hope for an afterlife; to read it into the passage is to sentimentalize it. They denote merely the deliverance from the evil that is life and express a bare and emphatic existential nihilism. The preacher of nothingness includes himself in the apocalypse. When in his last words Timon asks that with his own speech all utterance cease, "Lips, let four words go by and language end" (5.1.219), one remembers by contrast the painter's portrait in which imagination moved the lips in an all-embracing philanthropy. The man who thought that the world was but a word to give away by his breath and then strove to annihilate it by this very breath ends in silence. With the stifling of his powerful breath a soul of potential greatness is muted.

The word pattern most suggestive of Athenian indecency

and corruption is an ironic one, that of "honor" and "honesty." *Timon* ranks just below *Othello* in the relative frequency of "honest,"[9] and if to "honest" and "honor" are added their derivatives and synonyms, this is the most prominent word pattern of the play, one Shakespeare used nowhere else with such insistence. The philanthropic Timon has an old-fashioned belief in honesty and honor, and he is the first to use words from this group. He finds the servant qualified for receiving the gift that enables him to marry the old miser's daughter because the servant is "honest" (1.1.131). And when the old man demands that Timon "pawn" his honor (note the commercial metaphor), he pledges "My hand to thee; mine honour on my promise" (151). Although Timon is theoretically aware that "dishonour traffics with man's nature" (161), he treats those around him as men of honor and implicitly believes in their honesty.

Apemantus exposes the charade and gives this word pattern a satirical hue. The apostle of the simple life, he is also the advocate of plain honesty. He is on a campaign against Athenian dishonesty: he satirizes it by his "murderous" quest for the one honest Athenian, he points it up by revealing the poet and the painter as moral counterfeits, and he ironizes it by harping on "honest." For Timon's friends, honesty and honor are dissociated and both depend on the marketplace. To the crude Lucullus, honesty is of even less value; it is mere foolishness: "Every man has his fault, and honesty is his," he says, admonishing Timon's servant to be "wise" (3.1.27, 40). This is quite like Iago mocking Othello's "foolish honesty" or Edmund taunting his brother Edgar. The two villains Lucius and Sempronius fashionably protest their honor even as they dishonorably refuse to help Timon. The senators who capriciously banish Alcibiades set themselves up as judges in a matter of honor and mouth honorable maxims that are belied by their verdict. Nor is Alcibiades' pursuit of honor such as could be elevated into a universal moral law; his questionable idea of what is honorable is brought out by his triumphant conclusion " 'Tis honour with most lands to be at odds"—the country to be added to the list being his own (3.5.117).

Timon takes up the cudgel of Apemantus in the woods. It is he who now uses "honest" with ironic iteration. His treatment of the steward as the one honest man in Athens echoes the cynic's earlier satiric jest, and the misanthrope twists the whole idea into burlesque when he treats the poet and the painter as the only *two* honest men. Timon's quarrel with the world hinges on his friends' failure to keep promises, and therefore he will have no more promises. His rejection of Alcibiades' offer of help—one that we understand as being not altogether altruistic—demonstrates his revulsion to promise-breaking:

> Promise me friendship, but perform none. If thou wilt not promise, the gods plague thee, for thou art a man! If thou dost perform, confound thee, for thou art a man! (4.3.74–77)

Shakespeare took pains to confirm that promise-breaking is indeed still the trend of the times in the later words of the painter, which could come right from a page of an Elizabethan or Jacobean satirical tract:

> Promising is the very air o'th' time; it opens the eyes of expectation. Performance is ever the duller for his act; and, but in the plainer and simpler kind of people, the deed of saying is quite out of use. To promise is most courtly and fashionable; performance is a kind of will or testament which argues a great sickness in his judgment that makes it. (5.1.22–29)

For the painter, as for Apemantus, honesty and plainness are associated; but the practice is assigned to the lower classes, the plainer and simpler kind—one thinks of Timon's servants. We know, of course, whose the "sickness" is of which the painter speaks. We have thus no confidence in the fulfillment of Alcibiades' plea to the Athenians: "Descend, and keep your words" (5.4.64).

The main images that illustrate Athenian corruption belong to the categories of disease and animality, which are also prominent thematic images in *Hamlet, Troilus and Cressida*, and *King Lear*. In *Timon*, these images enter into alliances with the "honest" and "honor" patterns and add unpleasant associations to the ironies and sarcasms. Just as Athenian society feigns honesty and order, so its members express much spurious concern about each other's health and well-being. The play begins with the painter's greeting of his competitor in Timon's favor, "I am glad y'are well," and ostensibly everybody is interested in Timon's continuing bloom. Only Apemantus strikes a sour note when he introduces the disease imagery: "Aches contract and starve your supple joints!" (1.1.247). He highlights the abuse of friendship and the dishonesty of Timon's well-wishers when he says that the "healths" pledged to Timon will make his state "look ill" (1.2.56). Timon later takes up the cynic's claim that "ingrateful man, with liquorish draughts / And morsels unctuous, greases his pure mind . . ." (4.3.196–97). He amplifies Apemantus's strains when he wishes upon the Athenians a whole catalogue of diseases: itches, sciatica, blains, poisonings, and plagues. Once even a servant, Flaminius, chimes in when he calls Lucullus a "disease of a friend" (3.1.53) and hopes that the meat in the villain's stomach will turn to poison, a wish worthy of the misanthropic Timon. Such images contribute to making us feel the sickness of society. And this imagery also signals that the Athenian illness threatens contagion and death to the healthy. Apemantus's warning of Timon's future illness is prophetic; Timon, as it were, becomes quasi-ill when he is virtually confined to his house, beleaguered by creditors: "His comfortable temper has forsook him, he's much out of health, and keeps his chamber" (3.4.70–71). Simultaneously, the health of Alcibiades is threatened by the senators, who seek to inflict "wounds" on him (3.5.112).

The second part of the play depicts the struggle of Timon and Alcibiades to rid themselves of the disease. Timon tries to do so by leaving Athens, wishing the disease on the Athenians with multiplying force: "Of man and beast the infinite malady / Crust you quite o'er!" (3.6.94–95). However, his escape does not bring him health and sanity, and contagion follows him to his cave. He is so "sick of this false world" (4.3.378) that his "long sickness / Of health and living" can be mended only by the "nothing" that brings him "all things" (5.1.185–87). Alcibiades seeks to cure his disease by restoring the sick world to health according to his own prescription. He will make war the leech of peace and peace that of war—characteristically, the play that began with a comment on individual health ends with one on the health of the state. But Alcibiades' medical art is drawn into doubt, and the leech image with its unpleasant animal denotation is not reassuring. The ironic and disagreeable tone of the health and disease imagery carries through to the end.

A subspecies of the disease imagery, which becomes prominent in Timon's misanthropy, is that of sexual disease. It may seem surprising that Timon inveighs vehemently against the prostitutes and dwells sickeningly on venereal disease, since neither the disease nor prostitution has anything to do with his misfortune. We may say, of course, that Timon is himself diseased in some manner and that Shakespeare's audience was used to melancholiacs and madmen on the stage who suffered from sex nausea. Yet the sex-disease imagery also specifically supports the thematic patterns that point up the dishonesty of society. Unpleasant as Timon's behavior to the two prostitutes is, it breaks through the hypocrisy that shrouds his and his friends' sexual attitudes. Before his change, he is reticent about sexual matters, almost puritanically proper, although the letter the page carries from the prostitute to Timon hints rather strongly at his participation in common pleasures, which like other pleasures in this society have a pecuniary base. Timon is even fulsomely polite to the Amazonian ladies at whose promiscuity Apemantus jibes (1.2.148–50). When Timon later attacks the prostitutes.

he has divested himself of societal inhibitions and hypocrisies as has Apemantus before him. He recognizes now that the prostitutes, who pander love for gold, are infected by the same societal and human corruption as his usuring friends. He sees the venereal disease they communicate as emblematic of mankind's illness. Viciously, he exhorts them to spread it everywhere.

The disease imagery is joined by the animal imagery in invoking the unpleasant and disgusting aspects of Athenian and human life. Its pervasiveness has often been noted. There are, of course, the several dog images, which Caroline Spurgeon thought the leading imagery of the play and which, as William Empson has argued, contribute to the ambiguity with which cynicism is treated.[10] It is Apemantus's doglike existence that produces most of them. He is the first to use the word, and, like Diogenes, he knows how to turn the dog joke against his detractors, sometimes by playfully accepting their designation. When the painter calls him a dog, he snaps back, "Thy mother's of my generation. What's she, if I be a dog?" (1.1.201). In the mock banquet, when Timon assumes the role of Apemantus, he also adopts the cynic's leitmotiv. "Uncover, dogs, and lap" he shouts as he serves them the dishes with water (3.6.82).

In the debate with Apemantus in the wood, Timon demonstrates that he can turn the dog image against the cynic. Immediately upon the latter's appearance and his complaint that Timon imitates him, Timon barks: " 'Tis then because thou dost not keep a dog / Whom I would imitate. Consumption catch thee!" (4.3.202–3). Why Timon would want to imitate Apemantus's dog is hardly as baffling as Empson seems to think, and it is apt enough as an insult. Timon is saying that he would gladly imitate Apemantus's dog, if he had one, in preference to Apemantus, who is much less than a dog: a beggar, "bred a dog" and an "issue of a mangy dog" (253, 268). The insult mirrors Timon's dislike of having to imitate Apemantus; it does not refute the accusation that the misanthrope has adopted the cynic's idiom with his manners, which is really a quite justified accusation. But then, imitation was the Renaissance key to mastery of style.

Yet I do not think that the dog image has any great thematic significance. Nor do other specific animal images, such as the bird image, suggestive as it is of rapacious animalism. Characteristic of *Timon* is not the specificity, variety, or even the frequency of animal images—the play is outdistanced by *Troilus and Cressida* in these respects—but the prevalence of comparisons of men in general to animals. *Timon* has more such references than any other play[11]—all, of course, are unflattering unless one takes the phoenix as an animal. This imagery underlines human beastliness; as Willard Farnham has noted, the word "beast" occurs far more often in *Timon* than anywhere else.[12]

Apemantus's bitter comment that the strain of man has degenerated to baboon and monkey (1.1.249–50) is the first such generalization. The most odious is Lucius's hypocritical excuse:

> What a wicked beast was I to disfurnish myself against such a good time, when I might ha' shown myself honourable! . . . Servilius, now before the gods, I am not able to do (the more beast, I say!) . . . (3.2.43–48).

This is an insult to animals; it makes us uncomfortably aware that the true beast is man. As Apemantus says, "The commonwealth of Athens is become a forest of beasts" (4.3.350). All this recalls Montaigne's attack on the pride and presumption of man in believing himself superior to the animals—an attack echoed by Barckley, among others.[13] Shakespeare's misanthrope transcends even Montaigne's and Barckley's pessimism when he emblematically catalogues the passions and vices that make animals approach man in wickedness, showing that the beasts' too is a dangerous forest: it harbors the guile of the fox, the stealth of the lion, the stupidity of the ass, the pride and wrath of the unicorn, the hatred of the horse, the cruelty of the leopard (329 ff.).

The animal images, as we have noted, fuse with cannibalistic ones when eating is referred to. Even before the banquet, Apemantus makes this kind of association, to which he adds a sexual innuendo. As in *Troilus and Cressida*, a link between food, sex, and animality is thus established:

> *Tim.* Wilt dine with me, Apemantus?
> *Apem.* No; I eat not lords.
> *Tim.* And thou shouldst, thou'dst anger ladies.
> *Apem.* O they eat lords; so they come by great bellies.

> (1.1.203–6)

Timon later achieves virtuoso performances through similar linkages that expose the universal depravity. His awesome sermon to the bandits, for instance, begins with an animal-cannibal association, "You must eat men" (4.3.428), and plays variations on the themes of disease, dishonesty, and abuse, projecting them on a cosmic screen.

Of all word and image patterns, none is a more potent ingredient in the play's pessimistic milieu than that which clusters around gold. To my mind, gold never glows with the warm brightness and richness Wilson Knight ascribes to it in the hands of the philanthropic Timon bewitched by a "gold-mist of romance." Rather, the pattern is from the beginning harsh, ironic, and unpleasant. The first occurrence suggests not Timon's universal love but his foolishly energetic disposal: "He pours it out. Plutus the god of gold / Is but his steward" (1.1.275–76). The mythological metaphor ironizes Timon's lack of management; his actual steward is not Plutus but Flavius, who distributes his master's riches reluctantly and who knows that Timon is bankrupt, as we may suspect by this time. The senator who calls in his credit jests, "If I want gold, steal but a beggar's dog / And give it Timon— why, the dog coins gold" (2.1.5–6). Spurgeon would call this a dog rather than a gold image, but whatever the classification, there is something unpleasant, spurious, even scatalogical about the activity to which the image points. Apemantus calls the usurers' servants "bawds between gold and want" (2.2.63– 64), using a prostitution image that emphasizes the mercenary and degrading purposes to which gold is put. This is the tune Timon takes up later.

Timon actually never speaks directly of gold until he has arrived in the wood. In Athens, as much as he hands out talents and pearls and other gifts, he seems oblivious to the yellow metal. He is not, however, unaffected by its deification, which is rampant around him and which he later recognizes as idolatry. As R. Swigg has pointed out, Timon uses the computational metaphors that have become habits of speech in Athens.[14] When he enables the servant to marry the old Athenian's daughter, he says, "What you bestow, in him I'll counterpoise, / And make him weigh with her" (1.1.148– 49). He betrays even more clearly that, like his entourage, he thinks of wealth as the arbiter of affections when he says "I weigh my friend's affection with mine own" (1.2.214). This is the kind of measuring and weighing idiom that the Athenians continue to use throughout the play, and their hearts are in it. But Timon's is not, or he would not tip the scales in his disfavor. Later when he cries out "Cut my heart in sums," he protests against the commercial mentality with the commercial metaphor (3.4.91), and he uses it satirically from then on.

Timon's first reference to gold comes with the shock effect of an anti-lyrical use of "golden": "the learned pate / Ducks to the golden fool" (4.3.17–18). This is the age of gold, not the golden age. The first of Timon's two great speeches on gold follows immediately as he digs up the metal (4.3.25–45). This and the similar later speech (384–95) were much admired by Karl Marx, who wrote a lengthy gloss on them in his early years, condensing it later into a footnote of *Das Kapital*.[15]

His reading of *Timon* evidently played some small part in the evolution of his theory of money and wealth. It should be said that Timon's basic arguments against gold are quite traditional and hark back to medieval Christian protests; in milder moralistic or satirical form they were voiced frequently in the Renaissance. When Timon takes up the prostitution image and calls gold the "common whore of mankind," he adopts, together with Apemantus's tune, that of many Renaissance satirists and moralists. For instance, Agrippa of Nettesheim in his influential *De vanitate artium et scientiarum*, translated in 1569 (rpt. 1575), said that the "bawdry of gold brought about unlikely marriages, deflowered virgins, sold widows, perverted old nobility, and bought new titles."[16] Timon's addresses to gold are quite in this vein: "Thus much of this will make / . . . Base, noble; . . . place thieves, / And give them title . . . This is it / That makes the wappen'd widow wed again. . . . Thou ever young, fresh, loved and delicate wooer, / Whose blush doth thaw the consecrated snow / That lies on Dian's lap!" (28–39, 387–89).

These speeches have a highly ironic effect because of the incongruity between Timon's encomiastic tone and the horrors created by gold they describe. Shakespeare may have been influenced here by the similar technique of Ben Jonson in *Volpone* (1606).[17] For both Jonson's hero and Timon, gold is the great transformer: "Who can get thee, / He shall be noble, honest, wise—" (*Volpone*, 1.1.27). Jonson's Mosca later chimes in: "It transforms / The most deformed and restores 'hem lovely / As 'twere a strange poetical girdle" (5.2.100–102) —the latter figure being derived from "*cestus*: the girdle of Venus, into which were woven all her seductive powers," as Jonson explained in a learned marginal note. Timon likewise ascribes to gold the power of seducing and metamorphosizing; he addresses it as if it were a perverse Cupid: "Thou visible god, / That sold'rest close impossibilities, / And mak'st them kiss" (389–91). Whereas Jonson has his characters use unalloyed lyricisms and thus makes their dithyrambic praises into unconscious self-indictments, Shakespeare undercuts the lyrical effects by Timon's celebrating horrors, such as in "O thou sweet king-killer, and dear divorce / 'Twixt natural son and sire . . ." (384–85). Timon's mock-glorification of gold is, like Volpone's, an indictment of mankind.

These resemblances of thought and technique between Shakespeare and Jonson and the reliance of both authors on a moral tradition should caution us against claiming that Timon's speeches on gold are Shakespeare's individual manifesto. Both Shakespeare and Jonson were presenting one side of the story of gold, that is, its abuse, no doubt in the belief that the abuse was growing. As Bàrckley and many others said, "Gold and silver of itself is neither good nor evil, but the use or abuse maketh it good or bad."[18] And this brings up the interesting and significant association of the word pattern of "gold" with that of "use"—another word that occurs more frequently in *Timon* than in the other tragedies.[19]

The two terms are associated from the first gold image on, that of Plutus as Timon's steward. The lord who coins it continues with this further praise of the philanthropist:

> No meed but he repays
> Seven-fold above itself: no gift to him
> But breeds the giver a return exceeding
> All use of quittance.

> (1.1.276–79)

Of course, "use of quittance" refers to customary practice, but the phrase ironically draws attention to the uselessness of Timon's endeavor to bind his friends to him by gifts. For Shakespeare's audience, a further allusion suggested itself: they knew the word "use" as ubiquitous in discussions of the usury issue. Defenses of usury as well as attacks on it turned on the question of the proper use of money. Not greed but the need of putting their money to use made them charge high interest rates, said the usurers—an argument (not unfamiliar now) that their opponents attacked. An anti-usury tract accused the usurers of employing "use" as a euphemism for usury: these practitioners "will not call it usury lest the word shall be offensive or make things odious. But it shall be termed 'use' or 'usance' in exchange, which are smooth words as oil, never a biting letter in them."[20] Understood in this context, the lord's remark on the "use of quittance" exposes his noxious intention: he and Timon's other friends give in a usuring way because they expect him to remunerate them at a rate exceeding the usual way of borrowing. Laudatory of Timon as these words are on the surface, for Shakespeare's audience, primed to hate usury, they had opprobrious implications: Timon gives in excess of what is customary, and the resulting usury makes him an accomplice, hardly less guilty than the usurer.[21]

We shall take a brief look at the "use" patterns in general before returning to gold. Here again, Apemantus is a focal figure. The emphasis on "use," its synonyms, antonyms, and derivatives, together with semantically related words such as "want" and "need," surely suggested itself to Shakespeare in large part because of the doctrine of the cynics. For Apemantus, as for other members of this sect, the right answer to the question of what men's needs are is fundamental to the conduct of a happy life. This implies a testing of all goods and then rejecting those not absolutely necessary for life. Why does man need a house? Clothing more than to keep him warm? Delicacies and luxuries that merely make him sick? Gold that only makes him greedy for more? Renaissance moralists, enamored of ancient primitivism and the simplicity of the golden age, sometimes claimed that all problems would disappear if men reverted to the simple life: "Was there ever any man that, to suffice nature, had been constrained to sell his land or to borrow upon interest?"[22]

The cynics' question about the use of things is posed in *Timon* by the very presence of Apemantus. His choice of roots and water at the banquet points up Timon's prodigality and his friends' luxuriousness. Later, at the banquet of nature of which Timon partakes in the forest, the misanthrope proves himself a convert to Apemantus's view by adopting the simple life and by showing up the insanity of the uses of the world. Like a true cynic, he preaches to the bandits:

> Your greatest want is, you want much of meat.
> Why should you want? Behold, the earth hath roots;
> Within this mile break forth a hundred springs;
> The oaks bear mast, the briers scarlet hips;
> The bounteous housewife nature on each bush
> Lays her full mess before you. Want? Why want?
>
> (4.3.419–24)

But this is only the most basic way in which the dynamics of wants and uses work themselves out. The theme, carried forward through the ironic playing on "use" by Timon and his friends, develops beyond the rhetoric of cynical philosophy to probe the use and abuse of men even more than of things. This is most obvious in the case of Timon's friends. When they start to collect from him, they allege that their "uses" cry to them (2.1.20)—usurers' language again! And they make sly use of time, money, and men. Even the stranger lord who pities Timon adopts the linguistic usage and the hypocrisy of the times when he protests that he would have helped Timon "had his necessity made use of me" (3.2.84).

Timon does not base his actions on personal needs and wants as does the egotistic society around him; nevertheless, he contributes to the economic and moral malaise by giving to those who are not in need and who want more than they receive. Even his very conception of friendship is infected by the goals of his utilitarian society. He harps on friendship being based on need; friends would be the most "needless" creatures "should we ne'er have use for 'em" (1.2.92 ff.). When his debts catch up with him, he imagines that the uses of his society give him a special advantage; he opines that if he tried "the argument of hearts by borrowing, Men and men's fortunes could I frankly use" (2.2.182–83). When he sends out his servants for aid, he does so because "my occasions have found time to use 'em toward a supply of money" (195–96). He is "proud" that he has this "need" and can make this "use" of them!

All this changes in the mock banquet. Timon now prays to the gods that they "lend to each man enough, that one need not lend to another" (3.6.71–72). He goes on to strip himself before the walls of Athens in visible demonstration of his newfound belief that honesty requires the reduction of all human wants—a subject on which he waxes eloquent in the woods. His friends' ingratitude awakens him to the egotistic uses to which society subjects men and things, uses to which his prodigality contributed. His digging roots, like the mock banquet, is a mimetic and symbolic refutation of the conspicuous waste of the lavish entertainment he provided for his friends. Like Apemantus, he realizes now that gold is a bawd and that, in turn, it creates bawds, destroying genuine relationships. "They love thee not that use thee," he says to one of the prostitutes who will "do anything for gold" (4.3.84, 152).

The irony of fortune that makes Timon rich again by finding gold does not mitigate his hatred; rather, he turns the gold into demonstrative evidence of the world's perversion of uses and takes the offensive by making it do its "right nature," that is, ruin mankind (4.3.42–45). On a symbolic level, we might say, Timon's behavior dramatizes man's fall from the grace of the golden age to the pains of the age of iron, which satirists liked to call the age of gold. He leaves his utopian dreams and paradisiacal innocence for cursing and hard labor. In this symbolic reenactment of the history of mankind (which is suggested merely, not allegorized), Timon proceeds speedily to the apocalyptic stage by calling for the world's destruction.

Gold is the central image of the fourth act as I have defined it, that is, of all the episodes in which Timon confronts his visitors. Gold actually lies on the stage, and the word "gold" sounds again and again with pitiless insistence. Except for Timon's two great speeches, most of the word patterns are of the "give me gold" and "here is gold" kind and demonstrate the contrast between extreme greed and utter recklessness—a new kind of prodigality. When the issue of gold is raised now, it cuts two ways. On the one hand, Timon takes the cynic stance, making an effective point against the misuses of objects by men. His finding of gold while digging for roots to sustain his life already demonstrates the uselessness of gold by contrasting it with primary human necessities. And he rejects Alcibiades' offer of gold with "Keep it, I cannot eat it" (4.3.

102), evoking the mýth of Tantalus, the archetypical abuser of gold. On the other hand, Timon himself, prodigal and misanthrope, is the most spectacular abuser of this substance, an irony pointed up in his conversation with Apemantus. The cynic poses the question of the use of gold (indicating that, after all, he is not fully emancipated from wordly values): "Here is no use of gold." Answers Timon: "The best and truest;

For here it sleeps, and does no hired harm" (4.3.292–93). Timon knows how to castigate the evil employment men make of gold, but ironically he too seeks to use gold for "hired harm" when he distributes it for mankind's bale.

Nevertheless, as protests against the uses of the world, Timon's speeches and actions are impressive. He has no more use for these uses. Death in him is laughing at others' lives as if it were directing a danse macabre. When the senators offer him "special dignities which vacant lie / For thy best use and wearing" (5.1.141–42), he has a last jest and gesture for them that burlesques their obsession with using things: he invites them to hang themselves "in the sequence of degree" on the tree that "mine own use invites me to cut down" (205–7). It was their "use," the Athenians alleged, that necessitated repayment of their loans by Timon and prevented them from coming to his rescue. And it was through a specious adherence to "degree" that they disguised their rapacity.

This gesture of Timon's insultingly points up the illness of man and society, and so does Timon's final message to the Athenians, his epitaph. We can hardly doubt that his fellow citizens will shrug off the insults, transforming them, as Alcibiades is already in the process of doing, into a not-too-disturbing legend. Timon's protest will not stop the world from seeking and finding its accustomed uses. "I will use the olive with my sword," says Alcibiades in the last lines of the play.

8

The Ills of Society

What a god's gold

The many references to gold, together with such word patterns as those of "use" and "honest," are an indication of the significance of socioeconomic issues in the play. To a number of critics, *the* theme of *Timon*, overriding all others, has seemed to lie in this area.[1] However, I do not think that the play has a simple dominant social or economic theme, such as the decay of feudalism or the evils of usury. Like the other dramas of Shakespeare, this presents a dramatic case and situation to which the dialectics of ideas are subordinated. Yet the role of economic and social matters is certainly great, and the manner in which they are dramatized and discussed contributes very much to the pessimistic climate.

Timon breathes Shakespeare's awareness of the economic crisis of his time. So, of course, do *Lear* and some later plays. Corn riots and class struggle play a role in *Coriolanus*, the denunciations of gold in *Cymbeline* recall Timon's, and the plight of the weavers and unjust taxation figure in *Henry VIII*. But these are relatively minor issues. In *Timon*, the whole action is predicated on an economic disaster, the loss of a man's estate owing to his liberality and prodigality. This was a familiar occurrence in Shakespeare's England. Many a landowner was threatened by the greed and usury dramatized in *Timon*. Everybody must have heard about the kind of practices to which Timon falls prey, and many must have known people like Lucullus, Lucius, and Sempronius.[2]

To recover something of the flavor of the crisis as Shakespeare's contemporaries felt it, we must consider it in the moral frame in which it was discussed. We may begin with an analysis by Gerald de Malynes, a merchant and economic theorist, who was frequently consulted on trade matters by the governments of Elizabeth and James. Malynes, in 1601, published a curious allegorical account of English society and economics under the title of *Saint George for England*. Since so much of it sounds as if it were a description of Timon's Athens, the argument is worth summarizing here, and I shall give it largely in Malynes's own words (leaving out, however, his remarks on foreign trade, which are not relevant to our concern):

> The country of Niobla [i.e., Albion] is beset by a destructive dragon that has caused the ruin of many families, commonwealths, states, and kingdoms by enriching some and impoverishing others. It has disarranged society that previously lived in harmony. Since the hellhound has been raging, concord has been broken, charity has grown cold, and inequality has crept in through the falsification of measure. The general rule "Do as thou wouldst be done unto" is forgotten, free lending is banished, oppression flourishes, and no man is content to live in his vocation. Many now must buy what ought to be freely given, which makes them sell what they should freely give. Devoid of charity, some will lend no money but for gain, and give nothing to the poor. Gold and silver have jailed men's souls. Everywhere the laws are abused. Some pursue their debtors with bonds and counterbonds and enclose grounds unlawfully so that many are brought to ruin. A blockhead with a heap of gold can now control many who are wiser than himself. The dragon makes misers of some and profligates of others, who keep harlots, rob, and steal. He has one man spend his stock by prodigal riot and sumptuous fare while another fills his purse with the blood of innocents. He sets some to flatter and fawn like spaniels and others to devour one another. He incites many to oppose their betters, by whose help they have been advanced. He proclaims gold as the creed of the world and persuades some that they can hunt after gain and that honesty will take care of itself later. He leads people to believe that learning and wisdom are of no avail without gold. The dragon is like a cannibal because he eats raw flesh, especially that of men. But this same monster also feeds the wolves of the land.

From a modern point of view, this analysis is inadequate, as much as it makes the crisis appear quite real. It fails to distinguish properly between causes and effects, symbolizing both conveniently through a dragon. This monster represents at one time usury, at another covetousness, and then again prodigality; it stands also for whatever else the author considers amiss. The dragon is both the symptom and the disease.

The cure prescribed is simple only in allegorical terms: Saint George must slay the dragon.

Modern historians tell us that the crisis Malynes and others felt came from a profound socioeconomic change.[3] The static medieval society with its conception of the "just price" and the clearly definable status of persons was being replaced by a modern market society that permitted and encouraged a possessive individualism. The motivating force of men's behavior was no longer the love of God (or the fear of hell, as some would say) but expediency and utility, and the most desired goal was material success. The theoretical formulation of these new principles was slow in coming. But they can be seen budding, for instance, in Bacon's essays and philosophical writings. Thus in "Of Fortune" (1607–12), Bacon took note of the reality of a competitive society in which "the mould of a man's fortune is in his own hands" and "the folly of one man is the fortune of another." It is to the pursuit of fortune, Bacon said, that man's powers are to be marshalled (in the service of virtue, of course). Therefore, "When a man placeth his thoughts without himself [i.e., acts altruistically], he goeth not his own way."[4] The new principles did not find their full expression and defense until Thomas Hobbes's *Leviathan* (1651). Hobbes's title, like Malynes's, recognized the existence of a monster that controls all social activities; however, Hobbes's monster lets the dragonish urges of individuals work themselves out competitively and with minimal restrictions in the state united in one person. *Leviathan* may seem a rather longish way from *Timon,* but we may recall that Hobbes was about twenty years old when Shakespeare wrote the play. The society that Hobbes described was taking shape then, and *Leviathan* can throw light on Shakespeare's Athenian society, Jacobean English as this society is to the core. Although we can learn from Malynes what Shakespeare's contemporaries thought about the economic crisis, Hobbes can add to this some touches of the reality that escaped them. We shall orient ourselves therefore on both.

Malynes took the common conservative moral attitude toward the crisis: the dragon had destroyed the social harmony. He did not assume that this was a harmony without tensions, since a certain degree of tension, a balance of opposites, was thought basic to the body politic. Economically, this balance required free giving by those who had surplus to those who were in need. Thus Malynes still paid tribute to the classical-humanistic principle of *concordia*, in which friendship was basic to the fabric of society and the health of the state was undermined by ingratitude. As Sir Thomas Elyot had it, "amity" and "charity" are the ties of the commonwealth.[5] "Liberality and thankfulness are the bonds of concord," said John Bodenham in the immensely popular *Polyteuphia* or *Wit's Commonwealth* (1579 and twelve editions through 1630).[6] These natural bonds are torn in Shakespeare's Athens, just as many later Elizabethans and Jacobeans thought they were torn in England.

Usury was for Malynes and other moralists the most vicious of the dragon's activities. It must be understood that attacks on usury were often synonymous with attacks on interest-taking in general. The insufficiency of the money supply and the economic changes of which Malynes and others were not sufficiently conscious had brought an increasing need for money, a need either not met or else exploited by unscrupulous moneylenders. However, the need for loans was slowly breaking down the objections to what was loosely called "usury," and the first voices in its defense were heard. In 1625, the pragmatic Bacon was to defend it as "a concession to the hardness of men's hearts," i.e., to men's unwillingness to give and lend freely.[7] Bacon accepted here calmly the state of affairs that made Malynes unhappy and infuriates Timon.

In *Timon*, usury is endowed with its popular odium not only by the despicability of those who practice it but also by moral imagery and allusions by which it was castigated in Shakespeare's time, particularly in the anti-usury tracts. Such are the ubiquitous animal and cannibal images[8] and suggestions of Machiavellism, that ever-present devilish activity.[9] The first stranger speaks of the "policy" of Timon's friends (3.2.89), and the servant, of Sempronius's "politic" love (3.3.36)—terms that were applied to Machiavels. These terms are also appropriate in view of the connection between politics and usury in Athens—and not only in Athens. The mercantilist system with its alliance of politics and commerce encouraged usury and the taking of bribes by officeholders. Usuring counselors, comparable to the senators of Athens, were among the targets of moralists and satirists in England and elsewhere.

Attacks on usury as well as defenses of it such as Bacon's turned on the question of the "use" and "need" for money—key words in *Timon*, as we noted. Malynes said those who were of the dragon's party are content "to have money freely lent them, yet would lend none freely themselves, for, they say, 'I must make a gain of my money.' "[10] The use of money for its augmentation seemed rank abuse to the anti-usurers: money, they said, was not a commodity but only a means to obtain commodities. The Aristotelian objection was often quoted: to have money beget money was a perversion of its nature. As Louis Leroy commented, "It seemeth contrary to nature that a dead thing as money should engender."[11] The lord who gives to Timon because his gift "breeds the giver a return exceeding / All use of quittance" (1.1.278–79) evokes unpleasantly the old objection. A corollary to this objection was that the usurer enriched himself by using not only other people's money but also a commodity only God had a right to call his own, that is, time, since he took advantage of the interval between loan and repayment.[12] When Lucullus slyly suggests to Timon's servant that he can "use the time well, if the time use thee well" (3.1.36–37), he not only betrays an egotistic, opportunistic, and cynical attitude that tests men and relationships for what good they may do to oneself but he also confirms what the critics of usury in Shakespeare's time were saying. He speaks usurer's language. It is against the theory and practice of the usurers that Apemantus and, later, Timon assert that a man who lives according to nature's principles needs and uses little.

Malynes saw usury not as a profession but as an activity that supplanted the free giving when concord reigned, the giving in which Timon indulges. The practice of usury in the play corresponds much better to the norm in Shakespeare's England than the professional usury of a Shylock that is made even more exotic by his Jewishness. Early seventeenth-century society was essentially still in a pre-banking stage, and borrowing was done in an informal manner, often by aristocrats from other aristocrats, gentlemen from other gentlemen, or tradesmen from other tradesmen who possessed ready cash and had discovered an easy way of making it grow by charging high interest rates, usually more than the legal maximum of ten percent (later reduced to six). Frequently the lenders' resources came from businesses they ran as a sideline. It is true that there were also some wealthy merchants for whom usury was a more central occupation. But these are not in evidence in *Timon*. The primary agents of Timon's ruin appear to be wealthy men of approximately the same social status as his or, like the senators, above him. Timon, as has often been pointed out, is the equivalent of an aristocrat or at least of a member of the upper gentry in Shakespeare's England, a man whose wealth depends primarily on land. His friends, whom he lavishly entertains at his banquets and who leave him in the lurch, are the Athenian equivalents of the Jacobean gentry and aristocracy, well-to-do men who get wealthier by his means. Even those from whom he borrows, the Varros, Luciuses, and Isidores, are regular beneficaries of his munificence and guests at his table (see 3.4.50). They are gentlemen who use their capital to the greatest advantage by lending it out at a high interest rate; like the senators, they are part-time usurers engaged in various financial and commercial manipulations (3.2. 45–47).

These usurers conduct their nefarious business under the cloak of friendship; theirs is a "usuring kindness"—a demonstration of the way friendship becomes degraded. This, if we believe the satirists, was much the way in which such dealings were conducted in England. In *Diogenes in His Singularity* (1598), which, interestingly, places the narrative in an Athens that is a thinly disguised London, Thomas Lodge gave a satirical twist to this method:

> There is no word so common in Athens as "my friend." The usurer pretending cozenage will say "you are welcome." "My friend," saith the retailer, "it cost me thus much"; yet sells this man his soul for two pences and bobs thee out of thy coin with "my friend." It is an old proverb, and not so old as true, *amicus certus in re incerta cernitur*: a true friend is known in a doubtful matter, and what is more doubtful than when borrowing money a man finds no friends?[13]

The usuring friends of Timon are particularly disgusting because they are constant guests at Timon's table and devour his substance, "eat of my lord's meat," as the steward says. "Then they could smile, and fawn upon his debts, / And take down th' int'rest into their glutt'nous maws" (3.4.50–52). Shakespeare characterizes Timon's friends much as does Malynes the helpers of the dragon, who flatter and fawn like spaniels and devour others.

Timon's friends also use the dragon's method of pursuing their debtors with bonds and counterbonds until they have ruined them. The only "security" Timon can give for the loans extended to him under the cloak of friendship is his land—and Timon's friends and the senators, we are told, "love security" (3.1.43; 3.5.82). By the time the play opens, Timon evidently has already lost much of his large holding: "To Lacedaemon did my land extend," he says (2.2.155). The "bills" and "bonds" with which he is pursued were familiar instruments of moneylenders, notes of indebtedness valid for only a short time, usually six months, although they could be and often were extended for a lifetime. But when they were called up, and no payment was made, the "security" was lost. In unscrupulous hands, such as those of Timon's friends, these bills and bonds were deadly weapons.

This general practice of the transfer of land as security seems also referred to by the stranger-lord, who says that if he had been asked for help by Timon, he would have put his "wealth into donation, / And the best half should have return'd to him" (3.2.85–86). "Donation" was used as a euphemism for the loans that were given with usurious intent.[14]

By accepting them, many aristocrats in Shakespeare's England got into financial difficulties and some were bankrupted, as Lawrence Stone has pointed out.[15] In Malynes's words, the dragon was swallowing up many families.

Neither Malynes nor Shakespeare saw the enrichment of some by the impoverishment of many exactly as a class struggle. Timon is certainly not ruined by a rising bourgeoisie, even though this class was attracting greater wealth and power in England. Characters that can be assigned to the middle class, it is true, have a part in Timon's ruin. The jeweler tries to get the best price, probably an exorbitant one, from Timon for the jewel that he tenders flatteringly to him, and so do the poet and the painter for their works. But they are only minor feeders on Timon's extravagance. The one identifiable representative of the acquisitive and possessive middle class is the Old Athenian who wants a financially respectable husband for his daughter. He protests that he has always been "inclin'd to thrift" (1.1.121), and he aspires to the kind of economic and social advance for his progeny that has always been characteristic of the middle classes. However, the sum of three talents that he gets for his daughter is hardly more than a ripple in Timon's finances compared with the typhoon whipped up by his friends.

Timon's servants must be considered in this context. It is hard to say whether they should be assigned to the middle or the lower classes; Flavius probably belongs to the former. The remarkable thing is how sympathetically they are portrayed. One cannot attribute their benevolence merely to their choric function of underlining the pathos of Timon's fall; the devotion of a servant like the one who says, "Yet do our hearts wear Timon's livery" (4.2.17) goes beyond dramatic needs. Even the usurers' servants express unhappiness about the task for which they are used, and one, Hortensius, castigates his master's ingratitude (3.4.26–28). There is no breakdown in servant morality of the kind that Malynes and other critics of society found in England and that Timon proclaims in his craze for total upheaval: "Bound servants, steal! / Large-handed robbers your grave masters are, / And pill by law" (4.1.10–12). Yet, one cannot take much satisfaction in this goodness from below. Its most salient feature, after all, is its impotence, and it seems susceptible to perversion too. The second servant of Varro, when his master is called a knave by Flavius, rises almost to the level of his master's callousness: "No matter what; he's poor and that's revenge enough. Who can speak broader than he that has no house to put his head in? Such may rail against great buildings" (3.4.62–65). Flavius in the end will have the gold to put his head in a larger house and thus be subject to the temptations of fortune.

Poverty, in fact, provides no total immunity from these temptations. In speaking of the lower classes, we must not forget the bandits, these ferocious, if frank, pursuers of gold. Robbing and stealing, as Malynes said, were also activities of the dragon. I am at a loss to say where, in a class analysis, the prostitutes of the play belong. The one that deals with Timon, at any rate, can afford a page and a clown. Prostitution is associated with the perversions wrought by gold, and these perversions become greater the more the temptations and opportunities grow.

The temptations certainly are large for Timon, surrounded as he is by flatterers and basking as he does in the glory of his wealth. Aristocrats or members of the upper gentry, as Lawrence Stone has shown in detail, found it easy in this time of such economic pressures as rising prices and scarcity of money to, like a Timon, ruin themselves. The income from their lands remained static unless they found means—to the detriment of their tenants—to increase it, and their expenses soared. The Renaissance brought with it a stimulation for magnificent display that was not restricted merely to the courts. Status maintenance and status seeking, always aristocratic concerns, led to undue expenditures. Landowners were expected to be hospitable, and were praised accordingly; many put their energies into entertainments beyond their means. This was a particular temptation since these energies found no outlet in war during King James's time.

This is not to say that ruin for the aristocrats in this situation was automatic. As Stone shows, the factors that worked against the landed classes could be neutralized or made to work in the opposite way; there were examples of aristocrats and members of the gentry who through thrift and judicious investment achieved stability and growth.[16] But one wonders how many of these did so by adopting the method of Timon's friends or something like it. The ideal was to be both frugal and generous, as it is acclaimed in a contemporary play, *Hans Beerpot* (1610), by Dabridgcourt Belchier, an inexpert dramatist who lived for many years in the Low Countries. He looked to England for the ideal when he described a Dutch gentleman:

O there's a man lives bravely, keeps an house,
Relieves the poor, his gates he never shut;
His table's free, there's meat for honest men;
He lived in England, learned that country's guise
For hospitality; few such be here;
Yet frugal too, was never prodigal;

> Spends nothing more but what he well may spare.
> He borrows nought, nor lends on usury;
> Yet hath enough.[17]

If Belchier suggests that generosity and frugality were diffi-cult to reconcile, as he appears to do, he points up the dilemma that men of a status equivalent to Timon's faced.

But Timon's fall is not altogether attributable to social pressures. He is not exactly a feudal lord ruined by his duty to keep a bountiful and hospitable house, as J. C. Pettet has it;[18] nor is the play, à la J. W. Draper, an elegy on the ideals of chivalry that were succumbing to a capitalistic age.[19] None of the duties and reciprocal relationships of the feudal age are assumed: Timon makes the point that he gave "freely ever" (1.2.10). It is true that he is said to have served his country with distinction during war (4.3.93–96) and that in Shake-speare's time such service, even if not required, was looked upon as a moral obligation of the peerage. But there is no implication that this has anything to do with his financial problems; rather, it increases the Athenians' ingratitude. Timon is not depicted as the victim of a system, nor are his friends merely doing what the system gives them a right to do. All are put in a situation that tests their capacities as human beings even more than as members of a particular society.

To view this situation from the moral position of a Malynes means seeing Timon as both a maker and a victim of a soci-etal crisis. He too falsifies the measure and demonstrates that charity has grown cold. According to the definition of "charity" in Shakespeare's time just as in our own, Timon is not charitable. The play expressly urges us to judge him in these terms because he himself brings up the issue twice dur-ing the banquet, first when he emotes on his happiness to have given the "charitable title" of friends to his guests (1.2.89), and then when he says to Alcibiades, presenting him with a gift: "Thou art a soldier, therefore seldom rich; / It comes in charity to thee" (221–22). As preachers and moralists stipulated, one of the tests of true charity was for the recipient to be in need. Timon gives to those who have no need; even Alcibiades, entering as he does at the head of twenty men of cavalry, is not exactly indigent. To Jacobeans, he must have seemed the equivalent of a military captain or commander, a position that attracted knights and younger sons of aristocrats; although not lucrative, it did not make for starvation. We never see or hear of Timon giving to any-body that is poor. He fails to heed Sir William Cornwallis's maxim that "it is better to keep the poor from starving than to feast knaves."[20] Timon's later appalling advice to the steward to "show charity to none, / But let the famish'd flesh slide from the bone / Ere thou relieve the beggar" (4.3.531–33) comes from a man who has never notably practiced charity. The uncharitable nature of Timon's friends rather goes without saying, but it may be noted that the stranger who finds the soul of the world perverted and man monstrous in his ungrateful shape says that Lucius denies "what charitable men afford to beggars" (3.2.77).

We must see the situation in the context of the crisis of charity in England, which was part of the larger economic upheaval. As W. K. Jordan points out, the problem was one of transition from one system of charity to another: charity was no longer primarily a church function, as it had been in the Middle Ages; it was in the process of becoming the obligation of the whole body politic.[21] The breakdown of the old welfare system made many feel with Malynes that charity had grown cold and that men were becoming either misers or prodigals. If one believes the preachers, nobody was doing his share. The position of the aristocrats, of course, made their failure most evident. It should be said that many of them did better than Timon, but aristocratic performance was haphazard at best. It thus attracted criticism particularly from the frugal Puritans, who disliked the conspicuous consumption of the aristocrats and their imitators. Their abundant sermonizing and moralizing on charity would have sensitized Shakespeare's audience to Timon's deficiencies.

Timon clearly violates the safeguards of charity as sermons and tracts postulated them. The three major stipulations were that only those in need should be supported, that the giving should be according to means and not exhaust the substance of the giver, and that it should be done without ostentation and hope of reward. We have already noted Timon's curious conception of what is "need." Timon signally violates the second stipulation, one that is explained in a Jacobean tract on charity: "We must not let it flow out faster than it cometh in but still preserve the main stock."[22] Timon's wrongheaded giving is underlined by this same image of flowing (1.2.54–57; 2.2.1–3; 2.2.144–46). His lack of interest in management would appear even more irresponsible to those who compared him with a Jacobean landowner on whom a large entourage depended. "It is not baseness for the greatest to descend and look into their own estate," wrote Bacon.[23] Bacon, who bankrupted himself by extravagance, is proof that one could know the theory and fall short in practice.

Timon also fails the third test of charity, to "cast in secret, as on the waters, not to be seen and praised of men, for that is mere hypocrisy."[24] He gives ostentatiously, in a sweeping, quasi-royal vein, distributing, as it were, kingdoms to his friends (1.2.219). To give like a king in Shakespeare's time, one needed to be one, and a growing number of Jacobeans, unhappy about the extravagance of King James, thought that even he should reduce his expenditures. But we should perhaps not judge Timon too harshly in this respect; only the most self-effacing of large donors can escape the temptation of pride, and it might be argued that Timon as a man of the ancient world had no incentive to be a saint.

Yet even if liberality according to ancient notions becomes the measurement, Timon fails. According to Aristotle's discussion of this virtue in the *Nichomachean Ethics* (4.1–2), a discussion that influenced Renaissance notions of charity, liberality was the mean between the excess, prodigality, and the defect, stinginess: a liberal man is one who gives to the right people at the right time and fulfills the conditions of right giving. He will purchase and hold property as a necessary condition of having the means to give; he will acquire wealth inasmuch as it is a necessary condition of having the means to give. He will not deplete his substance unless it is to save his friends from ruin. According to Aristotle's definition, Timon cannot be called liberal; he practices the vice that is the excess of this virtue, prodigality.

But Timon is not the worst sort of such a prodigal, the debauched one. Aristotle said that the prodigal who wasted only his resources and did not become profligate possessed some of the qualities of the liberal character. Timon, in effect, wastes only his own property because even what he borrows from others they get back in gifts or securities. A prodigal who did not exploit others, Aristotle said, knew at least enough liberality to give to others and to refrain from taking, but he did not give in the right way. Aristotle thought that the defects of this kind of prodigal were curable and that, in any case, he was not directly harmful to others: "This is why he is felt not to be really bad in character; for to exceed in giving without getting is foolish rather than evil or ignoble."[25] Timon's defense after his ruin is not unlike Aristotle's of this prodigal: "No villainous bounty yet hath pass'd my heart; / Unwisely, not ignobly, have I given" (2.2. 177–78).

Thus, if we consider Timon's economic behavior, we are again faced with the dilemma of his paradoxical personality. We cannot help putting him in the dragon's party. His prodigality contributes to the societal discord, and he violates the canons of liberality and charity. Nor does he understand that a true concord depends on giving as well as receiving by all members of society: he refuses repayment from Ventidius and thus prevents the latter from doing his share. If Timon is not personally debauched, he is the cause that there is debauchery in others (see 2.2.161–67). He bears out the complaint of Barckley that prodigality was now mistaken for liberality.[26] By feeding the wolves, he provides the raw flesh that Malynes said was the food of the dragon. Yet, this flesh is his own; and he gives, if foolishly, from good motives. In fact, he is the only one who believes in the old concord of which Malynes speaks, according to which men must freely give. Quite in general, he is the only character in the play capable of unselfish acts of friendship. As the steward says, he is a "monument / And wonder of good deeds evilly bestow'd" (4.3.463–64).

We cannot consider Timon without reference to the society to which he belongs, a society we must hold responsible in large part for his shortcomings as a philanthropist. This is a dragonish tribe in which Timon's potential for liberality and friendship cannot grow effectively and which induces him to ruin himself owing to its false values; it elevates him to an artificial preeminence and dethrones him blithely when he does not serve its purposes any longer.

The dramatization of specious and shifting values is one of the subtlest touches of *Timon*. It links the play with the other "Greek" one, *Troilus and Cressida,* and makes both supreme documents of Shakespeare's reaction to the changing times. As W. R. Elton has shown, the pricing of men and commodities is a major theme of *Troilus* and permeates the imagery.[27] The theme is crystallized in the discussion of the value of Helen, who is treated as if she were a commodity to be bought and sold. A newfangled relativism is represented by Troilus's "What's ought but as 'tis valued"—commodities and persons are determined by their market price. This relativism is contradicted by Hector's traditional view:

> But value dwells not on particular will,
> It holds its estimate and dignity
> As well wherein 'tis precious of itself
> As in the prizer.
>
> (2.2.53–56)

Those who exploit Timon subscribe to the position of Troilus and try to get as much as they can for whatever they sell or give. The jeweler, for instance, urges the jewel on Timon with the argument that its value will be increased by Timon's wearing it: "Things of like value, differing in the owners, / Are prized by their masters" (1.1.173–74). As in *Troilus and Cressida,* the pricing embraces men as well as things. Timon's alleged worthiness, that is, his generosity, makes him a "rarity" in the world (1.1.4)—the juxtaposition of this evaluation with that of the jewel is telling. Timon himself accepts these inflationary arguments; he urges a jewel (the same jewel?) on the sycophantic first lord with the argument that it will be "advanced" by his wearing it (1.2.166)—only, of course, he gives rather than sells the jewel. This relativism is akin to that with which he accepts the practice of others who do not, as he does, prefer giving to receiving: "If our betters play at that game, we must not dare / To imitate them; faults that are rich are fair" (1.2.12–13). Such relativistic principles are practiced by the senators and his friends, who take from Timon what they can get and charge him for loans what the market will bear. As much as Timon acts counter to the practice of his entourage, he has unthinkingly accepted its commercial ethos.

Timon, as we have noted, combines the analysis of commercial meanness with a satirical examination of the world's conception of honor, and it bears out the elegiac complaint of Malynes, Barckley, and others that wealth was now the way to honor and reputation. Shakespeare, however, saw the connection between the "price" of a man and the honor bestowed on him much more clearly than his contemporaries. We have to look in Hobbes's chapter "Of Power, Worth, Dignity, Honor, and Worthiness" (*Leviathan,* pt. I, chap. 10) to find an insight comparable to his. The honoring and valuing in *Timon* proceed according to principles Hobbes saw at work in his society, where the standing of a man in the marketplace of honor was variable and where natural forces and instincts, as Hobbes mechanistically defined them, were working themselves out competitively.

Hobbes disregarded all conventional humanistic equations of a man's worth with his virtues and made a shrewdly analyzed "power" central to man's valuing of himself and others. This power, Hobbes said, lies in man's means to obtain some future apparent good, and it consists of a "natural power," such as strength, prudence, eloquence, liberality, and nobility, and an "instrumental power" acquired by these qualities or by fortune. This latter power is called instrumental because it enables man to acquire even greater power; it consists of "riches, reputation, friends, and the secret working of God, which men call good luck." This is the kind of strength that Timon's friends discern in him and that attracts them magnetically. Timon accepts their evaluation without realizing that it is founded not on his natural but on his instrumental power, that is, his wealth and apparent good fortune.

The Hobbesian scale of values prevails around Timon.

Human beings, like commodities, are estimated for what good they do to oneself, a procedure resembling Hobbes's contention that men were basing their estimates on the "power" of others: "to have servants is power, to have friends is power, for they are strength united. Also, riches joined with liberality is power and therefore is not absolute but a thing dependent on the need and judgment of another. An able conductor of soldiers is of great price in time of war present or imminent; but in peace not so." Hobbes unabashedly used the commercial metaphor: "And as in other things, so in men, not the seller but the buyer determines the price. For let a man (as most men do) rate themselves at the highest value they can; yet their true value is no more than is esteemed by others." Honoring is therefore variable and depends on fortune: "Good fortune (if lasting) is honorable as the sign of the favor of God; ill fortune and losses dishonorable. Riches are honorable for they are power; poverty is dishonorable."[28]

With the Hobbesian valuing of men and things in *Timon* comes the uncertainty and anxiety created by the dependence on market quotations. The uneasiness of Timon's friends about whom to honor and value shows itself in the trouble they have in deciding who is to take precedence at the banquets. Affected and prolonged courtesies, with which they urge each other to sit down first, precede the meal in each case. On the second occasion, there is also a kind of prologue before Timon's entrance, in which two lords nervously seek to read the barometer of Timon's financial health (3.6.1–24). Since status and place are not fixed, there are revaluations. Alcibiades, no less than Timon, is subjected to these. As Hobbes says, "An able conductor of soldiers is of great price in time of war present or imminent; but in peace, not so." Accordingly, the senators estimate the price of Alcibiades as low and think him therefore expendable; it takes Alcibiades' threat of war to convince them of his value.

In his optimistic phase, Timon accepts the homage of his friends and the senators, quite unaware of its uncertain and shifting nature. The two banquets demonstrate how quickly he who is valued today may be devalued tomorrow and, perhaps, revalued the next day. Timon has the chance of acquiring new and special "dignities" again when the Athenians, beleaguered by Alcibiades, need him (5.1.141). As Hobbes said, "The public worth of a man, which is the value set on him by the commonwealth, is that which men commonly call dignity"; elevating men to dignity is strictly a matter of self-interest: "To be sedulous in promoting another's good, also to flatter, is to honor, as a sign that we seek his protection or aid."[29] The misanthropic Timon, as if he had read Hobbes and disliked what he read, is not "witched" into new dignities based on such calculations.

Even when Timon mouthed the kind of relativistic principles about "our betters" on which his friends operate, he was an ethical absolutist at heart; he becomes an open absolutist when he makes his radical shift from treating the world as all good to knowing it as all evil. As much as we find his extravagant spending and his wild hatred extreme, we realize that both behavior patterns are protests, the first unconscious and the second conscious, against a society Malynes thought dragonish and Hobbes, more's the pity, natural.

9

The Uses of Nature and Art

Livelier than life

The concept of nature in Shakespeare often invokes the concept of art, generally contrastingly, and no more so among Shakespeare's tragedies than in *Timon*. This theme is developed not merely in the sense of a contrast between human skill, the most general meaning of "art" in Shakespeare's time, and the workings of nature, but art also figures in the predominant modern sense of the visual arts. This is a meaning it took in the Renaissance only accidentally, when, for instance, a painter spoke of his professional skill. A large part of the opening scene is devoted to a discussion between the poet and the painter about the works they are going to present to Timon, and the painter claims superiority for his art. This incident touches on a famous issue of Renaissance criticism, the parallel between poetry and painting as the humanists had drawn it by elaborating the Horatian phrase of *ut pictura poesis*, "poetry is like painting."[1] Even before the hero appears on the scene, we are given his image mirrored by the sister arts of poetry and painting. *Timon* does not merely parallel these arts; it integrates them, together with music, in the masque performed at the banquet. This kind of practical demonstration of *ut pictura poesis* was becoming the fashion at King James's court, a fashion that Shakespeare put to his own uses in *Timon* and in *The Tempest*, the two dramas in which the art-nature theme is strongest, with *The Winter's Tale* as a possible rival.

Shakespeare nowhere else engaged so explicitly in art criticism as he did in *Timon*. This matter is dealt with in the peculiar vision of this play; it is not decorative but woven into the dramatic structure and the thematic texture. Shakespeare made much of the poet and the painter's being, by the nature of their arts, illusionists; and this introduces the theme of appearance and reality, as W. M. Merchant has noted.[2] In some manner, this theme runs through all Shakespeare's dramas, implicit as it is in the very nature of his dramatic art, but in *Timon* appearance and reality are probed from a particular perspective that encompasses questions on the nature of art and the nature of man and reveals the strange ironies that arise in their interplay. The immoralists parade the moral purposes of their art; theirs is not, we feel, a "true" art. The art we can admire aesthetically is Timon's nihilistic rhetoric, but we cannot do so without moral reservation, although this reservation is of a kind different from that we have toward the artists' products. The play leaves us with vexing feelings about the uses to which men put art, uses that parallel their perversion of nature. The art-nature dialectic contributes very much to the pervasive pessimism.

The discussion of art and poetry in the first scene is carried on in a climate of gross flattery and deception. The very terminology reflects this climate by semantic ambiguities that unfortunately are mostly lost in modern usage (we are still aware of the ambiguity in "artful"). In Shakespeare's time, even the simple term "art" carried the now obsolete meanings of craftiness, cunning, and deceit. Timon later makes these meanings explicit when he says to the poet, "Thou art even natural in thine art" (5.1.84), that is, he calls the poet a born as well as a practiced deceiver. The art that nature makes cannot be better than that nature itself. "Artificial," which is generally pejorative in critical terminology now, meant "of art" as well as "deceitful." Therefore, for Shakespeare's audience, the poet's praise of the painting had an intriguing semantic ambiguity: "It tutors nature; artificial strife / Lives in these touches, livelier than life" (1.1.37–38). The painter may be striving to surpass nature by his art, but he is also engaged in a crafty enterprise—or so at least somebody alert to the two artists' duplicity would understand it. Even the painter's preceding remark, specious in its modesty, that the painting is a "pretty mocking of the life" (35) is subject to an ironic reading: it presents a good likeness, yet it is also a fraud of some sort.

Here and later, aesthetic criteria are in conflict with moral ones. Being livelier than life is praise as art criticism; it indicates that the portrait has not only the vividness that makes it a faithful rendering of the sitter's outside but also brings out his mental qualities—the painting has *enargaia*, the humanists would have said.[3] If we may believe the poet, the portrait of Timon does indeed have this, since it conveys an impression of Timon's gracefulness and imaginative power. But there was still an old prejudice about imitating nature closely and, in the process, making art triumph over nature. In Spenser's Bower of Bliss, nature is imitated and surpassed by an art designed to entrap man in sensuality and sin. An art that "tutors" nature, as the poet says the painting does, could raise a moral problem. In *Timon* this is a general problem; it goes quite beyond the two artists and their products.

The strategy of the artists is obvious: to impress the philanthropist that he is a huge and overpowering figure of benevolence so that they can more easily strip him of his money. All the interlocutors of the first scene, with the exception of Apemantus, are engaged in this con art. In view of the role that cosmic rhetoric later plays in Timon's misanthropic diatribes, it is interesting to note how the first scene of *Timon* is saturated with an artificial language of cosmic compliments. The painter, it is true, lightly touches on the decay-of-nature theme that Timon will develop powerfully later; but this offhand remark serves merely as a springboard for an outrageous compliment by the poet, who elevates Timon into a universal personality whose magic of bounty rises above the world's impermanence. All the sycophants around Timon participate in this deception, and they invoke all the elements of nature to emblazon it. Like the earth, Timon is awarded a magnetic field that attracts all spirits by the magic of his bounty (1.1.6–7). He is given an unending supply of air: he is so incomparably "breath'd" as to promise an "untirable and continuate goodness" (10–12). The pearl offered to him is luminous by its "water" (18), and poetry burns for him in a "gentle flame" (23).

In contrast to Timon, Apemantus sees from the beginning the reality behind appearances; he considers art not esthetically but morally:

> *Tim.* Wrought he not well that painted it [the portrait]?
> *Apem.* He wrought better that made the painter, and yet he's but a filthy piece of work.
>
> (1.1.197–99)

And, as to poets, Apemantus makes most of their lying—shades of Plato. The truest poetry is the most feigning, as Touchstone once said. In his misanthropic phase, Timon will imitate the Apemantian irony when he mutters about the painter, "Excellent workman, thou canst not paint a man so bad as is thyself" (5.1.30–31), and will say to him:

> Thou draw'st a counterfeit
> Best in all Athens: th'art indeed the best;
> Thou counterfeit'st most lively.
>
> (79–81)

The poet's "fiction" lends itself to the same irony: "Why, thy verse swells with stuff so fine and smooth / That thou art even natural in thine art" (83–84).

This latter phrase raises a question about man's natural condition. It appears to the misanthropic Timon that it is natural for these artists to deceive, just as it is natural for man to be evil. Earlier he saw in art proof of man's innate innocence: painting revealed for him the natural man, the good man unspoiled by the dishonorable traffic of the world (1.1.160–63). Shakespeare raises thus some vexing questions about man, nature, and art: is man innately good or evil, and is art a varnishing or an essentializing endeavor? Shakespeare wisely does not stay for an answer, but the play comes down strongly on man's degradation, whether by nature or by traffic or by both, and it shows that in a degraded world art is perverted too.

As to the specific relationship between the artists and their art, the play seems to be saying that it is difficult to disentangle the one from the other, the substance from the embellishment, the deception from the truth. The allegory is wrapped in a large compliment to Timon:

> His large fortune,
> Upon his good and gracious nature hanging,
> Subdues and properties to his love and tendance
> All sorts of hearts. . . .
>
> (1.1.56–59)

The poem eulogizes Timon for having the gifts of nature, grace, and fortune—everything a man can have—and warns him of the vicissitudes of fortune; but if we look at the quoted lines more closely we can also extract a different, ironic meaning: Timon's fortune is insecurely attached to him because he is giving it away in his great good nature. The thrust of the allegory is that of a warning against reversal of fortune; yet painter and poet are included among "all conditions, all natures" that pay tribute to the fickle goddess and to Timon, at least as long as he has her favor.

The poet, the more articulate of the two, is the more odious deceiver. His public remarks on his poetic inspiration are obscurantist because he poses as a creative genius of the most Wildean sort. He enters "rapt . . . in some work, some dedication / To the great lord." He coyly calls his allegorical poem "a thing slipp'd idly from me" and speaks of the "gentle flame" of his inspiration (1.1.19–25). It is impossible to reconcile his statement on his imagination moving in "a wide sea of wax" with his calling it also an "eagle flight" (45–50). Although a phrase or so went wrong with the text of the passage,[4] this contradiction and the tortured inflation of the language show clearly enough that the poet is merely pretending. To his brother-in-spirit, he reveals a simpler spring of his creativity in simple language: "Then do we sin against our own estate, / When we may profit meet, and come too late" (5.1.40–41). The profit of which he speaks ironically points up his signal perversion of the Horatian demand of *aut prodesse* that Aristotle and the Renaissance humanists thought was the poet's function.

The artistic prelude of *Timon*, in which a discussion of poetry and art exposes the commercial prostitution, turns on a triad of values whose places were often discussed in the Renaissance: Nature, Art, and Fortune. The two former were generally looked upon as forming a defensive alliance against the fickleness of the latter. One of Alciati's emblems, for instance, showed Art (Mercury) as the helper of Nature (*ars naturam adjuvans*) in rejecting the advances of Fortune (*adversus vim fortunae est ars facta*).[5] Perversely, the poet subordinates himself to Fortune in her attack on Nature and thus violates the Renaissance triad, changing it from a harmonious relationship into a subversive hierarchy: Art above Nature, Fortune above Art.

Before pursuing the subject of the artists' subservience to Fortune further, we may take another look at the poet's claim that the painter's "artificial strife" imitates nature. This phrase may be interpreted not only as meaning "strife of art with nature" but also, according to Johnson's suggestion, as referring to the contrast of colors in the painting. This second meaning, disregarded or rejected by modern commentators, is very much in accord with Renaissance notions of the imitation of nature by art. The contrast of colors was looked upon as one of the creative tensions that, like that of the elements, produced harmony and stability, the *discordia concors* by which art imitated nature. To quote from John Norden's *Vicissitudo rerum* (1600):

> All arts have discords, yet in unity
> Concording as in music; high and low,
> Long and short, these compose the harmony.
> The painter does by contraries forth show
> By lively hand what nature doth bestow
> By colors: white, black, red, green, and blue;
> These contraries depaint right Nature's hue.[6]

The two artists' "artificial strife," the imitation of nature under the aegis of fortune, does not produce this *discordia concors*. It contributes to the disharmony of society.

This, I think, is the significance of what would otherwise be an odd topical concern of Shakespeare with a contemporary quarrel of the practitioners of different arts, particularly of poetry and painting, for supremacy, the *paragone*.[7] The quarrel is reflected in the painter's insistence that painting more vividly than poetry depicts the adversity of fortune:

> 'Tis common.
> A thousand moral paintings I can show
> That shall demonstrate these quick blows of Fortune's
> More pregnantly than words.
>
> (1.1.91–94)

Shakespeare evidently knew about the rivalry between poets and painters concerning which of their respective arts was superior in the imitation of reality, although the *paragone* seems not to have been waged in England—somehow he knew about all major intellectual and artistic currents. The humanists had given poetry the prize, but Leonardo in his *Paragone* emphasized the superiority of the eye above the ear and consequently protested that painting ranks above poetry:

> And if you, oh poet, tell a story with your pen, the painter with his brush can tell it more easily, with simpler completeness, and so that it is less tedious to follow. . . . Though the poet is as free to invent as the painter, his fictions do not give so great a satisfaction to men as painting, for though poetry is able to describe forms, actions, and places in words, the painter employs the exact images of the forms and represents them as they are. Now tell me which comes nearer to the actual man; the name of the man or the image of man. . . . And if a poet should say: I will write a story which signifies great things, the painter can do likewise, for even so Apelles painted the Calumny.[8]

At first sight, the painter's claim for his art seems to be not unlike Leonardo's, a claim ratified by Timon when he says that the penciled figures are even what they give out to be and that they depict natural, that is, ideal man—Leonardo speaks of "the image of man." But poet and painter are not in competition about the first rank of the arts in the imitation of nature; they belong to the society at the base of Fortune's hill that competes for gold. As much as we are tempted to mention the two artists in one breath, they are not Concordia personified; and if their art can be said to imitate nature, it is not the ideal nature of harmony and proportion but one that has lost these qualities. There is indeed talk in the play about "bonds"—a word that elsewhere in Shakespeare signifies the integration of man into the world order—but these are financial bonds. Only for Timon do human bonds matter, and even he is obsessed with the idea that gold threads run through their fabric: "To build his fortune I will strain a little, / For 'tis a bond in men," he says when endowing his servant (1.1.146–

47). More even than the strain the gift puts on Timon's wealth, we feel here the strain in his belief that he can tie the parasites to him by feelings of gratitude. This idyllic delusion is rudely shattered when he is beset by "clamorous demands of debt, broken bonds" (2.2.43)—the dissonances become audible. The very speech of Timon's senatorial friends suggests them when they answer his request for aid with "hard fractions"—broken rhythms that are superbly imitated by the steward (2.2.208–17). And the collapse of Timon's house leaves his servants mere "broken implements" (4.2.16). These images conjure up the picture of the fragmented world as the pessimistic moralists of Shakespeare's time saw it, the world that, in Barckley's phrase, resembled "a chain rent in pieces, whose links are many lost and broken that they will hardly hang together."[9]

The concord of nature has been broken by an ingratitude that Timon conceives as monstrous. Ancient and Renaissance ethics were here on his side. "Nothing does more unknit and pluck asunder the concord of mankind than that vice," said Seneca in an Elizabethan translation of *De beneficiis*, still a fundamental book on giving and liberality in Shakespeare's time.[10] Flattery and pursuit of fortune constitute now "the world's soul," (3.2.65)—the stranger's comment gives a strongly pessimistic twist to the old idea of the *anima mundi*.[11] It is a topsy-turvy world in which those rejected by Fortune fall downward, head over heels. The Athenians dance to Fortune's tune—emblematic fashion[12]—and they value and revalue as they perceive these strains. Timon's friends, who first adore him as a wealthy man, reject him when they discover him to be a pauper. His invitation for the banquet makes them think that he still has money, and they come once more to pay him tribute; but his behavior convinces them that they were right before and that he is merely a mad pauper. Yet the senators, who abandoned Timon in need, would fain have his help later when besieged by Alcibiades.

The dance-of-fortune motif is highlighted by the two banquets. At the first, art once more communicates a truth different from what it is designed for. Timon's masque ends in a dance, interpreted by Apemantus as symbolizing the quick changes brought about by fortune: "I should fear those that dance before me now / Would one day stamp upon me" (1.2.139–40). Timon, however, still spins his euphoric dream to the accompaniment of lutes and oboes. Not until the demands for repayment have reached a fortissimo does he perceive the disharmonies around him. The trumpet sound with which he has the second banquet opened signals his awakening to the harsh realities. He produces now his own Apemantian anti-masque when he knocks his guests and they fall over each other as they seek to recover their

jewels, coats, and hats. Before the overturn of all order becomes Timon's constant theme, he glaringly exposes the
disorder that reigns in Athens.

Banquets that reveal social disorder occur elsewhere in
Shakespeare's later plays. In *Macbeth*, Banquo's ghost with
his góry locks creates havoc at Macbeth's celebration of
kingship. In the banquet of *The Tempest*, which most resembles that of *Timon*, Ariel under the direction of Prospero first
serves and then snatches away a banquet from the hungry
Neapolitans. The banquets both in *The Tempest* and in *Timon*
are, in a sense, banquets of art (and Prospero's, being served
in nature, offers a clear nature-art contrast) since they are designed by their creators to make meaning visible. In both,
social disturbers are mocked; in both, the hosts play, as it
were, Fortune. But *The Tempest*, as I shall note later, has some
significant differences from *Timon* in its art-nature-fortune
associations.

That art, nature, and fortune are central to the thematic
movement of *Timon* has been well recognized in an engaging
essay by Paul Rheyer. Rheyer rightly places *Timon* in the context of the later Renaissance, when, as he says, the assurance
about the proper placement of nature and fortune in the
scheme of things was losing itself "in the night of the times."
Not only Shakespeare but contemporary moralists and satirists believed that this was happening. In *Timon*, Shakespeare
gave his heroes two contrasting careers, one of fortune and
one of nature. The Timon who is Fortune's darling, Rheyer
says, is spoiled by her gifts; although theoretically he knows
that man tries to conceal his true feelings, he is naive about
his friends and accepts their facade as their true essence, incapable of understanding how much fortune and gold have
denatured them. Only when he turns toward nature in the
wood does he gauge these perversions. He realizes now that
being favored by fortune is enough to make a man forget all
human obligations, reverse his relationship to others, and disregard all inherent merits and priorities: "all's obliquy," i.e.,
all is oblique. Ingratitude flourishes because fortune and nature are not assigned to their separate spheres but have become inseparable: "Not nature, / To whom all sores lay siege,
can bear great fortune, / But by contempt of nature" (4.3.
6–8). Timon's plunge into nature teaches him also that there
exists a nature outside of man that is not affected by the
corrupting society and that enjoins a contempt for fortune.
He prefers this sane and unadulterated, yet rough and rude,
environment to the company of man. His turn away from
fortune and toward this harsh but unspoiled nature is symbolized by his choosing his grave at the seaside, where it is
visited each day by the tumultuous flood.[13]

This analysis is fine as far as it goes, but it describes primarily the Apemantian influence on the misanthropic Timon's attitude toward nature. Reyher himself indicates that there is a further turn when he notes a "more original" strain in Timon's rhetoric that is evidenced in his encouragement to the robbers to steal and plunder because the sun, the moon, and the sea are also wholesale thieves. Timon does not merely experience the harshness of nature but feels empathetic with it, feels one with this nature. He undergoes, as it were, a seasonal change. At the outset, it appears to him to be summer in his life; but the steward warns of a coming change when his friends will abandon him: "one cloud of winter show'rs, / These flies are couch'd" (2.2.175–76). When the senators refuse to come to his aid, they answer his plea for help with the excuse that they are "at fall" (2.2.209) —"fall" was then used in England for the autumn as it is now in America, and this is surely one meaning here. When it is "deepest winter" in Timon's purse (3.4.15), he realizes what "summer birds" his friends are (3.6.30–31). He views the nature into which he withdraws as a winter landscape: those who "numberless upon me stuck, / Do on the oak, have with one winter's brush / Fell from their boughs (4.3. 265–67). His rhetoric of wrath that calls on nature and the elements to undertake his revenge is a counterblast to the storm created in his life by men who have left him "open, bare" (267–68). After participating unknowingly in a dance of fortune and symbolizing it first unwittingly in the device of his masque, then consciously in the mock banquet, he asks nature to perform its own dance of destruction.

Although Timon is not a philosopher and no clear line in his thought is discernible, we can see a general hardening of his feeling that nature is potentially so cruel that it can be invoked to destroy man. It is for this purpose that Timon in his different way also "tutors nature," becoming an artist of destructive and nihilistic rhetoric—of course, it is ultimately the creator of Timon, Shakespeare, who is the real artist. Nobody before or since has ever drawn up such awe-inspiring rhetoric, and the question arises regarding what resources Shakespeare drew on for this art. None of the dramatic antecedents has anything like it. The curse of destruction in tragedy, it is true, has a tradition.[14] There are characters in Senecan tragedy who in anguish or in anger call for the overthrow and ruin of the whole universe; but these are isolated and fairly simple outcries that lack the scope of Timon's curses and his repertory of diatribes. Lear, of course, goes through a nihilistic stage when he feels part of nature's destructive impulses as does Timon and calls on the lightning: "Strike flat the thick rotundity of the world! / Crack

nature's moulds, all germains spill at once / That makes ungrateful man!" (3.2.6–9). But again this is a passing, if impressive, phase.

Shakespeare's success in the rhetoric of cosmic destruction, I believe, derives to a large degree from his skillful adaptation of Christian pessimistic traditions of nature and their
incorporation into the cosmic curses conventional in tragedy.
Harold Wilson is on the right track when he notes that in
Timon "Shakespeare has chosen to write his *contemptus mundi*
without affording any ground of reconciliation or compromise
in the explicit context of the play itself"; Wilson adds that it
is idle to speculate from what motive or out of what mood of
personal bitterness Shakespeare did so.[15] Shakespeare's motives need not concern us here except for the artistic need to
deepen Timon's misanthropy into the strongest pessimism
imaginable. Wilson is certainly correct in seeing an analogy
between Timon's rhetoric and the *contemptus mundi;* it was
from this tradition and the allied idea of nature's decay that
Shakespeare drew the substance of Timon's tirades.

Shakespeare, of course, had to make some changes when
adapting this Christian tradition to the pagan milieu of his
play. He could not have his Timon ascribe the malignancy
of nature to man's fall and continuing sin in Christian theological terms, although he could have him hint at a causal
connection between man's degradation and nature's severity.
Similarly he could not explicitly make Timon see nature's
unkindness to man as the result of God's punishment; but
again, he could hint at such a connection. The *contemptus
mundi* described the elements as the executors of the wrath
of God against sinful man, and analogously Timon appeals
to their destructive power against wicked Athens. Already
Timon's first soliloquy outside Athens, when he addresses the
walls, implies that he attributes to the four elements this
function: the *earth* is to swallow the wall, youth to *drown* itself
in riot, *breath* to infect breath, and a contagious fever to *sear*
the Athenians (4.1.1 / ff.). In Timon's next soliloquy, when
he has stationed himself in nature, he calls more explicitly
on these elements:

> O blessed breeding sun, draw from the earth
> Rotten humidity; below thy sister's orb
> Infect the air!

(4.3.1–3)

At least once Timon hints that this deterioration of nature is
to happen in analogy to God's use of nature against sinful
man. He thus admonishes Alcibiades to become the Athenians' Nemesis:

> Be as a planetary plague, when Jove
> Will o'er some high-vic'd city hang his poison
> In the sick air.

(4.3.110–12)

The role envisaged for Jove here somewhat contradicts the usual passive one Timon attributes to the "perpetual-sober" gods, and resembles that of the Christian God of Wrath. As Boaistuau, for instance, pointed out, God could use war for the punishment of mankind, and He could make the air, so indispensable for human life, into man's poisoner.[16] Timon's next notable soliloquy, which addresses the nourishing earth and demands that it engender poisons and beasts noxious to man (4.3.179–94), is analogous to arguments on the potential role of the elements as instruments of divine vengeance. Shakespeare may well have adapted it from Boaistuau. (See the Source Appendix.)

Besides apostrophizing the elements, Timon's soliloquies call on the cosmic bodies to bring about man's destruction. And here the literature of the decay of nature, which allied itself with the nature pessimism of the *contemptus mundi*, provided the pattern. Timon's call for the sun to leave its course and infect the air of the sublunary zone drew substance from the fear that the ordered courses of the celestial bodies were weakening. Even some of Galileo's discoveries seemed to be pointing to the decay of the solar system, as the apocalyptic preachers were not slow in discovering. Thus Thomas Gardiner warned in the *Doomsday Book* (1606) that "the constitution of the celestial orbs is weakened, the sun not so many spaces different from us as it was wont to be. . . ."[17] What were conceived as warnings in this literature become fervent wishes in Timon's rhetoric. To Shakespeare's audience, they must have seemed far from impossible of eventual fulfillment.

The greatest, most original, and fiercest of the speeches in which Timon parallels nature's destructiveness with human wickedness is his sermon to the bandits:

> I'll example you with thievery:
> The sun's a thief, and with his great attraction
> Robs the vast sea; the moon's an arrant thief,
> And her pale fire she snatches from the sun;
> The sea's a thief, whose liquid surge resolves
> The moon into salt tears; the earth's a thief,
> That feeds and breeds by a composture stol'n
> From gen'ral excrement; each thing's a thief.

(4.3.438–45)

For Shakespeare's audience, aware of how these cosmic relationships were supposed to work, the speech had an added fascination. Each of the cosmic bodies and elements was supposed not only to take something from another but also to give to some other in return and thus produce a cosmic *concordia*—the reciprocity was analogous to the free borrowing and lending that cemented the stable society according to old-fashioned humanism. From this point of view, Timon might appear to be merely ignorant or willful. But we must see this speech against the background of the decay-of-nature ideas that drew the proper working of the natural harmonies into doubt. Further, we must consider it in the context of feelings inspired by the economic crisis that was dissolving societal bonds. Both developments made the old commonplace of the harmony of nature appear outdated. Writers even could poke fun at it, as did Sir William Cornwallis when he spun a lengthy analogy between man's commercial activity and the operation of sun, moon, stars, and earth; everybody acted now, he said, as if "without debt and loan the fabric of the world will be disjointed and fall asunder into its first chaos."[18] Timon sees this activity as a one-way street, as exploitation and robbery; and so indeed it must have appeared to many of Shakespeare's contemporaries. The kinetic metaphors of robbing, snatching, and surging in Timon's speech vividly convey the impression of a violent disruption of order and decency. Timon projects this societal degeneration onto the universe in a monomaniac obsession with the denaturing, that is, humanizing, of nature.

Besides drawing on the elements and the celestial bodies, Timon's rhetoric of nature outdoes Apemantian pessimism in denying that animals are better than men and in seeing them as participating in the general corruption. The conventional misanthropic position has always been to disparage man in favor of the animals or at least some animals, such as Swift's rational and temperate horses. Apemantus similarly prefers animals to men. Timon accepts this idea at least initially upon turning misanthrope: "Timon will to the woods, where he shall find / Th' unkindest beast more kinder than mankind" (4.1.35–36). By the time he comes to debate Apemantus, his hatred of man has become so ingrained and his view of life's malignancy so obsessive that he sees no kindness any longer anywhere, not even in the animal world. The distance he has traveled shows when he exposes the sentimental core in the cynic's position. He asks Apemantus the loaded question: "Wouldst thou have thyself fall in the confusion of men, and remain a beast with the beasts?" (4.3.325–26). When Apemantus answers affirmatively, Timon proves that animals are engaged in the same war of everybody against everybody else as are men: "If thou wert the lion, the fox would beguile thee; if thou wert the lamb, the

fox would eat thee . . ." (329 ff.). So far this is perhaps
not too unusual a statement; but Timon gives it a unique
turn when he sees this enmity not merely as setting one
species against another or one individual animal against
another but as pitting each particular creature against itself: "If thou wert the ass, thy dulness would torment thee
. . . if thou wert the wolf, thy greediness would afflict thee
. . . ; wert thou the unicorn, pride and wrath would confound thee and make thine own self the conquest of thy
fury . . ." (333 ff). This goes quite beyond the preachers'
saying that "every creature since sin entered into the
world is become an enemy to another like enemies in war."[19]
And it even goes beyond what Hobbes was to say later when
he saw this general hostility as the natural state, no longer
worrying about any human sin that might have created it.
There are deeper fissures than these in Timon's discordant
universe and they leave nothing sane and whole. The animal world appears to him now humanized, that is, stripped
of all that is benevolent, just as man has become beastly.
The misanthrope's pessimistic view takes wing from the
Renaissance traditions.

Timon's tutoring of nature for self-destruction is a gigantic
enterprise, but it is also utterly useless. In his own way, as
Swigg notes, Timon, like the poet and painter, is better in
promising than in performing.[20] His lack of effect on the
world's uses is highlighted by the last nature image he creates, his seaside grave visited by the flood. He cannot control the symbolism with which he seeks to make it a denunciation of, and separation from, mankind. The lash of the
turbulent surge, by which he seeks to symbolize the force of
his hatred of mankind, is artfully tamed in Alcibiades' "rich
conceit" of Neptune's tears: the powerful flood image becomes translated into mythological embroidery.

If the world does not take Timon's misanthropic message
seriously, neither does it really pity him. The "droplets" that
Alcibiades describes as falling from "niggard nature" are a
"brains' flow" rather than an effusion of the heart. We are
reminded of the real tears, the few touches of a benevolent
nature in the play, when Timon wept for friendship's sake
and the steward for the folly of his master. The eyes of
Timon's exploiters were dry then, and there are no real tears
now for the stilling of the breath whose very epitaph is a
curse. The rich and mighty will not look on Timon's work
and despair.

It is tempting to contrast the vanity of Timon's destructive
and nihilistic art with the success of Prospero's optimistic
and life-affirming one. Prospero, we might say, translates his

vision into reality because he works with a benevolent nature; Timon, attempting to whip nature into malignancy, ends in a solitary grave, his message disregarded by the world. Yet, this comparison is unilluminating for several reasons. First, it uses "art" in two different meanings, those of Prospero's powerful magic and Timon's nihilistic rhetoric. Nobody really assumes that Timon could bring off his desire to destroy man and nature. Second, the comparison exaggerates the gap between Timon's failure and Prospero's success. Prospero knows that supernatural powers are not man's to wield and that cloud-capped towers do not last forever: he goes back to Milan with the intention of giving every third thought to his grave. Fortune is not brought irrevocably under the control of art, since the possibility of Prospero's failing again as a ruler is not excluded. Third, the comparison is inappropriate because the worlds of the two plays are entirely different. Athens is not Prospero's magic isle: we cannot transfer Timon to the isle or Prospero to Athens. Had Shakespeare been a philosopher, the contrast between the world of *The Tempest* and that of *Timon* might have been a flaw in his system; as an artist he could create without contradicting himself two such worlds, the one animated by a benevolent nature, the other doomed by a malignant one. We may perhaps take these two visions together as expressing Shakespeare's hopes and fears for mankind and perceive the one world as a Utopia, the other as a warning.

It should be said also that, unsuccessful as Timon is in persuading Athens, he triumphs as a verbal artist. He, not the mediocre poet nor the flattering painter, is the true artist of the play, and he soars in eagle flight, even though this is a flight into nihilism and madness. If Timon does not succeed in speeding up the world's conflicts and bringing about an apocalypse, at least he conjures up the picture of a world that deserves such an apocalypse: a world of deceit, discord, chaos, and deadly illness. In this sense, he accomplishes what many Renaissance moralists and satirists who no longer touch us tried to do, and he succeeeds because of his, or rather, Shakespeare's art.

10

Fortune and the Globe

All broken implements of a ruined house

Although the poet's allegory of Fortune is trite by itself, it is highly significant for the meaning and quality of the play. Not that it is really revelatory of Timon's tragedy beyond the mere outward movement from fortune to misfortune. Rather, it functions as a kind of prologue that puts the action, as it were, under the aegis of the goddess Fortuna and invites the reader or spectator to view it from a pessimistic perspective.

Fortuna was a Roman goddess of older origin—the Greeks knew her as *Tuche*. She had become somewhat uncertainly acclimatized to the Christian scheme of things in the Middle Ages, and she continued and enlarged her dubious reign in the Renaissance.[1] From a strictly Christian point of view she had no legitimate role except as Divine Providence. But it could hardly be denied that she represented something real that was going on in the world, something to hope for or feel threatened by even though its connection to the will of God was often opaque. In *Timon*, Fortuna presides, as it were, from the allegory onward; her influence is attested by the frequency of the word "fortune" in the remainder of the play. It occurs particularly often in the plural form, in which it primarily referred to wealth, estate, and possessions.[2]

Although the worship of the goddess is not unknown in our own time, allegories about Fortune—along with allegories in general—have lost their appeal, and it is therefore under-standable that a few years ago *Timon* was performed without the poet's recital of his composition. Director or designer in-vented an ingenious substitution: a female statue, suggestive of the goddess, became visible on the stage when the curtain rose; later it gazed in a lurid light at the ruins of the mock banquet.[3] One hopes that the audience sensed the significance of this prop, a prop that Shakespeare's audience, familiar with Fortuna iconography and alert to its occurrence not only in the allegory but also in the play at large, did not need. Since the Middle Ages, literature and art had worked to-gether to draw Fortuna's picture; it is not fortuitous that the miniature *paragone* between the poet and the painter erupts on who can better depict the goddess.

However, the painter's self-important assertion that he can show the poet "a thousand moral paintings" that demon-strate the blows of fortune more pregnantly than words is disingenuous. Although there were Renaissance and baroque paintings of Fortuna, her major impact came from the area somewhere between literature and art, from emblems and from symbolizations in *trionfi*, pageants, and processions. It is to the emblems, in particular, that the poet's allegory and the allusions to fortune in the play offer parallels. Since the emblems, like drama, were a *picta poesis* combining word and picture, they had a mutually fruitful relationship with the stage. Shakespeare's stage and the acting on it, as we have come to see, were in some manner emblematic. Through using the symbolic *donnée* of the Elizabethan-Jacobean stage and augmenting it by props, groupings of characters, movements, costumes, and even sound effects, the dramatists created a symbolic language; Shakespeare was as much a master of this language as of the verbal idiom. Moreover, he could and did make the verbal images suggest conventional visual ones to give a graphic extension to the text or provide an ironic commentary. I shall in this chapter try to re-create the the-matic patterns that arise from this interplay of literary and visual suggestiveness in the Fortuna allusions of *Timon* by drawing on emblems and processional symbols. We must be satisfied here with a plausible reconstruction; we cannot witness a Jacobean performance of *Timon*, nor can we put ourselves in the minds of Shakespeare and his audience and say definitely that every single association was intended or perceived. Their total effect is beyond doubt.

First the allegory and its immediate implications for the play. The poet says, "I have upon a high and pleasant hill / Feign'd Fortune to be thron'd" (1.1.65–66). We are struck here, at first, not by a likeness but by a contrast between the poetic image and the usual visual images of Fortuna in the emblems.

"Fortune," says Shakespeare's Fluellen, "is painted blind, with a muffler afore her eyes, to signify to you that Fortune is blind, and she is painted also with a wheel, to signify to you, which is the moral of it, that she is turning and inconstant, and mutability, and variation: and her foot, look you, is fixed upon a spherical stone, which rolls, and rolls, and rolls" (*Henry V*, 3.6.30–36). Fortuna seated on a throne does occur in literature, but rarely, it appears, in art, and then with a symbolism different from that in *Timon*.[4] Likewise, one can find a hill of Fortune in medieval romances and in miniatures illustrating them, such as in manuscripts of *The Romance of the Rose*,[5] but I have failed to locate this hill in Renaissance emblems or paintings. Shakespeare evidently was aware that poetry and painting, although sister arts, sometimes choose different iconographic details.

Shakespeare's Londoners, however, had seen a symbolic hill of Fortune of sorts a few years before *Timon* was presumably written and performed. It crowned one of the triumphal arches through which King James passed during his coronation procession in 1604 (which, ironically, had been delayed because of the outbreak of the plague in 1603). The fifth "pegme," or structure, entitled *Hortus Euphoriae* (Garden of Plenty), showed Fortune standing on top of a little temple or palace, which in turn was on top of a hill, a "high and pleasant hill" like that of the Fortune favorable to Timon. Moreover, the device made the dependence of man's fortune on material prosperity evident: under Fortuna "sat two persons, representing gold and silver, supporting the globe of the world between them."[6] But this hill lacked the allegory's slippery slope down which Fortune's rejects slide. Shakespeare's hill of Fortune, as we have noted, is a variant of the conventional visual and literary wheel of Fortune, and this conception of the wheel accentuates the structure of the play.

In this context, the poet's reference to the throne of Fortune has an interesting stage symbolism. The throne, of course, was a frequent stage prop, particularly in the history plays, which often began with a king seated on a throne that he later lost or relinquished by death, a dramatic emblem related to the iconographic tradition of an enthroned king on top of Fortune's wheel.[7] The reference to a throne in *Timon* draws attention to its absence on the stage, and it underlines Timon's foolishness in dreaming of dealing kingdoms to his friends (1.2.219). He emulates, as David Cook says, "the indiscriminate giving of an abstract goddess like Fortune."[8] It is *Fortuna Bona*, the benefactress of mankind, with whom Timon comes close to identifying himself; he dreams, we might say, of sitting on her throne. And this, naturally, is a kind of hubris.

Timon's hubris makes it impossible for him to have anything more than a kind of collegial attitude to the gods. Even
so, he and Apemantus are the only Athenians in the play
who recognize the gods and pray to them, odd as their prayers
are. By contrast, the merchant's god, as Apemantus says, is
"traffic." Later Timon says much the same thing when he calls
gold the Athenians' "visible god" (4.3.389). Religious or
spiritual feelings of any kind are inconceivable in Athens.
The pursuit of fortune is the only worship there; the loss of
fortune, the only hell: "Let molten coin be thy damnation,"
says Flaminius to Lucullus (3.1.52).[9] To his credit, Timon does
not worship the Athenian ersatz gods; but he is unable to
call on the gods for anything more than the expression and
affirmation of his own desires. When he thanks them in
prosperity, it is for having so many friends who will help in
need. When he leaves the city, he removes the gods from the
human scene so that they will escape contamination, just as
he removes himself. Timon's gods resemble the gods of
Epicurus and Lucretius; like these they are quite superfluous.

Chummy in his attitude toward the gods, Timon scatters
gifts and favors from what he assumes to be an inexhaustible
treasure, a cornucopia of the kind from which *Fortuna Bona*
distributes her riches in the emblems. We must not balk at
the identification of Timon with Fortuna because of his sex.
The mythographers noted that the ancients represented
fortune sometimes as a young man, presumably because of
the association with *Chairos*, the Greek god of opportunity,
and they recollected from Pliny that the Romans erected a
statue of a male Fortuna.[10] This conception was also embodied
in an illustration of Vincenzo Cartari's influential *Le Imagine
dei Dei degli antichi*, an illustration that has an intriguing resemblance to Timon's situation. The woodcut shows two
Fortunas: one, Felicitas-Fortuna, is seated at the left, with a
cornucopia, as the presiding goddess, and a male Fortuna
hovers in the air at the right with the Roman attributes of
plenty—a dish, an ear of corn, and a poppy—in his hands.
This latter image represents the extravagant dream of the
winged struggler beneath on Fortune's wheel, whose feet, like
Timon's, are on the wheel that will sometime turn down.
On the right, Adulation, like Timon's friends, adores the
favorite of Fortuna. An emaciated Envy stands next to the
struggler, the Envy that always looks unfavorably on anybody
who does not fear her.[11]

Timon's eminence, like that of this struggler on Fortune's
wheel, is not merely a self-projection but also the making of
his adulatory friends. They do their best to nourish his delusion
that he sits on Fortune's throne. When one of them says that
"Plutus the god of gold / Is but his steward" (1.1.275–76), he

casts Timon in a Fortuna role since Plutus was generally conceived to be Fortuna's helper and companion. In a typical emblem drawn by Jean Cousin, a blindfold Plutus holds a blindfold Fortuna by her hand.[12] Timon's flatterers, in fact, act as if he commanded the globe with its four elements: they make earth, water, air, and fire attest to his glory. Such symbolic reign was traditional in Fortuna iconography. The Londoners saw it depicted on one of the structures through which King James passed during his coronation procession: the central device of the sixth pegme, entitled *Cosmos Neos*, was a globe presided over by Fortuna, her foot treading the turning circle that contained the insignia of the various estates; the circle itself was turned by four allegorical figures that represented the four elements.[13] One is reminded of Coriolanus's phrase "O world, thy slippery turns!" (4.4.12), and one wonders whether all viewers accepted the official iconography of the device, that is, the promotion of virtue and justice by fortune. The circle must have suggested to thoughtful observers the inexorable wheel on which those who are carried up will also be carried down.

The poet's allegory in *Timon* certainly emphasizes the bipolarity of Fortune, and Timon's career is its manifestation. When Fortune is described as wafting Timon to her with her "ivory hand" (1.1.72), the implication is, as Samuel Chew proposes, that she has an ebony hand with which she will turn him away later.[14] In emblems, Fortuna was presented as having opposite sides and qualities, and sometimes she was shown as half-light and half-dark.[15] In his two banquets, Timon enacts the antithetical behavior of the goddess: at the first he distributes, Fortuna-like, lavish gifts; at the second he serves his friends symbols of their worthlessness, stones and lukewarm water. He calls them now "fools of fortune, trencherfriends, time's flies" whose "perfection" is smoke and lukewarm water (3.6.85–92)—smoke being a symbol of the vanity of the world's glory.[16] The discomforted guests have a point when they feel he acts like an ambivalent Fortuna: "One day he gives us diamonds, next day stones" (3.6.115). The goddess was similarly depicted in emblems as scattering crowns, scepters, tiaras, and precious objects with one hand, worthless things like stones and foolscaps with the other.[17] She is also shown distributing gifts with one hand while holding a whip or rod in the other.[18] The two banquets bring out Timon's assuming these polar roles of Fortuna as rewarder and punisher; it is likely that Shakespeare conceived the contrast of the banquets, which has no equivalent in the sources, so to point up these roles.

From the second banquet, Timon impersonates solely *Fortuna Mala*, an enemy of man and a frequent subject of the image-makers. In her punishing function, she was often identified with Nemesis. It is in practice difficult to distinguish the two figures in art; Dürer's famous engraving has been called both *Nemesis* and *Great Fortune*. One might say that Timon's earlier career aspires to be a Triumph of Fortune, his later a Triumph of Nemesis—the contrasting pageants that were pictorial motifs.[19]

The most vivid feature of the poet's allegory, one that has much correspondence in the visual arts, is the bipolarity of the Fortuna landscape, the luxuriant slope of *Fortuna Bona* and the steep and barren one of *Fortuna Mala*—a change of setting as it is symbolized in Timon's career. In the emblems, the change is sometimes one from an urban center, such as Timon's Athens, to a woodland like that of Timon's later days.[20] Trees, as Werner Habicht points out, were generally associated with Fortuna.[21] The symbolism of the movement from the city to the wood in *Timon* is the more significant since it was Shakespeare's own interpretation of the story. None of the sources has anything like it; in them, Timon lived in Athens or in a hut of the fields. Timon moves, like two figures in an emblem by Denis Lebey de Batilly, from a walled city on the left, symbolizing prosperity, to a wood of adversity on the right. The two men are propelled in this direction by the wind of Fortune above them; but while one of them resolutely marches on without turning his back, the other foolishly turns around and attempts to blow back the wind toward the heavenly force: necessity must be obeyed, says the text.[22] Timon's gesture on leaving Athens goes against this commonplace Fortuna moral; and his mighty stream of condemnation and defiance of the Athenians, who have created his adverse fortune, is quite a different matter from the weak breath of Batilly's wanderer. Shakespeare was not interested in convenient little morals.

The Fortuna iconography of *Timon* raises the question of for what theater the play was written. Several scholars have argued that its particular theatrical qualities indicate that it was intended for an indoor stage. J. M. Nosworthy, though not rejecting the possibility of a Globe performance, thinks that the spectacular scenes with the masque as central interest may have been assembled to provide an entertainment at court.[23] E. A. J. Honigmann suggests that *Timon* (and *Troilus and Cressida*) may have been intended for an evening performance at one of the Inns of Court; it would have appealed to young lawyers, and the emphasis on food and drink and the masque would carry a warning against their prodigality.[24] In her intriguing reconstruction of the play's first performance, M. C. Bradbrook claims that it was an "experimental scenario for an indoor dramatic pageant" with which Shakespeare's company opened their new Blackfriars Theater.[25] What a subject for an opening!

None of these arguments seem to me plausible enough to deny the play to the Globe, where Bernard Beckerman puts it.[26] There is no reason to think that *Timon* required the special properties of an indoor theater if one assumes that the style of the performance was emblematic: a table and benches for the banquets, a stage tree for the wood, and a small stage rock for the cave would have been quite sufficient. For the rest, the bare Globe stage provided some excellent emblematic possibilities, such as for the house of Timon, the city walls of Athens, and the heavens above. Banquets and masques were not inappropriate for the public stage, and it is quite gratuitous to suggest, as does Bradbrook, that a waterworks or wave machine may have been employed for Timon's watery grave; it is offstage, and, in any case, the ending provides that Timon's joining of Neptune be transformed into a conceit rather than a bath. The Fortuna symbolism of the play suggests to me strongly that the public playhouse was the setting of Shakespeare's vision when he wrote. This does not exclude the possibility that the play was also intended for performances in the private theater, but I believe that the Globe had a definite edge in producing the appropriate pictorial suggestiveness.

There is, first of all, Timon's actual house. Much of the earlier action takes place either in front of it or within; all of act one and, except for the first very short scene, of act two plus a large portion of act three are set here. Although Shakespeare's plays do not require definite localization, the Globe stage in this case made the house setting fitting. The pillars that carried the roof of the stage would have helped suggest such a setting to the audience's imagination; they imitated classical architecture, and they may have been painted to look like marble if they were like those of the Swan Theater.[27] The movement of the actors from the forestage to the area under the pillars or through the tiringhouse would signify their entering Timon's mansion, or, for that matter, their passing from one part of it to the other. The banquets would be served "indoors," that is, under the pillars; tables, chairs, and dinnerware carried in by the servants would provide the setting. When Timon hides himself from the creditors in his house, that is, behind the tiringhouse facade, the pillared stage would appear like a portico.

In conformity with Timon's impersonation of Fortuna, his house would also evoke emblems in which the goddess in her smiling mood is associated with a building, a large palace or spacious house, "Fortune's hall," as it is called in *Troilus and Cressida* (3.3.134). For that matter, Fortuna was also at home in the theater—a symbolism to which we shall turn later. Interestingly, in Lydgate's *Fall of Princes*, Alcibiades was said to have dwelled in "Fortunys halle" during his prosperity;[28] and a house of Fortune had been put on the stage in a masque-like morality play, *The Contention between Liberality and Prodigality*, performed about 1576 and printed in 1602. When Timon impersonates the goddess, his house takes on a duality similar to the house of this morality: it is a real dwelling but also an illusion created by the people who worship Fortune. The tall pillars of the Globe would appropriately suggest a hall worthy of the goddess. Under its roof, that of the stage, are enacted scenes symbolic of her allurement, such as banquets and dances—emblems associated both activities with the goddess.[29] Of course, the house of Fortune carries a warning: splendid today, it may be a ruin tomorrow.

The liberal and symbolic meaning of Timon's house is brought home by strong verbal emphasis. When Timon says of his servant, "To build his fortune I will strain a little" (1.1.146), the strain on his property can be felt. Later, when Timon's great house, so hospitable and so freely accessible before, becomes his retentive jail, a servant coins the convenient Fortuna moral: "Who cannot keep his wealth must keep his house" (3.3.43). This moral resembles an emblem by Batilly in which a man takes cover from the storms of Fortune behind the thick walls of a house[30]—Timon, of course, rather than remaining in the shelter, breaks forth violently. We are made aware not only of Timon's house but also of the houses the others keep because these structures are a measure of their standing with Fortune. The fool offers a wittily relevant paradox when he compares the house of his mistress, the prostitute, with those of Timon's usuring friends: "When men come to borrow of your masters, they approach sadly, and go away merry; but they enter my mistress's house merrily, and go away sadly" (2.2.102–5).[31] Fortuna was often called a hussy because of her promiscuity; and the userers' houses as well as the house of the prostitute share in the function of the house of Fortune in which the sad are transformed into the merry and the merry into the sad, according to the whims of the goddess. The inhabitants of Timon's house, in which the fool turns his paradox, will soon be transformed from happiness to misery.

The world judges Timon by the house he owns and reverses its judgment when he loses it. Keeping "so good a house" appears to Lucullus the essence of nobility (3.1.23). When the substance is gone and the house lost, the nobility of the owner is foreclosed too. The magnificent houses of the creditors, enlarged with spoils of Timon's, now support their preeminence as one of their servants snobbishly reminds the steward: "Who can speak broader than he that has no house to put his head in? Such may rail against great buildings" (3.4.63–65). But building to great height is apt to lead to disaster, as one of La Perrière's emblems warned and as Timon's fate shows.[32]

In the mock banquet, Timon's turn toward misanthropy is accompanied by the rejection of the house in which he has presided: "Burn, house! Sink, Athens! Henceforth hated be / Of Timon, man and all humanity!" (3.6.100–101). This "unhousing" is followed in the next scene by undressing: house and clothes imagery are linked here as they are in *Lear* and climax in the hero's dramatic gesture of stripping himself. In his allegory, the poet speaks of Timon's "large fortune, / Upon his good and gracious nature hanging" (1.1.56–57); but Timon's estate, like a garment, "shrinks from him" and he is "shrunk indeed" (3.2.7, 62). After leaving Athens, he lives with the naked creatures "whose bare unhoused trunks, / To the conflicting elements expos'd, / Answer mere nature" (4.3.231–33).

Timon's gesture of tearing off his clothes as he glances back at the city walls has the configuration of a Fortuna scene:

> Nothing I'll bear from thee
> But nakedness, thou detestable town!
> Take thou that too, with multiplying bans!
>
> (4.1.32–34)

The image here, doubly impressive because it is both verbal and mimetic, resembles one of Batilly's emblems in which a naked man leaves a city that is on fire. ("Burn, house!" said Timon at the mock banquet.) Yet the moral of the emblem is quite different: the man leaving the city is naked because a wise man puts no trust in the goods of Fortune, as the motto says.[33] In contrast, Timon's gesture accompanies his attempt to free himself from the causality of Fortune in which a dishonest world seeks to cloak him. What for the emblem figure is an act of deliverance undertaken with a composed mind is for Timon a rage in which he violently tears off the lie that men are better than beasts. The clothes are left behind not because they are a ballast for the wise man but because they are symbols of a rotten civilization, the corruption of which Timon's rage wishes to "multiply" to the destruction of society.

The mood is that of pathos rather than rage in the next scene when the steward and the servants intone an elegy on the fall of master and house:

> Such a house broke?
> So noble a master fall'n, all gone, and not
> One friend to take his fortune by the arm,
> And go along with him.
>
> (4.2.5–8)

Timon's house is deserted by its former guests, "familiars to his buried fortunes," who slink away as if its owner had been thrown into his grave; Timon's servants are now mere "broken implements of a ruin'd house" (10–16). These images have a general resemblance to emblems that, like two of Jean Cousin's, symbolize the blows of Fortune by broken columns or a falling house; in one of the drawings, a falling ceiling is in the process of burying a victim underneath.³⁴

After Timon's departure from Athens, all evocations of a dwelling, be they through the stage location or verbal imagery, have a way of recalling contrastingly or ironically Timon's splendid house. When that foremost implement of the broken house, the steward, sights his ragged and savage former master, he visualizes him as a ruined edifice: "Is yond despis'd and ruinous man my lord? / Full of decay and failing? O monument / And wonder of good deeds evilly bestow'd" (4.3.462–64). Timon reciprocates the steward's solicitation with gold and with the advice to use it in order to "build from men" a house of hate where charity is shown to none (530–31). The phrase is a sad reminder of what Timon said in his house of plenty when he sought to build his servant's fortune even if it diminished his own.

In the wild, wooded region that Timon inhabits in exile, his dwelling becomes a cave. On Shakespeare's stage, the contrast between the earlier spacious and illuminated house, practically equivalent to the stage itself, and the dark and narrow cave, presumably represented by the small discovery space behind an intimated rock, must have been visually impressive. Like the wood, the cave was Shakespeare's addition to the Timon legend, and he chose it surely for its association with fortune and despair. In Spenser's *Faerie Queene* (1.9.44), the Cave of Despair serves as a refuge from the world in which "fickle fortune rageth strife." As in Spenser, irony overcomes the pathos: the cave proves no haven. The heap of Timon's newfound gold in front of the cave symbolizes the allurement that again draws those who seek fortune to his abode.

By the kind of imaginative transformation that Shakespear's stage made possible, the roof over it became now literally what it was called figuratively, that is, the heavens. Shakespeare availed himself of this bit of theatrical illusionism when he made Timon ask the earth to "Teem with new

Fig. 1.   Emblem 35, "Sinistrae Fortunae Exemplum," in Jean Cousin, *The Book of Fortune*
[Liber Fortunae (1568)], ed. Ludovic Lalanne (Paris and London: Librarie de l'art,
1883).

monsters, whom thy upward face / Hath to the marbled mansion all above / Never presented" (4.3.192–94). I do not think that the image of heaven as marbled, a common idea, had an application to the Blackfriars; it is mere speculation to say that it had a ceiling painted in imitation of marble.[35] If the Globe had marble columns (admittedly also a speculation, but one made more likely by those of the Swan), the description would have been fitting for the "mansion" above, particularly if the lower part of the columns was covered with stage trees. In any case, the significance of the marble is metaphorical and emotional: the mansion with its cold and hard marble is the dwelling of "perpetual sober gods" remote from mankind and indifferent to it. This mansion, however, cannot fail to suggest another contrast to Timon's once radiant and now ruined Athenian house, symbol of his fortune. Another such contrast is suggested poetically in Alcibiades' tribute to the dead misanthrope: "Timon has made his everlasting mansion / Upon the beached verge of the salt flood" (5.1.214–15). The narrowness of Timon's last mansion is an apt reminder of the spaciousness of the Athenian palace he once inhabited. The pulsating sea, vividly described by Alcibiades, evokes the up-and-down movement of his life. Lapped by the waters that change and obliterate, his grave is a powerful symbol of the ultimate fortune to which all men must come: death.[36]

Besides the house, another architectural structure is significant in the play's Fortuna iconography: the walls of Athens. Fortuna was the guardian of the cities: emblems showed her above or in front of walled cities. In one of Cousin's, she stands before the gate with a lock and a key in her hands.[37] The theatrical ambiance of Shakespeare's public playhouse would have made the city walls an appropriate feature to evoke; the playhouse was itself surrounded by a frame that resembled such walls. When the stage represented Timon's house or some other location in Athens, Shakespeare's audience could consider themselves inhabitants of that city and could empathize with its fortunes. The satirists who used ancient Athens as a pseudonym for Shakespeare's London encouraged such typological identification; Thomas Lodge, for instance, with an unmistakable reference to London, made Diogenes say: "Good lord, what a city Athens is: here are fair houses, but false hearts."[38] With this identification, the ironies, the pathos, and the fears inspired by Fortune in *Timon* must have had a strong topical relevance.

The freedom of visualizing diverse locations on Shakespeare's stage made it possible to change quickly the imaginative orientation when action and circumstances required it. Such is the case when Timon leaves Athens. Until this time, the tiring-house facade would have suggested a wall in or on Timon's house. When Timon leaves Athens, the situation changes and, with it, the significance of the facade, as W. M. Merchant has well noted: "For the feast we have an elaborate interior scene; with the removal of the banquet and the helpless search of the affronted suitors for the jewels, caps, and gowns, the function of the setting is literally reversed: without a break in the action, Timon emerges to address the walls of Athens."[39] The outer walls of the Globe now assumed the meaning suggested by the theater's emblematic name: they became the frame of the world, and the back wall of the stage, the tiring-house facade, took over the function of the city walls.

In this imaginative climate, Shakespeare's Londoners would have had good reason to refer Timon's valediction to the walls and his cry for their fall not only to Athens but to all cities, particularly their own:

> O thou wall
> That girdles in those wolves, dive in the earth
> And fence not Athens!
>
> (4.1.1–3)

This, I think, is a moment when for Shakespeare's audience, or at least for many of them, the impression of Fortune's ironies and of the pathos engendered by her frown must have given way to awe. Accustomed as they were to think of the fall of Athens as a warning example, Timon's words must have had a credible application for their present and future. The prophetic ring of these lines would have been even more awesome to those who were aware that the walls of Athens did indeed come down when, after the death of Alcibiades, the Athenians razed them at the request of the victorious Spartan general Lysander. Stephen Batman spoke for the apocalyptically inclined when he had them come down at the blast of a trumpet, like those of Jericho.[40]

With this orientation, the final appearance of Alcibiades before the walls of Athens—the tiring-house facade again—gains an ironic perspective beyond the ordinary Fortuna associations. Alcibiades' appearance before the walls Timon left behind emphasizes the contrast between his and Timon's fortunes, and it demonstrates the familiar turn of the wheel: once Timon was the city's protector, now Alcibiades is its master.

It remains finally to speak of the Fortuna imagery in Timon's rhetoric of condemnation. However unwise his own position toward Fortuna, he knows now how to draw graphic characterizations of those congregated at the foot of Fortune's hill. He begins with fairly traditional iconography in his first soliloquy in the wood, backing up his call for universal destruction by pictures of the wholesale perversion of men through fortune: "Raise me this beggar, and deny't that lord, / The senators shall bear contempt hereditary, / The beggar native honour" (4.3.9–11). This resembles an emblem like Cousin's "Sign of Fortune's Inconstancy," in which a blindfolded Fortune sits in the middle of the beam of a see-saw; a senator is carried upward on one side while a scholar dips downward on the other.[41] If Timon's image puts the beggar in the place of the scholar, his subsequent words about the "learned pate" ducking to the golden fool (18) glance at the latter.

Timon refurbishes the traditional imagery by imbuing it with various associations, such as those of flattery in "If one be [a flatterer], / So are they all, for every grise of fortune / Is smoothed by that below" (15–17) and again in "The sweet degrees that this brief world affords" (255). The allusion here, of course, is to the conventional ladder of Fortune, that same ladder by which Fortuna climbs to her seat at the beginning of *The Contention between Liberality and Prodigality*.[42] It is, however, in fusions with nature images that the Fortuna imagery becomes most allusive and brilliant, as, for instance, when Timon identifies himself with a tree—appropriately in the presence of the advocate of the simple life of nature, Apemantus—and remembers that

> The mouths, the tongues, the eyes and hearts of men
> At duty, more than I could frame employment:
> That numberless upon me stuck, as leaves
> Do on the oak, have with one winter's brush
> Fell from their boughs and left me open, bare,
> For every storm that blows.
>
> (4.3.263–68)

Images of the seasons, of fortune, and of flattery are conflated in this speech. Timon likens himself to the tree of life, now stripped bare by the blast of winter. This tree also resembles that in Ripa's emblem where Fortuna on its top shakes down, as if in a storm, the crowns, scepters, miters, and jewels like ripe fruits.[43] The leaves on Timon's tree of Fortune, however, are not her gifts but the tongues and hearts of the flatterers who have left him in the lurch.

Sun and moon furnish other images of multiple allusiveness in which Fortuna looms large. Timon's career is appropriately likened to that of the sun, and both suggest the analogy to the wheel of Fortune. Even when Timon appeared to be in his glory, Apemantus warned, "Men shut their doors against a setting sun" (1.2.141). After his fall, a creditor's servant moralized that a prodigal's course is "like the sun's, / But not, like his, recoverable" (3.4.13–14)—the word "sun's" is here suggestive of the sums lost by Timon. Timon takes up this latter idea in an image that identifies him with the moon, a frequent symbol of Fortuna's inconstancy.[44] To Alcibiades' question of how he came to be changed from prosperity to adversity, he answers:

> As the moon does, by wanting light to give.
> But then renew I could not like the moon;
> There were no suns to borrow of.
>
> (4.3.68–70)

Timon thus hints sarcastically at the sums that are the suns of the world of Timon's friends—sums-suns they keep to themselves. His identification with the moon here gives him a Fortuna persona; but paradoxically, he obtains through the quirk of the figure the constancy of a permanent eclipse not undergone by the changeable moon, whereas the reproach of inconstancy is attached to his former friends.

Timon's last speech climaxes in the apocalyptic demand "Sun, hide thy beams" (5.1.222). Whatever associations may be evoked by the phrase, foremost is surely that of an extraordinarily powerful sunset as Timon's course comes to a halt. The light that formerly illuminated Athens is extinguished, and with it an unrealized potential for generosity and friendship. As Cicero said in a sentence that became proverbial, "They seem to take the sun out of the universe when they deprive life of friendship."[45] When Timon spoke his final words on Shakespeare's stage, it was late afternoon or evening, and the sun would indeed soon be setting on the theater open to the skies, the theater that symbolized the world. The shadows were descending over the wooden frame that in the medieval-Renaissance view suggested the idea of the universe as a structured and bordered organism. New philosophy had drawn this view into doubt, and prophets only somewhat less vehement than Timon had declared the world to be ripe for destruction. Like the new microcosm, Shakespeare's Globe now looked like a less stable structure; it was after all a fragile thing easily subject to destruction; in fact, it burned down a few years after *Timon* was written. Shakespeare's audience would have found the theater a fitting setting for the apocalyptic strains of the play.

Timon is a play of fortune; from the beginning to the end, Fortune is evoked with strong pictorial suggestiveness: the verbal patterns, the images, and the configuration of the stage bring to mind again and again the goddess, her settings, her attributes, and her influence. It is almost as if

Shakespeare had appropriated the motto of the Fortune Theater, then in competition with his Globe. But the Fortune had no monopoly on the idea of an association between Fortuna and the theater. "Fortune is like a theater" reads the motto of one of Cousin's emblems, which depicts the outside of a theater.[46] The kind of play performed in such a structure is emblematically depicted by Boissard and Batilly: it is a tragic pageant of the misery and wickedness of mankind under the aegis of the Fortuna seated on the stage.[47] So, in a sense, is Timon. This orientation of the play is one of the main features that takes it beyond Renaissance drama in the direction of the baroque, which was to prevail on the Continent in the seventeenth century. The trend was from the Theatrum Mundi to the Theatrum Fortunae.[48]

But it would be a mistake to assume that Timon is a didactive lusus fortunae or moral fable on the working of the goddess. Timon is not the poet's allegory writ large: it does not instruct us about the ways of fortune; it illuminates one particular way. The moralists and emblematists of the Renaissance acted as if they knew the enigmatic goddess and her activities well; so do Shakespeare's poet and the painter. But Timon, a drama of ideas without being a drame à thèse, shows that one cannot really know her. The play presents us with an imaginative experience of what men call Fortune; if we try to abstract it, we lose the experience for a simplistic generalization. We may, of course, say that Fortune is the grand illusion for which men strive and for which they exploit others. We may say that a world in which, in Thomas Nashe's phrase, "gold is the controller of fortune"[49] is a world of villainy and hard hearts. We may also say that he who, like Timon, tries to impersonate Fortuna is apt to be overtaken by her ironies and to come to a premature end. But this gets rather away from the tragedy of the philanthropist turned misanthrope, and it leaves unanswered the important questions with which we are vexed when we consider the action morally and philosophically, such questions as whether Fortuna represents an agent or force in a purposive design or a willful and random spirit and whether the human struggles, victories, and defeats for Fortune's sake make sense. The play, as we see and read it, gives Fortune an imaginative reality; it leaves her meaning and purpose a mystery, a dark and rather threatening mystery.

APPENDIXES

Stage History, 1816—1978

By Gary Jay Williams

The director who choses to stage *Timon of Athens* is apt to be regarded as unwisely brave, if not perverse. He can be forgiven if it is a matter of fondly doting on even this, one of the least of the poet's plays; or he can be tolerated for supposing that intensity of language will compensate for the lack of dramatic action. Should he actually be interested in Shakespeare's misanthrope, he may be altogether suspect. *Timon* has been one of the least produced plays in the canon, with probably only *Pericles, Titus Andronicus,* and the *Henry VI* plays staged less frequently. Since Edmund Kean acted the relatively restored version of the play in 1816, there have been, according to my checklist, twenty professional productions on the English-speaking stage (twenty-six if university and non-Equity summer festival productions are included).[1] As we shall see, when it has been produced, critics have often expressed a constrained admiration for the attempt but ultimately doubted that the play has proved stageworthy. Still, interest in the play in this century has gradually increased. There have been more productions of *Timon* in the last thirty years than there were in the previous one hundred and thirty. As in the case of the other rarely seen plays, some of the attention *Timon* has had from producers is owing to dutiful completions of the canon at the Old Vic and Stratford-upon-Avon. Some of the recent interest may be due to the overexposure of the familiar plays in the Shakespeare festival industry. But *Timon's* rough text and problem protagonist will not yield to the casual, dutiful, or novel commitment. What is more promising (ironic word) is the increasing receptiveness to the play, which suggests to me that our age may be seeing in Timon a recognizable man, one without spiritual resources in a mean-spirited world, who makes his fiercest commitment of all to despair.

My purpose here is to provide an account of the major productions of *Timon* from Edmund Kean to the production of Peter Brook in Paris in 1974. This is not a search for an ideal *Timon*, for, in the theater especially, each age, to a considerable extent, impresses upon Shakespeare its own image. It is hoped that a fuller account of the play's performance history than has been available may stimulate further interest in it. The account is informed with my own enthusiasm for the play's dramatic values and theatrical possibilities in our time, including the belief that its dramatic interest must derive in some measure from the very size and intensity of Timon's pursuit of misanthropy.

The chief case the nineteenth century made for a theatrical revival of *Timon* was that it offered a good moral, an exemplum all the more valuable for coming from Greek history through Shakespeare—both were touchstones of middle-class Victorian education. This moral case could be earnestly advanced as compensating for the play's defects, so long as the necessary considerations of propriety were met and the second half of the play curtailed. On the occasion of Kean's revival in 1816, the *Theatrical Inquisitor* strained to make the case.

> [Timon's] confusion, his sorrows, and his misanthropy abound with didactic lessons, they afford but little amusement, yet convey much instruction; and the failure of the stage can hardly be lamented, in the consumation of [the] moral excellence it so happily sustains.[2]

On the Victorian stage, the play was realized in idealized and sentimental terms. Those two noble Athenians, Timon and Alcibiades, were seen as the victims of greed, corruption, and ingratitude. Timon was a good and generous man, driven to hate and madness by the inhumanity of unworthy friends, but avenged in the end by the stalwart Alcibiades. Neither the shallowness of the early Timon nor the intensity of his later satire and nihilism was squarely faced. Also, Alcibiades was simplified and made a noble hero, though it is not clear, to say the least, that he is a promising candidate for a just and temperate ruler who will bring better days to Athens.

The version of the play by George Lamb that Kean acted was correctly advertised by Lamb as much less altered than previous versions. Chiefly, this meant it was without the women characters that Restoration and eighteenth-century adapters had added to provide the play with some romantic or familial interest. Romantic critics were now championing the restoration of Shakespeare's texts, and, by the second quarter of the century, conscientious managers such as William Macready, Elizabeth Vestris, and Samuel Phelps were offering Shakespeare relatively whole. Still, Victorian productions distinctively shaped the plays. Lamb's 1816 version was an attempt, he said, "to restore Shakespeare to the stage with no other omissions than such as the refinement of manners has rendered necessary."[3] Necessary was the omission of Alcibiades' camp-following prostitutes, Phyrnia and Timandra. This served not only the purpose of excising a few sexual epithets; it improved upon Alcibiades' stature. It also removed one of the most invidious of Timon's misanthropic attacks—the scene in which he throws gold coins into the outspread skirts of the women and exhorts them to spread the gold like venereal disease. Elsewhere, too, sexual references in Timon's imprecations were omitted, such as in his curse upon the city (4.1).

Lamb still found it necessary to carry over from Richard Cumberland's 1771 adaptation a major adjustment in the play's ending. In Lamb's version, after Athens has yielded its keys to Alcibiades, the victor says, "Yet all's not done: Vengeance must work. Where is that loathsome crew, / Whose black ingratitude corrodes the heart / Of Athens' noblest son?"[4] Penitent Athens then brings the Lords Lucius and Lucullus before Alcibiades, and they are stripped of their riches and banished. Alcibiades declares that final approval of this merciful sentence must come from Timon, whose death is then reported. Thus Lamb brings the play to a morally tidy conclusion with particular villains who are publicly punished; justice and mercy are administered on Timon's behalf and right order restored.

Lamb shortened the second half of the play by curtailing the exchanges between Timon and the visitors to his cave, especially the bitter clash between Timon and Apemantus. The visit of the poet and painter is omitted, "mercifully eliminated," exclaimed George Odell.[5] Yet, their return brings the play full circle. These opportunists, who deal in flattering outward images of their patrons, are the first we meet in Timon's lobbies at the opening of the play. Having heard Timon has gold, they return to ride Fortune's wheel upward again. Audiences laugh in recognition as they enter. Timon overhears them, emerges saying, "I'll meet you at the turn," and satirizes them out of sight (5.1.46 ff.). Always the ironic illustrators of their own lines, in this last encounter they exemplify the way of the world described in the lines with which they open the play:

> Poet: I have not seen you long; how goes the world?
> Painter: It wears, sir, as it grows.
> Poet: Ay, that's well known.

(1.1.2–3)

Not only are they comic reminders of an unregenerate world in the final scenes; they also function to alert Timon—and us —to the similar self-interest of Timon's next visitors—the subtler senators, who come to beg Timon's assistance against Alcibiades with unctuous, verbose ceremony. In both episodes, we see Timon firmly sealed in his commitment to a kind of irregular greatness, to a self-consuming rejection of an insincere world. But the Victorian stage was determined that Timon be simply a noble victim. Leigh Hunt regretted Lamb's omissions,[6] but many contemporaries approved, including two stage historians. John Genest thought Lamb's text "a model of the manner in which Shakespeare's plays should be adapted to the modern stage," and W. C. Oulton agreed that the courtesans "were not calculated to entertain a polished audience."[7]

Edmund Kean had admired the play,[8] and the role of Timon offered, of course, more than a few opportunities for the emotional intensity that was his special power. "To see him act," Coleridge remarked, "is like reading Shakespeare by flashes of lightning."[9] The slight young actor with blazing black eyes had electrified London within these two years with his Shylock, Hamlet, and Richard III. Audiences who had respectfully worshipped the neoclassical John Philip Kemble were now fascinated by Kean's new naturalistic display of emotion, with "the wonderful truth, energy, and force with which [he] strikes out and presents to the eye this natural working of the passions of the human frame."[10] (See figure two.)

He made a considerable impact in the role of Timon, but contrary to the wishful reports of several modern theater historians,[11] his performance cannot be said to have sustained the play. The production had a modest seven performances over three weeks and was never revived thereafter.[12] Timon did not become one of the roles Kean repeated in his career, nor did his revival bring the play into the standard Shakespearean repertoire. Leigh Hunt gave Kean's genius its due but thought the role itself wanted "sufficient variety and flexibility" for Kean's talents.[13] One of Kean's contemporary biographers found in Kean's Timon the bitter skeptic but not the easy, lordly prince.[14] The lightning flashes of intensity or insight were not the hallmark of a consistent and seamless

Mr. KEAN as TIMON.

Nothing I'll bear from thee,
But nakedness, thou detestable town!

London. Pub.ᵈ as the Act directs, by J. Roach. Rußel Court, Drury Lane, Nov.ʳ 4. 1816.

Fig. 2. Edmund Kean in the role of Timon. From the Art Collection of the Folger Shakespeare Library. Reprinted with permission.

characterization. In the early scenes, Kean presided with a stately languor rather than "ardent animal spirits,"[15] and he lacked in the banquet scene, for example, the affection that could overflow into indulgent tears. Kean's first burst of passion came with Timon's confrontation with his creditors. With his final line in the scene, "Here, tear me, take me, and the gods fall upon you" (3.4.98),

> Mr. Kean gazed at the bloodhounds who were preying on his existence, tore open his vest to enforce the offer he had made, and at length broke from the clamour his distractors could not silence, with an imprecation of tremendous horror on the throng that assailed him.[16]

In the mock banquet, Kean unsheathed the caustic edge that had served him in the role of Richard III. It was in his delivery of Timon's curse at the city that George Cruikshank elected to draw Kean, legs defiantly set apart, eyes fierce, fists raised, flinging off his cape on "Nothing I'll bear from thee / But nakedness, thou detestable town!" (4.1.32–33).[17] But too often, said Hunt, Kean offered vehemence rather than intensity, an anger louder than it was deep, though he pleased the galleries. At times, Kean clearly worked for pathetic effects. He "breathed the very soul of melancholy and tenderness" into Timon's reproach of Apemantus, "But myself, / Who had the world as my confectionary" (4.3.259–67).[18] Early in the wilderness scenes, the staging created a visual contrast between the pathetic misanthrope and the proud Alcibiades, which Hunt thought one of the production's best effects.

> First you heard a sprightly quick march playing in the distance; Kean started, listened, and leaned in a fixed and angry manner on his spade, with frowning eyes . . . he seemed as if resolved not to be deceived. The audience were silent; the march threw forth its gallant note nearer and nearer; the Athenian standards appear, then the soldiers come treading on the scene with that air of confident progress which is produced by the accompaniment of music; and at last, while the squalid misanthrope still maintains his posture and keeps his back to the strangers, in steps the young and splendid Alcibiades, in the flush of victorious expectation. It is the encounter of hope with despair.[19]

The production offered other spectacle. Timon aimed his curse at a handsome distant view of Athens painted on a backcloth. Whether for the Athens of *Timon* or *A Midsummer Night's Dream*, the nineteenth-century pictorial stage illustrated Shakespeare with uplifting historical splendor. The banquet masque was given a Homeric theme. Oscar Byrne, well-known dancing master, choreographed a piece in which he danced as Hercules (the Folio stage directions call for Cupid) amid twenty Amazons who clashed swords and shields (rather than playing lutes as the Folio prescribes). Its intent puzzled Hunt, as well it might since the masque is intended to honor Timon as patron of the senses. Modern directors usually make this dance climax the feast with a debauch to provide the image of the vain and insincere society that Apemantus here prophesies will betray Timon. But a decadent Athens, broadly drawn, was as out of the question on the Victorian stage as were the two prostitutes for the noble Alcibiades. So, too, the retribution for the two particular Athenian villains at the end of Lamb's version is a far cry from a modern broadly cynical vision.

Hunt appreciated the Drury Lane revival effort but predicted (correctly) that Kean's Timon "will not rank as one of his first performances," and that the play would not run long. His reservations about the play itself are those still to be heard when it is revived: the scenes of dramatic interest were too few, especially after Timon's fall, and the moral was too obvious and too easily anticipated. A reader could, however, "weigh every precious sentence at leisure, and lose none of the text either by the freaks of adapters or the failure of actors' voices."[20]

John Kemble may have considered producing Timon,[21] and William Macready certainly did. Macready's diaries record his assessments on two separate occasions. He believed it "could not be made interesting on the stage," that it was "not complete enough, not finished . . . with the requisite varieties of passion for a play; it is heavy and monotonous."[22]

But a mid-century production by Samuel Phelps won the admiration of his followers and achieved a respectable total of forty-one performances in its premiere season of 1851 and in the revival of 1856.[23] Phelps took early advantage of the lifting of the patent restrictions by the Theatre Regulation Act, and at Sadler's Wells, out beyond the circle of the West End's fashionable theaters, produced thirty-one of Shakespeare's plays between 1844 and 1862. His operation was modestly financed and his company not exceptional, but thoughtful attention to intrinsic dramatic values rather than lavish scenery or star performers won him a loyal following. None of this is to say that Phelps's vision of the play was not a nineteenth-century one. Phelps's idealism alone might have led him to stage the neglected *Timon*, but he was probably influenced in his choice of the nearly all-male Timon by the practical factor of the loss of his talented actress, Isabella Glyn, just before the 1851 season began.[24]

His text was the most complete yet to have been produced, and there were no added scenes. Phelps's promptbook shows he cut about twenty percent of Shakespeare's lines (463 lines), a percentage not uncommon in the century.[25] This included the omission of the fool scene (2.2.51–127), commonly omitted in this century and our own, and of the poet-and-painter sequence of the fourth act. Explicit sexual references were, of course, cut from all Timon's curses. Phyrnia and Timandra were present, though their exchanges with Timon were well expurgated.

Phelps's major alteration occurred at the play's end and involved scenic effects rather than textual changes. It employed the panorama, a continuous painted canvas unwound across the stage that, as nearly as could be done before the cinema, created a moving picture. After Timon had scorned the pleading senators and they had exited, the panorama began to unroll, and Alcibiades' army entered marching on Athens, accompanied by music and the moving canvas. Frederick Fenton's movable painting brought them to the city walls, with "Alcibiades and soldiers discovered on raised platform, backed by his officers and men looking down into the town."[26] One promptbook records that there were "troops painted on canvas to join those discovered," a not unusual device.[27] After Alcibiades had settled his accounts with Athens, word of Timon's death was brought. Alcibiades commanded that he be conducted to Timon's tomb, and this one promptbook describes.

> Troops face about and mark time. Panorama moves on slowly and closes them in; they descend platforms and a woody opening in the panorama shews them on the march. They are again closed in, and the panorama works entirely off—shewing Timon's tomb—a sunset backing and rolling waters.[28]

Here Alcibiades read Timon's epitaph, and after muffled drums ("Let our drums strike"), his twenty soldiers, arranged in two ranks perpendicular to the footlights, lowered their pikes in grief, as light rippled on the sea in the stillness.[29]

There was more here than picturesque spectacle for Phelps's audience, and there are more than quaint scenic conventions for us to understand. These two pictorial sequences clearly add moral and dramatic values to Alcibiades' victory and Timon's death. They bind the main plot and subplots together and tend to idealize both figures. Alcibiades' march on Athens is translated into the coming of a righteous, avenging conqueror. The *Athenaeum* tells us Henry Marston's Alcibiades (1851) in bearing and costume "looked truly an historical portrait."[30] His march to Timon's tomb provides a final ennobling of the fallen man, a rite of honor that in turn recommends Alcibiades to us as a future leader. The play ends with a visual coda, a meditation upon the death of Timon, which in the text some find unsatisfyingly abrupt. Out of the tragedy of his misanthropy and death, the suggestion seems to be, a new knowledge has been born. It is understandable how Henry Morley could praise Phelps on the occasion of Timon for making scenery serve his author. "Shakespeare's plays are always poems, as performed at Sadler's Wells."[31]

Yet, as Shakespeare's play stands, it is less neat and less idealizing. I am not convinced that either of these conditions should be construed as evidence that the play is structurally defective, or that extensive rehandling of the fifth act is wanted. As this is an issue touching productions from Phelps in 1856 to Michael Benthall in 1956, it will be useful to examine it now.

There is nothing in the final act to indicate that Timon's misanthropy and death have changed matters in Athens. If anything, the opposite is suggested—an imperfect world will wear on. The peace between Athens and Alcibiades is an enforced one; there is little here to inspire our confidence in a bright new future born in the ashes of tragedy. There seem to be contradictions within the prolix pleas of the senators. One says to Alcibiades, "Nor are they living who were the motives that you first went out," and the other invites him to "cull the infected forth, / But kill not all together." In between these appeasements, they offer another—the traditional killing of one in ten: "Take thou the destin'd tenth, / And by the hazard of the spotted die / Let die the spotted" (5.4.26–44). This is the facile rhetoric-for-all-occasions of politicians, not principled men. Alcibiades is well-meaning, but we are given reason to doubt that the captain is a stable man of absolute principles. There is charity and kindness in his treatment of Timon in the wilderness. But it is no simple, hearty field officer who speaks in this exchange at Timon's banquet:

> *Timon*: You had rather be at a breakfast of enemies than a dinner of friends.
> *Alcibiades*: So they were bleeding new, my lord, there's no meat like 'em; I could wish my best friend at such a feast.
>
> (1.2.75–79)

The senate before whom Alcibiades later pleads for the release of a companion in arms may be complacent and corrupt, but Alcibiades' argument that murder should be winked at because of his friend's military service amounts to a cynical appeal from mutual convenience, not justice. He is no more loyal to Athens than a mercenary. His banishment "is a cause worthy my spleen and fury," and in his vanity he can justify his vengeance with "Soldiers should brook as little wrongs as gods" (3.5.114,118). Add to these considerations the baggage of Timandra and Phyrnia, and it must be said that Shakespeare has made it difficult for us to see in

Alcibiades an ideal hero upon whom the leadership of Athens should devolve.

The future of Athens at the end of the play is, then, not one that permits us to be condescending and comfortable in our pity for the misanthrope when word of his death is brought. If Timon's misanthropy and death effects Athens's redemption at the end of the play, as it did in Michael Benthall's production in 1956, this is not only an ironic twist at Timon's expense; it diminishes Timon's despair. So far as self-interest in Athens is made a temporary and local matter subject to such a sentimental remedy, so far will Timon's misanthropy appear a peculiar perversity and his death a simple object lesson. Shakespeare seems too earnest and intent in his exploration of the misanthrope to let us leave him without some awe for his commitment, fear for the truth in his vision, and pity for his suffering. He has not made Timon wholly sympathetic, but he has given Timon's commitment to despair a magnificent intensity. Certainly he has made him greater in it than all those about him, made him achieve a kind of irregular heroic greatness. Beside Timon, Alcibiades and Athens appear small indeed.

Of Phelps's own performance as Timon, it will not surprise us to find Morley saying he "treats the character as an ideal, as the central figure in a mystery."[32] John Oxenford of the *Times* said, "Mr. Phelps never loses sight of the inherent dignity of the misanthrope," and he and others found it useful to compare Phelps's aristocratic, noble misanthrope with the "low-born snarler," Apemantus, neatly realized as a foil in the performances of both George Bennett (1851) and Henry Marston (1856).[33] In Phelps's performance, the misanthropy of Timon seemed affected, "something alien to his disposition, the expression of which severely tasks his capacity and is but ill accomplished after all," said the *Athenaeum*.[34] "We cannot but mourn over a naturally noble nature thus upset," said critic H. G. Tomlin; "his confiding nature, his simple heart, his unwordly mind is [*sic*] overwhelmed by the discovery, and he cannot recover the shock."[35] This describes a pathetic, suffering misanthrope, and the descriptions are also suggestive of qualities associated with Phelps's general acting style, such as his deliberate, thoughtful manner and slow delivery. It is difficult to imagine that Phelps achieved any fierce intensity in the bitter scenes; references to this are conspicuously few. Tomlin assured his readers that in Shakespeare there is "nothing morbid," and noted that "we are never led to feel that Timon is right in his indiscriminate denunciation of mankind." Thus, the loyal Flavius's encounter with Timon in the woods is "the redeeming part of the drama," and "Flavius, accordingly, was greeted with more plaudits than any other person in the play."[36]

The Phelps production enjoyed an exceptional thirty-one performances in the 1851 season. In 1856, there were ten, though it was on that occasion (for which there were some scenic improvements) that Phelps received from critics some of the highest praise of his career for his system of management in which the scenery and acting served the play.[37] Reading of the hushed and reverent audiences at Sadler's Wells, one cannot doubt that Phelps created an effective interpretation and staging of the play in the terms we have seen. Perhaps no other production of Timon pleased its time as much. Yet it does not seem that the admiration for the Phelps production resulted in a wider admiration for the play. There were only two minor revivals in the next half-century, and London did not see the play again until 1904.

In Manchester, actor-manager Charles Calvert produced the play in 1871 at the Prince's Theatre, where, from 1864 to 1874, he mounted a series of Shakespearean productions after the elaborate manner of Charles Kean in London. The sources suggest there were major omissions and rearrangements of the text, but the *Manchester Guardian* approved: "Mr. Calvert has cut out everything which is certainly not Shakespeare's, a great deal of what is doubtful and all the coarseness."[38] This would mean at least the absence of Phrynia and Timandra. We learn from the *Guardian* also that Calvert had Timon die in the arms of his servants, and that at some point "his unhinged mind recover[ed] its balance under the warmth of their affection." One must assume that Timon's final defiances, if given at all, were superceded by this sentimental effect.

Calvert arranged the text in three acts and employed eight tableaux. On the rising of the curtain in each scene the characters remained grouped in tableau for a few seconds before the action began, a device obviously intended to frame the play as a moral allegory. The staging and scenery received no other special notice except for the ballet that replaced the masque and the rather too-spirited melee that ended the mock banquet. Calvert's Timon was most effective in the quieter scenes, as in his incredulous response to Flavius when faced with the reality of his indebtedness: "To Lacedaemon did my land extend." The Manchester production had twenty-four performances,[39] but Calvert did not, as one critic supposed, rescue the play once and for all from "the limbo of the unacted drama."

It was next produced in a reduced three-act version by Sir Frank Benson at Stratford-upon-Avon in 1892. In the one-century history of the spring and summer festival, *Timon* has been produced at Stratford only three times. It was first chosen as the birthday presentation—which meant three performances—and its production fell to Benson, who was often responsible for the festival productions in over two decades. The earnest, athletic young actor's approach must have been simple and vigorous. He himself remembered that

> the points we laid stress on were: Banquets, dancing girls, flutes, wine, color, and form. Then comes the contrast of the sour misery, the embittered wisdom, the impotent rage against false gods, and the end of the man who yearned for truth and wisdom and love. . . . I love the play and the part.[40]

Benson was credited for his acting, but the production did not make a persuasive case for what a critic described as a "one-man play, without lovers and love scenes, without plot or counterplot."[41] Two endings were tried; the one nearest the original was reportedly the more effective. But Benson found no way to sustain the "long and dragging scene in the woods where visitor after visitor arrives and departs."[42] Lady Benson remembered the production being received with scant enthusiasm.[43]

J. H. Leigh produced a three-act, reduced version, reportedly based on Benson's text, at London's Court Theatre in 1904, and Frederick Warde took a free adaptation of the play on tour in the United States in 1910. Neither seems to have overcome the reputation of the play as a thorny curiosity. Leigh was said to have had "neither the experience nor any qualifications for the role of Timon,"[44] though his company performed zealously and had the strengths of Hermann Vezin's Apemantus and Frank Cooper's Alcibiades. The *Times* noted the roles of Timandra and Phyrnia were "reduced to dumb show," and found compensation in the banquet scene, which offered, instead of a masque, "a lovely ballet and a Cupid who might have strayed out of Offenbach's *Belle Hélène*."[45]

Frederick Warde was a respectable American tragedian whose acting style was of an older school by 1910. He had frequently toured and had achieved some stature in cities in the South, Midwest, and West.[46] As a young man, Warde had played Flaminius in Charles Calvert's production, which he remembered being received with interest, "though I cannot assert that it was a popular success."[47] Still, Warde, at fifty-nine, determined to try the play on a regional tour, and he opened his production at the Fulton Opera House in Lancaster, Pennsylvania, in the fall of 1910.

Warde said he followed Calvert's example in the handling of the text. His promptbook shows an extensive reworking of the play by a painstakingly conscientious, if uninspired hand. The nature of the changes is familiar. Timon and Alcibiades are idealized; the misanthrope scenes are greatly reduced. At the end of the play, the "senators, citizens, women and children of Athens" have come out to Timon's cave to beg his assistance against Alcibiades when Alcibiades and his army enter. The captain demands that the Athenians kneel and promise to restore Timon to honor and wealth. A soldier seeking Timon finds him dead in his cave, and his body is then borne off with a long procession of Athenians behind.[48] Warde freely rearranged scenes or rewrote them, interpolating lines from other plays of Shakespeare. In one case, he provides some background on the Timon-Alcibiades relationship by making it clear that Timon had "furnished forth the sinews" of Alcibiades' latest battle. There is the usual laundering of sexual references and the omission of the more bitter of Timon's curses. Over thirty percent of the text is omitted and most of this from the last two acts.[49] Warde's promptbook instructions make clear his portrayal of Timon as a pathetic misanthrope. For the scene with Flavius and the senators, Timon is to enter from his cave "weak and ill," and from this entrance to the end of his final speech there is to be "Music theme for Timon pathetic, to continue until 'Timon hath done his reign' and exit." Warde and his company, which included his son, Ernest, as Apemantus, won critical respect for the attempt, especially for careful elocution.[50] But Warde wrote in his biography that the play, being unfamiliar to the public, did not attract audiences. After about a dozen performances over several weeks, he withdrew it "at a great financial loss," and offered the more familiar *Julius Caesar*, which could be mounted with little change in costumes and scenery.[51] Warde's was not the first American *Timon*. In 1839, one N. H. Bannister produced it at New York's Franklin Theatre, a small theater to which the press paid less attention than its rivals, the larger and more fashionable Park and Bowery theaters. That production had only two performances.[52]

Between 1910 and World War II, the continuity of the play's performance history improves. Robert Atkins produced *Timon* at the Old Vic in 1922 as part of Lilian Baylis's five-year project of staging all the plays in the First Folio to mark the tercentenary of its publication. W. Bridges-Adams staged the play in 1928 in the Stratford-upon-Avon's temporary festival home in the Picture House (the original theater burned in 1926). Both Atkins and Adams were disciples of William Poel, whose religion it was that Shakespeare's texts should be played uncut upon an open platform no more scenically adorned than the Elizabethan stage. In these years, there were attempts to leave behind the pictorial and declamatory traditions of nineteenth-century Shakespearean production; following the example of Poel, Harley Granville-Barker and others emphasized the poetry and swift continuity of the plays, a development that entailed less-cumbersome scenery and that turned to more impressionistic stage décor or Elizabethan economy.

At the Old Vic, a forestage, proscenium doors, curtains, and some changeable stock scenic units sufficed.[53] One might expect that, in the absence of noble views of the Acropolis and with more of the original text, Timon's misanthropy might have been less subordinated to idealizing and sentimentalizing effects. But among the "blemishes" that friendly critic Herbert Farjeon found in Atkins's production was "the intermittent tableau tendency, which led to the introduction of an additional scene at the finish, undreamt of by Shakespeare or his collaborator, with soldiers and senators saluting Timon's grave."[54] In Atkins's performance as Timon, there was "something too ponderous," said Farjeon; "one looked for the flash of lightning in that 'Methinks I could deal kingdoms to my friends,' and one heard only a distant rumble of thunder." Mention is made of the Fool—not seen before and seldom since—and Hay Petrie made the Poet a notable character. In these years there was little coverage of Stratford's country festival. One would like to know more of the performances under Bridges-Adams of Wilfred Walter as Timon (he had provided an acid Apemantus to Atkins's Timon), George Hays's Apemantus, Roy Byford's Lucullus, and the Sempronius of Francis L. Sullivan.[55]

Nugent Monck's 1935 production at London's Westminster Theatre left critic James Agate tied in a double knot of frustration over the inadequacies of both the play and the production. He was at some pains to demonstrate the play was not *King Lear*. Timon was not as sympathetic a figure; the play was not as rich in incident, character, and language; and it was structurally defective, with all interest ending at the end of the mock banquet. The rest was "interminable talk."[56] For one who found so little to admire in the play, Agate was wonderfully indignant about Ernest Milton's Timon. "Timon must be drawn to heroic size," said Agate who found the mannered Milton too meticulous and too lightweight physically and vocally. "It is a part for a great actor, as great acting was understood before lesser actors began to drag brains into it."[57] He invokes Phelps's name where other modern critics often invoke Kean's. It is a commonplace in modern theater criticism that the play requires the services of an extraordinary actor not only to meet the role's vocal demands but also somehow to compensate for the play's ostensible inadequacies. This may be intended as fond faith in actors, but it leaves the problems and possibilities of Timon's character unexplored in a way no actor can afford. Actors reveal character by the choices and the pursuits of courses of action, both particular and general. The principle is not only Aristotelian; the pursuit of clear objectives is also essential to the actor's imaginative engagement in the play.

Herbert Farjeon was sad the seldom-seen play had not been done justice in the Monck production. He and other critics found Milton's delivery fast, erratic, and indistinct at the emotional crests. J. C. Trewin remembered "the rustle in the Harcourt Williams's voice softened the misanthropy of Apemantus."[58] Among Monck's directorial ploys were a ballet for the masque, which Farjeon thought much protracted, and a court-martial arrangement of the scene of Alcibiades before the senate, which Agate thought had "a fine, warlike frenzy." Benjamin Britten, then twenty-one, provided music that Agate found too literal an underscoring of the scenes. Monck did cut the text and, one suspects, not always judiciously. In a program note, he praised Shakespeare's stagecraft, calling the play "better than those who have only read it are able to realize." But he cut "certain comic scenes that are obviously not by Shakespeare," (the Fool scene and more?) and condensed "other repetitive scenes."[59] Among the regretted losses was Timon's curse upon Athens (4.1).

The first *Timon* after World War II was the "modern dress" production of 1947 by Sir Barry Jackson's Birmingham Repertory Theatre, directed by Willard Stoker. Timon was dunned by modern Athenian businessmen, and Alcibiades and his men were costumed as modern Athenian soldiers. Apemantus was portrayed (with some excess of relish by the actor) as "an out-at-elbows Bohemian of the Aldous Huxley period—a discharged reporter, insolvent artist or ham actor" who worked crossword puzzles.[60] The latter half of the play took place beside a bomb crater overlooked by a huge howitzer. When the company performed in makeshift, scenery-less conditions in the Stratford Conference Hall for a Shakespeare conference, reviewers found the play "gained enormously" from performance, "and particularly performance in modern dress." John Phillips played Timon with authority, speed and ease, and in the tirades "revealed a power of acceleration, of changing gear, of taking a hairpin bend worthy of a champion motor-cyclist in a cross-country trial." This did not, apparently, help sustain the latter half of the play which these reviewers described as "closet drama," and "a rhetorical indictment of man as a social animal" in which "pity is shouted down by wrath."[61]

The experiment with *Timon* as a social satire continued with the Old Vic production of 1952, directed by Tyrone Guthrie. Characteristically, Guthrie's resourcefulness meant some broadly theatrical effects; given this particular play, critics were more than usually tolerant of them, even enthusiastic. He approached the play not as a tragedy but as a satire against materialism.[62] His senators were "a covey of harried grotesques"; the jeweler was sinister, and the poet (John Blatchley) was effectively rendered as an eager, pretentious, amateur art critic. Around the open-handed Timon of the play's first half, there was a "golden turbulence of movement . . . gold on the pillars of Timon's house . . . gold in Timon's hair and in Timon's clothes, and Mr. André Morell gives his hero a golden smile."[63] The set and lighting design of Tanya Moiseiwitsch clearly was intended to speak to the imagination in subjective and suggestive ways. Timon moved in a bright world of wealth surrounded by darkness, "an enveloping gloom," out of which the sycophants and friends emerged. "Timon lives on a minute island of teeming magnificence in a world of blackness, which suddenly swallows him."[64] The *Times* described Morell's Timon as assured, radiant, and never breaking stride, but others found no stature in him. Roy Walker described him as a "devout peasant who had won a chariot-pool and set up as a one-man Athenian arts council, a fool and his money soon parted."[65] It is clear that neither Morell's performance nor Guthrie's satirical animus sustained the play in acts four and five. The *Times* said, "The latter part of the play may be said to lapse into one tremendous grouse." When Leo McKern's Apemantus accused Timon of affecting his misanthropy, it seems to have removed any sympathy there was for Timon and any reason for further interest. Basic to Guthrie's development of the play as a satire was his conviction that "Timon is not a hero in whose sufferings we are supposed to share with pity and terror. He is the spoiled Darling of Fortune whom Fortune suddenly spurns."[66] Guthrie's view of Timon is an understandable one and a welcome, sharp rejection of the idealized Timon, but it can account theatrically for only the first half of the play.

Guthrie shows little interest in the play at precisely the point where Shakespeare seems most in earnest, where Timon reaches for the most intense and imaginative expressions of rage and despair. The view precludes deeper exploration of acts four and five, which comprise forty-three percent of the play (971 of the play's 2,254 lines), the forty-three percent that, as this history shows, requires the most resourceful attention to sustain in production.

One further impression made by the Guthrie production deserves note. Harold Hobson writes that, at the end of the play, "one emerges from the theatre hardly recovered from the unexpected speed of Timon's demise." The impression that Timon's death is not marked clearly is one a performance may leave more strongly than a reading of the play wherein one can dwell upon the implications of Timon's last speeches. The actor and director must use means that leave little doubt that Timon shakes his fist at the sun and dies.

The Old Vic's production of 1956 was an ambitious but conspicuous failure. Although it remains in memory today as a major reference point in the play's performance history, it had only thirty-seven performances. Where Guthrie had banked upon a broad concept and the whirl of staging effects, director Michael Benthall built upon the personality and reputation of a major actor, Sir Ralph Richardson, then fifty-four. Of even greater consequence, Benthall also reworked the text to an extent that his was probably the most altered version seen in the century since the 1910 Frederick Warde production (based on Calvert's text).

With approximately five hundred lines cut and a resulting playing time of two hours (including one fifteen-minute interval), the omissions were considerable.[67] Of most interest was Benthall's handling of the end of the play. Timon chiseled his epitaph on a huge stone slab set atop a rock by the sea like a huge grave marker as he ended his interview with the senators, "Come not to me again . . ." (5.1.213). The senators' report back to Athens was cut, and only the first few lines of the soldier's discovery of Timon's tomb were given. At that point, Alcibiades and his army entered before Timon's tomb and were confronted there by the frightened, pleading senators and citizens of Athens, who entered from the opposite side of the stage. Roy Walker described the new sequence (which he praised):

Alcibiades rejected the Athenian pleas for mercy and ordered the assault; but at this moment the Soldier, who had climbed up to read the inscription, called urgently to him and Alcibiades halted to read the epitaph himself. It was this reminder of human mortality that melted the banished general to pity, a bold rehandling of the end of the play which at least tied the main and sub-plots together in a theatrically effective way.[68]

In spirit, this idealizing ending seems not unlike those of the nineteenth century. The misanthrope was reduced to being chiefly a motive for the rather sentimental conversion of Alcibiades. Like others before him, Benthall was determined to make something out of nothing. Not only was there the particular irony that Timon's death was the cause of the salvation of Athens, but the ending also quite generally advanced the premise that men can be redeemed, and so, with some dispatch, it canceled out Timon's misanthropic vision—shades of Nahum Tate's *Lear*. In Benthall's ending, Timon was mourned as a formerly noble man gone mad; his despair discounted, he was to be pitied as one might pity the death from rabies of a pedigreed dog.

It follows that in the cutting Timon's curses lost the fiercest of their lines. In the curse flung at the city wall, eighteen lines were omitted, from "Matrons, turn incontinent!" to "And yet confusion live!" (4.1.3–21). In his charge to Timandra and Phyrnia, the lines from "Crack the lawyer's voice" to "quell the source of all erection" were cut (4.3.155–66). Timon's soliloquy after Alcibiades' exit, in which he digs for a root to eat, was omitted (4.3.178–98), as was his disquisition on gold, "O thou sweet king killer" (4.3.384–99), and his caustic attack on the senators, "Thou sun, that comforts, burn!" (5.1.130–33). The exchange between the two misanthropes was trimmed, and throughout the play many of Apemantus's lines were omitted, including his running commentary during the banquet. There was little sympathy for Timon in this production, and Roy Walker attributed this (perhaps too much) to the omission of most of the poet and painter's opening discussion of Timon and the shift and change of Fortune's moods. One may doubt that the presence of the tall statue of the goddess in Timon's house was a recognizable replacement for a modern audience. A further alteration should be noted: the roles of Timon's three major servants were condensed into one—Flavius.

Richardson gave Timon his own easy, genial manner in the first part of the play. He was, in the creditors scene, able to "let fly with tremendous force," but, said Muriel St. Clare Byrne,

> he simply cannot bring himself to believe in the last two acts. On his own view of life, generosity, tolerance, a sweet reasonableness, and a natural philanthropy will keep breaking in, judging from knowledge of this well-loved player in his many parts, which as the *Times* critic remarked, turned the last scenes into a meditation, not a curse, and presented us with a Timon "as gently intoxicated as Richard II."[69]

Kenneth Tynan characterized the production as not so much a "study of benevolence warped by ingratitude" as "the story of a scoutmaster betrayed by his troop."[70] The critics were unanimous in their displeasure with Richardson's delivery. He made an ingenious attempt to replace fury with irony ("His invective was silky and detached," said the *Times*), but his delivery was badly marred by personal eccentricities. There was the hammered emphasis on each syllable, as in lines such as "This it is that makes the wappen'd widow wed again." Or, to use Tynan's example, there was Richardson's thanks to the Amazons for enlivening the banquet: "You have added," he said distinctly, "worth, and toot, and lusture" ["worth unto't and lustre"]. The *Times* was impressed with Richardson's originality in the role, but Byrne strenuously objected to Benthall's free handling of the text and contrasted Richardson's "easy, genial manner" with the "giant misanthropy" of the play, its "fearful, unmistakable violence and bitterness."[71] Tynan, who had recently praised the visiting Berliner Ensemble under Bertolt Brecht, soon to influence English staging of Shakespeare, found that by comparison English acting and directing such as that in *Timon* was "sickeningly laden with curlicues and excess baggage."[72]

Leslie Hurry's setting for Timon's house was dominated by a large door upstage center, which remained in that position for scenes outside as well as inside the house. Heavy draperies and lush colors of gold and magenta, yellows and greens suggested a wealthy and decadent community. The banquet ended in a general debauch from which the lecherous senators departed with one or two young women each. Tynan objected to the company's "epicene intensity." In the masque, Sir Ralph descended from his dais at the entrance of Cupid and "graciously allowed a bevy of girls to pepper him with tiny arrows, standing in their midst with the smile of a foolish emperor."[73] These women served him at other times in the play. Flavius entreated Timon's friends for help in the public place outside Timon's house. Lucullus was called from a drinking bout to speak with him, and a pudgy, bejeweled Sempronius was carried on in a palanquin with a giggling mistress. In the act one scene of the Old Athenian and Timon's servant, an actress provided the young daughter (for whom there are no lines). In the scene of Alcibiades before the Senate, Benthall clarified the question of whom Alcibiades is defending by bringing on a soldier in chains. Timon served steam at the mock banquet, overturned tables in the path of the bewildered guests trying to escape, and knocked over the tall standards in which the lights were burning. He next appeared on the forestage for his curse outside Athens's walls which were depicted on a semi-transparent drop. Behind it, the ruins of the banquet were seen in the light of flickering flames. The wilderness scene was a tangle of green around Timon's cave, but in his last scene, in which he carved his epitaph, he was found atop a rock with a Charles Kean seascape behind him.[74]

The play was again dressed fit to kill as a modern satire in the Stratford, Ontario, Festival Theatre production of 1963, conceived and staged by Peter Coe and Michael Langham. Timon was played by John Colicos, an interesting and intense if sometimes too theatrically efficient leading actor of the company. Howard Taubman of the *New York Times* described the "modern dress" production as "so preoccupied with effects of contemporaneity that it seems to call attention to its cleverness rather than to Shakespeare." In the first half of the play, Taubman wrote,

> there is so much concern with apt correspondence between the Elizabethan text and our epoch that each time a fresh modern conceit is invoked it becomes the core of interest, and produces a burst of applause.[75]

Timon hosted his banquet in a dinner jacket of red brocade, and his fashionably dressed guests were entertained by a combo playing suave jazz that Duke Ellington composed for the production. A trumpeter moved among the guests, serenading them. Apemantus (Douglas Rain) was a detached, cynical newspaperman with a cigarette on his lips and a photographer in tow. His asides from a balcony during the banquet provoked Alcibiades (William Hutt) to whip out a revolver and fire a shot at him. There was later business with ticker tape, Jewish bill collectors, and Timon's servant seeking out Lucius in a steam bath, attended by a masseur and a podiatrist. None of these flash-bulb effects seems to have illuminated the play, but they did create a certain notoriety for the production. It was taken to the Chichester Festival Theatre in the spring of 1964, the quadcentenary year. The London *Evening News* critic reported:

> While the first part strikes home—the banqueting scene with tired businessmen twisting with hostesses is magnificent—the second part, with Timon in the wilderness, comes properly to life only after his death.[76]

The focus, it is clear, was on the life of the great Gatsby rather than the misanthropy of Timon. The *Daily Worker* called the production a triumph and cited Marx's comments on the play, and a critic for the *Times* believed that its disillusion and cynicism were themes to which modern audiences were responsive.[77]

The 1960s brought the new Royal Shakespeare Company, headed by Peter Hall, Peter Brook, and Michel St. Denis, whose avowed and controversial intent it was to see Shake-

speare's plays afresh and to inform them with the spirit of
contemporary culture. In essays on the modern director and
Shakespeare, directors Hall and Brook argued for the freedom
to depart from conventional theatre-of-illusion practices and
standard interpretations, which they suggested were often
more Victorian than Elizabethan.[78] Although, on the whole it
seems not to have been a radical departure, the RSC's 1965
production of *Timon* with Paul Scofield reflected the new
directions. It enjoyed considerable interest that season, in
part perhaps because of an increasing public interest in the
play, to judge from the newspaper reviews, but mostly because
of Scofield. He came to the role of Timon at forty-three after
his portrayal of Lear in the renowned and controversial production directed by Peter Brook in 1962, which conceived of
the play as a tragedy of modern despair in a meaningless
universe. It bore the marks of Brecht's non-illusionistic staging
techniques and Jan Kott's existential reading.

Director John Schlesinger created a hard-edged, realistic
portrait of Athenian society and Scofield, a central performance of some magnitude. There seem to have been some
disparities between the two. John Russell Brown thought
Schlesinger had attended chiefly to pictures of the *dolce vita*
in ancient Athens and left Scofield to render a sometimes
psychologically subtle interpretation of Timon, with a resulting lack of structural strength.[79] Scofield created throughout,
however, an impression of power and authority. His early
Timon was a noble innocent rather than a foolish prodigal.
For both the host and the misanthrope, he drew upon his
considerable technical vocal powers. The *Times* said:

> But if Mr. Scofield's delivery—the inconsolable broken phrasing,
> the unresolved cadences, the sweetness of his top register—
> sometimes seem externally applied to the lines, much marvel-
> lous speaking remains. His way of handling verse often suggests
> a man struggling to lift a heavy weight, or being carried along
> by its momentum; and this part gives stupendous exercise to his
> technique.[80]

Robert Speaight and others saw in Scofield's Timon the
passion and power that had not been in his Lear. Many of
the responses suggest an increasing receptiveness to the play.
Speaight reports, for example, that in Scofield's playing of the
later scenes, "the excess of his misanthropy was the measure
of his growth."[81]

In Ralph Koltai's setting, red-tiled walls slid apart to reveal
the interior of Timon's house; two leprous beggars were
propped against them during the banquet scene. Servilius
found Lucius at the Athenian barber's, attended by a masseur
and a manicurist, "writhing in his chair in mixed agonies
of physical and moral discomfort."[82] For the wilderness scenes,

Timon's cave was set in a barren waste with a single gnarled tree, reminiscent for audiences of Samuel Beckett's *Waiting for Godot*. A new *Timon* was scheduled for the RSC's 1971 season but was canceled.[83]

The 1971 production of *Timon* in Joseph Papp's New York Shakespeare Festival in Central Park was a disappointing trial of this play so rarely seen in America. Walter Kerr characteristically complained of the play's structural weaknesses and blamed director Gerald Freedman for failing to make a firm attack on it. "A play with its own built-in fatigue cannot really afford any fatigue in the mounting," said Kerr.[84] Timon was played by Sheppard Strudwick, a familiar actor in contemporary stage and television plays, here unequal to the verse and the role. Clive Barnes observed: "He was unable really to suggest the folly of misplaced idealism or the rancor of misanthropy, and concentrated on a rather stiff brand of nobility."[85] Michael Dunn created a fierce, spitting, dwarfed Apemantus inordinately proud of his plain-dealing. But, on the whole, the American company was below the mark of giving all the verse intelligibly. Ming Cho Lee's metal scaffold-and-stairways setting for the outdoor Delacorte Theatre featured a trio of cloth kite buzzards flopping quietly in the winds above the towers.

The production of *Timon* to create the most interest in this decade to date is that directed by Peter Brook in Paris in 1974 as one of the experiments of his International Center for Theatre Research. The production was created in the shell of an abandoned Victorian theater, the Théâtre des Bouffes-du-Nord, north of the Gare du Nord in an area Brook's supportive critics liked to call a working-class section of Paris. A key element in the production was a translation of the text into modern French, prepared for Brook by Jean-Claude Carrière, French film scenarist best known for his work with director Luis Buneul. Brook's previous efforts to make Shakespeare accessible to modern audiences had included the commissioning of a modern English version of *King Lear* by poet Ted Hughes, which Brook decided not to use for fear it would call attention to itself. He chose *Timon* for the French experiment because, he said, "dans Timon, en anglais, les valeur musicales sont très peu importantes." Brook argued that the play's "langage archaïque ne fait plus sur le public une impression directe comme à l'époque élizabethaine."[86] One sample of Carrière's text may suffice here, Timon's final speech, which he rendered in somewhat regularized verse:

> Ne venez plus me voir. Dites à la cité
> Que Timon a bâti sa demeure éternelle
> Sur le bord d'une plage auprès de l'eau salée.
> Chaque jour une houle nouvelle

La couvrira d'écume et de mousse. Venez
    Voir votre oracle sur ma pierre.
Lèvres, laissez partir les paroles aigries.
    Que le langage soit fini
Que toute infirmité trouve sa guérison
    Dans la peste et dans le poison.
Que l'homme ait le tombeau comme unique chantier
    Et la mort comme seul salaire.
Soleil, que tes rayons se cachent de la terre
    Timon a fini de régner.

The difficulties of translation granted, one still misses here the intensity of Timon's rage, the extravagance and power of the diction. As to the play's structure, there was, interestingly, no significant alteration with the exception of the omission of the Fool sequence.

Brook made use of the Théâtre des Bouffes-du-Nord as it stood after a fire a quarter of century ago—the cavernous shell of a once red-and-gilt Victorian theater, pocked and fire-scorched, with a gaping, curtainless proscenium that exposed a deep cavity where the stage had been. Most of the action took place in a semicircular area in the orchestra in close proximity to the audience, which sat around it on backless bleachers. The actors also used a pipe-railed walkway running high across the bare, scarred backstage wall, and emerged from steps out of the cavity that was once the stage. Said one reviewer of this setting for *Timon*: "Every spectator at once knows that he is sitting inside a symbol of the decline of the West."[87]

Brook spoke of Timon as like a modern man whose illusion of well-being has collapsed, as an affluent man suffering the deflation of his world, even as an emblem of the West rudely awakened from the dream of the consumer's society by the oil crisis. In an interview, Brook commented:

> Pour chaque spectateur, devant l'univers entièrement saccage de Timon et devant le monde naissant d'Alcibiade, une question vitale se pose: qu'est-ce qui est à détruire? Qu'est-ce qui à sauver? Cela aussi fait partie de l'actualité. Shakespeare ne fournit pas le réponse.[88]

Elsewhere, Brook described Timon as a failed liberal, a disillusioned altruist who withdraws from the world and dies in confusion without reaching any transcendent understanding.[89]

The informal staging did not stress modern relevancies heavily, although it was in "modern dress." The prevailing tone of the young company's performance was that of a group of friends assembled to perform a play for a friendly audience in an open town square. Any semblance of illusion or conventional theatrical effect was eschewed; the play was a *jeu* to which actor and audience contributed imaginative engagement. This was not a theater of genteel illusion-making. Floodlights illuminated actors and audience equally; actors came and went visibly on the perimeter of the unlocalized playing area. In the playing area, scenes were acted with taut concentration. At the opening of the play, a smiling young Timon in a white suit moved across the playing area and through the spectators, amidst a fluttering covey of young admirers. "Lords" wore nondescript white capes over shirts and slacks. The banquet scenes were done in Roman style on a round golden cloth spread on the floor, circled with brocaded cushions. Timon and his guests lounged in extravagant flowing capes in glittering pastels. The entertainment included a dancer who weaved Timon's circle of fair-weather friends together with a large ball of colored twine—perhaps a vestige of folklore from the company's recent experiments in the Near East. Later, the bill collectors appeared in coats, ties, and black fedoras, each carrying an attaché case. They knocked on the old proscenium doors to serve their due bills. Alcibiades (Bruce Myers) was the model of a modern Mediterranean general in a severe black military tunic, edged in red. Apemantus, played by a young black man (Malick Bagayogo), appeared in an Army surplus overcoat and boots, resembling an Algerian street beggar familiar to French audiences. The senators of Athens visited Timon in morning coats and top hats, and were shielded from the sun by black umbrellas held by aides. Timon's wilderness was a Beckettian desert defined by sprays of sand over the playing floor. Timon sprawled in the ragged remnants of his white suit and a filthy trenchcoat. The staging of the final scene made it pictorially clear that Alcibiades' triumph was one achieved by force and intimidation. The Athenians sprawled in prone supplication at the proscenium edge, seeking mercy from Alcibiades, who stood high on the rear stage wall catwalk, across the gulf of the stage cavity, looking down on them, his red cape casually over one shoulder.

The production was received enthusiastically by the French press, who were especially impressed by the staging methods. Audiences filled the small-capacity theater during the runs of the play in the fall of 1974 and the spring of 1975. My over-all impression was of a rather leveled, simplistic rendering of the play in which one was engaged by the young company's anti-traditional methods and collective sincerity. There was an unevenness of talent, and some of the international company had learned their French merely phonetically. If the theme of the fall of Timon the disillusioned materialist was effectively set amidst the ruins of the Bouffes-du-Nord and underscored by the altruistic denial of conventional, elaborate, expensive production methods, there was also an elaborately contrived naiveté. A youthful Timon, such as was that of François Marthouret, can project an image of the vulnerable, credulous, and impetuous host. But youthfulness alone will not sustain any size of misanthropy, and it did not in this production.

Brook's unflinching view of the play's ending has much to recommend it. Yet his concept of a confused Timon contained curiously little compassion for, or interest in, the intensity and dramatic size of Timon's commitment to despair. Like the previous treatments of the play as a satire on materialism, this production seemed to leave the tragic misanthrope essentially unexplored, the man of whom Alcibiades says at the close of the play, "Yet rich conceit / Taught thee to make vast Neptune weep for aye / On thy low grave, on faults forgiven" (5.4.77–79).

Text

According to the presently prevailing opinion, the text of *Timon* in the First Folio reflects a not-quite-finished manuscript of Shakespeare. This opinion may be stated in Charlton Hinman's characteristically judicious words:

> [*Timon*] is consistent in mood and temper; the execution of all its parts seems firmly governed by a single general scheme; the same patterns of image and idea recur throughout; details which all critics have found characteristically if not uniquely Shakespearean are scattered through the very passages which are in other respects so far below the expected standards, and the flaws which mar these are by no means peculiar to them alone. The play is of a piece, and Shakespearean. Yet it undeniably contains hosts of such relatively small anomalies as . . . metrical irregularities, signs of false starts and of alterations planned but not made. The simplest and most satisfactory explanation of these is that the manuscript used by the Folio printer was, in the sense of the word already suggested, unfinished: substantially complete but not yet what could forthwith be made the basis of a promptbook and of stage presentation.[1]

The theory that an unfinished manuscript of Shakespeare was the basis of the Folio text may be the right explanation, but we should be wary of letting it harden into orthodoxy. Unless accompanied by an insistence on the essential unity of the play such as Hinman's, this theory can be, and has been, outrightly harmful for critical appreciation. Implications have crept in that somehow *Timon* is not worthy of the critical attention given to other plays and does not warrant a faithful rendering on the stage. The evidence presented by the Folio text is complex and ambiguous, and some features do not seem to me to fit into the unfinished-play concept.

First, it should be said that the textual problems do not set the play apart from the others. Every type of problem occurs in some "good" text; they are merely more crowded and more acute here. Also, as Honigmann warns, the state of the Folio should not bias our attitude toward the play as a whole; a better text than the present one may have existed at one time, and it would be a great mistake to suppose that the text we now have proves Shakespeare's dissatisfaction with his own achievement. Opportunity for a considerable post-Shakespearean corruption existed in the printing house since the text was set by the less-careful of the two main compositors of the Folio, the compositor B, probably together with some even less-expert help. If they were working from a badly legible, perhaps damaged, manuscript, they would have introduced numerous errors.[2]

It should also be said that the text is not as bad as it is sometimes made out to be. Editors and critics have a tendency to see symptoms of incompleteness in cases where in other dramas they look for dramatic exigencies or even discover felicities. Thus arose the notion that *Timon*, in Una Ellis-Fermor's influential and damaging verdict, is "roughed out, worked over in part, and then abandoned; full of inconsistencies in form and presentation, with fragments (some of them considerable); bearing the unmistakable stamp of [Shakespeare's] workmanship throughout."[3] It is salutary to be reminded of Coleridge's contrasting opinion: "as originally written, he apprehended that it was one of the author's most complete performances."[4]

The theory of *Timon* as in some manner unfinished, which goes back to Ulrici and was developed by Wilhelm Wendlandt in 1888, has taken the place of the now-defunct theory, also of nineteenth-century origin, that Shakespeare was not the sole author.[5] The older belief had died of its own even before the advent of the new bibliography.[6] But many of the discrepancies that the keen eyes of these detectives spotted here, there, and everywhere have been used by those who declare the play to be unfinished. We should also be warned that even apparently objective conclusions about the nature of the text may be influenced by subjective reactions to the play's pervasive pessimism. One senses that E. K. Chambers's feeling that this somber play was a product of Shakespeare's temporary neurosis made him underestimate its literary qualities and declare that "the structure of *Timon* as a whole is incoherent."[7] Consistent with this view, his diagnosis of the text stressed its faultiness and all-too-readily made him conclude that the play was left unfinished.

I have argued that the structural deficiencies disappear when we consider *Timon* from the point of view of regular Renaissance tragedy; we must make allowance, of course, for the particular nature of the play. The lack of relatedness and of interaction among the characters, to which Ellis-Fermor drew attention, is appropriate for the emphasis on the theme of isolation, which, in agreement with other scholars, I have found characteristic. Even Ellis-Fermor had a hunch that this theme may have been partially determinative of Shakespeare's dramatic conception, but she rejected the idea because she felt that the theme was not developed. I think it is, threading itself as it does through the play from the beginning to the end. The flatness of characterization that Ellis-Fermor censured is the result of streamlining for dramatic emphasis. All that is needed is there. We do not really have to know who Timon's parents were, when they died, how he was brought up, and where his wealth came from. Such background details would merely clutter up the plot and detract from the most significant developments, the loss of Timon's wealth and the consequences of this loss. These and similar alleged deficiencies could have been removed only by Shakespeare's writing a play totally different in kind.

Other inconsistencies of plot structure and loose ends exist merely in the imagination of the critics; some are even subtleties of dramatization. I have already dealt with the delayed entrance of the poet and painter, which occurs almost two hundred lines after they are first sighted near Timon's cave; rather than being a defect, I see it as a plot device that underlines the acceleration of the visits to Timon and gives the arrivals an impromptu appearance. I have similarly argued that the apparent inconsistencies in Alcibiades' account of what he knows about Timon's misfortunes (4.3.56–57, 78, 93–96) come from the general's caginess. If it is claimed that the episode with the fool in 2.2 is not sufficiently integrated into the play, as much could be said about other appearances of fools in tragedy. It is true that Shakespeare generally found better use for them; but as Frank Kermode has noted, there is no more point to the fool's contribution in *Othello*[8]—I would say that there is less.

Timon's speech in 4.3.377–95 offers an example of a passage that a modern editor, H. J. Oliver, considers indicative of the play's lack of finish but which is quite defensible on dramatic grounds.[9] Here, after Timon and Apemantus have engaged in insults, Timon expresses his disgust with the false world, speaks of his grave, and then erupts in a denunciation of gold. Timon, says Oliver, begins what "reads" like a soliloquy: "Then, Timon, presently prepare thy grave . . . " (380). Oliver argues that Apemantus does not seem to be needed for this passage, so the reader is surprised to find him still present after the end of the speech; he therefore suggests to put an "exit" for Apemantus after line 377 and have him reenter about line 392. Thus he overhears Timon's final words and interrupts to bring the news of the bandits' approach.

The trouble with this argument is that it is a reader's argument. On the stage, Timon's forgetfulness of Apemantus's presence makes an effective point. Timon's disgust with the false world includes Apemantus; he will love nothing but "the mere necessities upon't" (379); as he now realizes, the only necessity left for him is the grave. As Timon, self-absorbed, ponders the reduction of his wants and expresses his desire for death, his thoughts fix themselves on the deadly object of human desires: the "sweet king-killer" gold. The incident dramatizes the shrinking of Timon's desires and interests; the point is emphasized by his forgetting the presence of the apostle of minimal needs, Apemantus, who has to pull Timon back to reality.

Something too much has been made of the roughness of the language. The unevenness in some of Apemantus's speeches, as I have argued, is characteristic of his purposely rude and boorish manner of speaking. Similar reasons of dramatic propriety account for some metrical and syntactical irregularities in speeches by other characters, such as in Alcibiades' defense against the senators. Ellis-Fermor and Oliver think the speech mere jottings, intelligible in its thought but not yet made into firm verse paragraphs. If we realize that it shows Alcibiades' anger rising when he is rudely interrupted by a senator, we shall find the slight irregularity of the lines emphasize his clipped accent, irritated questions, and the stinging axioms he throws at the senators.

Alcibiades begins with a metrically regular first line— he tries to be reasonable—but then stops short, leaving the second line incomplete:

My lords, then, under favour, pardon me,
If I speak like a captain.

(3.5.41–42)

The pause is dramatically appropriate; it betrays Alcibiades' growing anger, which vents itself in the series of rhetorical questions that follows. I see nothing really irregular in these until Alcibiades comes to the end:

To be in anger is impiety;
But who is man that is not angry?
Weigh but the crime with this.

(57–59)

The last two lines, a tetrameter and a trimeter, show how Alcibiades' breath is getting short as he justifies his anger. One feels him choking, and the senator's ensuing comment is therefore suitably sarcastic: "You breathe in vain." Regularizing these lines would do only harm.

The case for incompleteness is thought to be clinched by an alleged confusion in the text about the value of the talent. It has long been noted; advocates of the theory of multiple authorship used it to support their claims. The main problem is that the numbers of talents mentioned early in the play, the five talents Timon gives to Ventidius and the three to the old Athenian, seem small compared with later figures and with what appears to be Timon's total indebtedness, which the senator calculates as 25,000 talents (2.1.3). Then there is the matter of apparent irregularities concerning the three-times fifty talents Timon sends his servants out to borrow from his friends. In 3.2., "so many talents" is thrice used instead of the fifty talents specified earlier, and this phrase has been thought a stopgap. It has been considered strange that the servant asks Lucius for "so many talents" (35) and that the latter answers: "He cannot want fifty five hundred talents" (37)—so the Folio has it, without the hyphen or dash that editors usually put between "fifty" and "five hundred." Oliver and others explain this puzzle as originating from Shakespeare's writing both 50 and 500 (probably in figures) as alternatives and forgetting to strike out one of them.

An intriguing explanation of this "talent muddle" has been devised by Terence Spencer, who argues that Shakespeare did not know the value of the talent when he started out, became confused about it, and therefore sought and obtained the correct information. He then began to revise the figures, and in some places got them right. According to this explanation, the three and the five talents of the first scene are the correct sums, and the later, larger figures are the sums he had used before. The phrase "so many talents," Spencer argues, represents the stage when Shakespeare became uncertain; he did not get around to supplanting it with the correct number.[10]

There are problems with this explanation. For one, the allegedly revised figures seem too high if the ancient talent is rated according to its comparable value in Shakespeare's time, that is, something between £120 and £180. At a time when a manual laborer could expect to earn no more than

£10 or £15 a year and a playwright got as little as £6 for a finished play, a Jacobean audience would surely have found it hard to swallow that this Athenian landowner endowed his servant with about £450 as an advance gift for matching his bride's father's "all"—whatever this may be. Another objection to the idea that the early figures are revised comes from their resembling those in Lucian and the *Timon* comedy, Shakespeare's presumable sources. Both Bradbrook and Bulman have suggested that Shakespeare took over these sums as well as the confusion from the comedy; Timon here releases Eutrapelus from a five-talent bond, the exact sum of Timon's loan to Ventidius. The author of the comedy, although expert in Greek, did not seem to know the value of the talent either or he would not have had his Laches bring in sacks filled with talents.[11] In fact, this author refers to pounds in a way that makes it impossible to gauge their exchange value with talents. There is no proof that Shakespeare ever learned or cared to learn the exact value of the talent. It is symptomatic that in a later occurrence of "talents" in *Cymbeline*, 1.6.80, the word stands merely for an indefinite, large sum.

By focusing on the value of the talent, it appears to me, critics have both understated the extent of the "money muddle" and made it appear as if it had dramatic significance, which, I think, it has not. The muddle is even greater than is generally realized since Shakespeare referred not only to talents but also to "crowns" and "pieces," and it is impossible to ascertain their value. To Varro, Timon is said to owe 9,000 talents (2.1.2), but also, elsewhere, 3,000 crowns (3.4.29), and the latter sum cannot be reconciled with the former if the crown is given its English value; the confusion is increased when one realizes that French and Flemish crowns of differing values were also circulating in Shakespeare's England. And a "piece" could be any kind of coin. We do well to look at these and other figures not from the point of view of a financial expert but from that of Shakespeare's audience, who did not know the value of the talent any more than he; for that matter, a modern audience is as blissfully ignorant about it. The reviewer of a recent performance who asked that the exact value of the talent be stated in the program evidently did not suspect that the sums were inconsistent. I think that they do have a sufficient surface plausibility and dramatic consistency provided one does not know the value of the talent and assumes it to be in some manner larger, but not hugely so, than the pound in Shakespeare's time.

Shakespeare seems to have begun with the figures of the talents in Lucian and the *Timon* comedy in mind without knowing exactly what they stood for in terms of pounds. He could not have thought about their value as anywhere near their actual rate in ancient Greece since he hardly wanted Timon's loan to Ventidius and endowment of his servant to represent exorbitant sums but rather show his everyday extravagance that by this time has built into a huge deficit. Let us assume, for argument's sake, that Shakespeare operated with the idea that a talent was about five pounds. Ventidius's indebtedness would then be about £25, and Timon's gift to the servant £15, plus the promise of another and larger gift in the future. Certainly, these monetary expenses, together with the remunerations for the poet's and the painter's works, the purchase of a pearl, the rich entertainment of the banquet and the gifts distributed there, constitute enough of a day's effort toward financial ruin. If this ratio of one to five for talent and pound or a similar one is assumed, all other figures come nearer to being reasonable. Timon's total indebtedness as estimated by the senator would be £125,000, a huge but not unbelievable sum in Shakespeare's time. To list only a few spectacular examples of financial losses of Elizabethan-Jacobean aristocrats, as chronicled by Stone: the earl of Oxford, between 1575 and 1586, sold all his property for over £70,000 and had nothing to show for it in the end; the earl of Northumberland incurred a debt of £15,000 in eighteen months between 1585 and 1586; and the earl of Dorset ran through a marriage portion of £17,000 and through £80,000 from the sale of land in the ten years from 1614 to 1623.[12]

As to the sums Timon tries to borrow from his friends, he does what was not and still is not unusual in such circumstances. He does not acknowledge his total indebtedness, and he tries to tap a number of sources for smaller amounts. The three-times fifty talents (£750 in our hypothetical model) are mere pebbles to throw at a dike about to burst; but we must add to these the 1,000 talents (or £5,000) Timon tries to borrow from the senators and the 1,000 "pieces" (whatever these are) he has sought from the lords (3.6.21–26). The total effort amounts at least to an attempt at stopping the rising flood by sandbags, and he might have succeeded temporarily had he obtained these sums. By the time we hear one creditor's servant demand 3,000 and another 5,000 crowns (3.4.29–30), we realize that the dike has burst; I do not think that is is important that we learn the exact amount of these demands. What with the addition of new creditors' names and new and larger figures, we get the feeling that Timon's indebtedness must be greater than the senator calculated earlier and we thought. The three occurrences of the phrase "so many talents" and the "fifty five hundred" do not prove that Shakespeare was becoming uncertain about the value of the talent and penned them in embarrassment. "So many talents" is first used by the stranger as the sum Timon has sought to borrow from Lucullus (3.2.11); the stranger is apparently ignorant of the exact sum, but the audience, of course, knows it to be fifty talents. Lucius, not knowing the exact amount, would naturally repeat the phrase: "I should ne'er have denied his occasion so many talents" (23). Thus he blithely implies his unlimited generosity. When the servant then also asks for "so many talents," as Steevens suggested, he may be showing Lucius a note with the figure on it—there is humor in his unconsciously using the phrase by which Lucius has protested his generosity. But it is also possible that the compositor slipped and used the words he had twice before set to precede "talents" instead of the "fifty" that may have been in Shakespeare's manuscript. Lucius's answer, of course, must indicate that he knows the specific sum asked of him, and it does indeed show this if a pause is put between fifty" and "five hundred": "He cannot want fifty—five hundred talents" (37). As Deighton explained in the Old Arden Edition, Lucius means that no sum, however large, "fifty or even five hundred talents," can add significantly to Timon's already large wealth—the nuance of Lucius's thinking that five hundred talents would save Timon is ironic. The servant's answer keeps strictly to the request for fifty: "But in the meantime he wants less, my lord" (38).

It is certainly hazardous to conclude from this "talent muddle" that Shakespeare was engaged in a revision of the figures that he failed to complete because he abandoned the play. The figures as they stand add to the impression of Timon's violation of number, weight, and measure, and they bear out the merciless exploitation he is subjected to even if they do not allow us to judge the extent of his debt accurately. They would not be satisfactory in a currency exchange, but provided the audience is ignorant about the exact value of the talent, they are effective enough in the theater where complicated financial calculations are impossible.

Nor does the often-invoked duplication of Timon's epitaph in 5.4.70–73 prove that Shakespeare abandoned the play before fully revising it. In fact, the repetition could be used to argue the opposite. The customary explanation is that Shakespeare copied down both epitaphs as Plutarch quoted them, the one attributed to Timon himself and the other to the poet Callimachus, even though they contradict each other, and that he failed to expunge one of them later. But in similar scenes of duplication with variation, such as *Love's Labor's Lost*, 4.3.280–362, and *Julius Caesar*, 4.2.143–58, 166,

181–95, textual scholars have usually thought that the explanation lies in a revision of the original lines by Shakespeare; somehow, both the first version and the revision remained in the manuscript and were printed. This could also have been the case with the epitaphs. The epitaph of Callimachus may have seemed to Shakespeare to express better what Alcibiades calls Timon's "latter spirits" and he may have thought that evoking Timon's name at the end, as it does, was a good idea. Perhaps Shakespeare wrote Timon's own epitaph first, and then during a revision remembered the more fitting lines of Callimachus; he turned once more to Plutarch in order to paraphrase them, and somehow both epitaphs got into the printed text.

Ellis-Fermor and others seem to me at least partially right about the defectiveness of the fifth act. Even as the act stands, it brings the play to a logical conclusion; the large design, at least, is complete. But there is a certain unevenness and jumpiness in the movement; something appears to be left out. I have already noted that I incline to think that cuts were made for purposes of performance. If so, the possibility also exists that one of the two versions of the epitaph represents a revision for theatrical reasons by Shakespeare or somebody else.

It is unfortunate that the textual problems have generally been discussed with the underlying conviction that the play was never performed in the theater. This questionable thesis sometimes has been thought to be supported by the play's irregular placement in the Folio. I have argued that this placement does not indicate that the editors were in doubt as to whether *Timon* was a tragedy; similar reasons militate against the assumption that they considered it not to belong to the regular repertoire. When they placed *Timon* between *Romeo and Juliet* and *Julius Caesar* in the gap left by the temporary withdrawal of *Troilus and Cressida*, it was surely not because they needed a play—almost any kind of play, even a mere fragment—to save themselves the embarrassment of a gap in the pagination (and they did not save themselves this embarrassment altogether). *Timon* must have been from the beginning intended for some place in the Folio; there is no reason to think that the editors disbelieved that they had one of "the true and original copies" of Shakespeare's plays here, the plays they were presenting to the public "perfect of their limbs." They may have made the mental reservation, of course, that these copies were as true and original and as perfect of their limbs as they could obtain them.

The absence of any record of performance of *Timon* in Jacobean times should not be taken to indicate that the play was never performed. No records exist that *Antony and Cleo-*

patra and *Coriolanus* were performed, but who would doubt that they were? It is indeed possible that the lack of a performance record for all three of the last tragedies points to their being less popular than the preceding ones, but it is extremely unlikely that any one of the three was withheld from the stage. Until the fantasy arose that *Timon* is Shakespeare's spiritual autobiography, editors and critics took for granted that the play was performed in Shakespeare's time, and they attributed the corruptions to the actors; Coleridge, among others, did so. In 1905, Deighton still opined that there was "some player, to whom the editors, failing to find portions known once to have existed, had entrusted the task of putting together the incomplete material."[13] The new bibliography, with its sharp distinctions between good and bad quartos as well as foul papers and promptbooks, has made such arguments unfashionable. But for *Timon*, at least, these distinctions may set up too rigid a frame to explain all peculiarities of the text. If indeed the manuscript was very defective and recollections of some stage version existed, would it not have been likely for the editors to seek reconstruction of missing or deficient parts through assembling a text in whatever way feasible, the kind of procedure often assumed to be behind the "bad quartos"?[14] In this case, the text would reflect Shakespeare's "foul papers" as well as a stage version, perhaps one considerably altered from Shakespeare's original manuscript.

We should therefore consider three possibilities for the true textual deficiencies: one stemming from Shakespeare's failure to polish his autograph, the second deriving from compositors' errors, and the third owing to attempts to reconstruct defective or missing passages through the actors' memories or even through one or the other of their parts that had been preserved.

In practice, it is not easy to assess the probabilities even in apparently simple cases. The mislineations, the printing of verse as prose and prose as verse could have come about by the compositors' working from a badly legible manuscript; but memorial reconstruction could also have occasioned some of these. A compositor may have been responsible for the mistake of "Flavius" instead of Flaminius in 2.2.189; the manuscript perhaps had merely "Fla". But Shakespeare was not beyond slipping in such minor matters. Likewise either the compositors or Shakespeare himself may have spelled some names inconsistently: Apemantus (Apermantus), Ventidius (Ventigius, Ventiddius, Ventidgius), Phrynia (Phrincia), and Timandra (Timandylo). But renaming by the actors is also a possibility.

Lines that are excessive or defective metrically and passages that are neither quite verse nor prose are generally explained as due to Shakespeare's failure to finish or polish the play. I find this not always plausible. For instance, I am unable to accept this explanation for the strange condition of the steward's elegy on his master's fall (4.2.30–51)—an example used by both Chambers and Oliver. Chambers says that the speech impresses him as "not so much un-Shakespearean as incompletely Shakespearean." But very little would have been required to "finish" it, and I wonder therefore why Shakespeare should not have done so at the first try. Consider the lines:

> Who would not wish to be from wealth exempt,
> Since riches point to misery and contempt?
> Who would be so mock'd with glory, or to live
> But in a dream of friendship,
> To have his pomp and all what state compounds
> But only painted like his varnish'd friends?

> (4.2.31–36)

Obviously, the first and the last two lines are complete and "finished." The third line could be made into a regular and more speakable line with a stroke of the pen, and the fourth line requires only a small addition to make it metrically and syntactically regular. For example, (with apologies to Shakespeare):

> Who would so mock'd with glory be to live
> But in a dream of friendship? Who would wish
> To have his pomp and all what state compounds,
> But only painted like his varnish'd friends?

"Ein Federstrich," Tschischwitz said long ago, was all that was needed in most cases of deficiencies of the *Timon* text.[15] I find it hard to believe that Shakespeare, whose reputation was to have never blotted a line, would not have supplied these touches immediately. More plausible than the text's here representing an unfinished draft appears to me the intrusion of some kind of post-Shakespearean corruption; but I find myself unable to decide between the alternatives. It is certainly possible that the manuscript was so illegible through some damage that the compositor left out a few words and made some errors. But it seems to me also possible that the speech was reconstructed with the help of an actor's faulty memory. The kind of garbled speeches one finds in *Timon* occur in the "bad quartos," which may have been assembled texts, granted that even the best of these is inferior to the *Timon* text.

The feature of the *Timon* text that makes me most incline toward believing in some influence from a stage version are the stage directions. They have, of course, generally been taken to prove the derivation of the text from Shakespeare's "foul papers." Yet critics also have often noted that the directions are unusually detailed and explicitly realized. Thomas M. Parrott, who still thought that Shakespeare was not the sole author of *Timon*, said: "One of the characteristics of the Folio text is the fullness and specific character of the stage directions. This would seem to me to indicate that the manuscript had been carefully annotated for performance."[16] Even Chambers, as much as he felt that the play was textually and structurally unfinished, noted the special theatricality of these directions: "There are some elaborate stage directions resembling those of *Coriolanus*. Occasionally . . . a touch seems superfluous for theatrical purposes, but in the main there is nothing which an author, wishing to give careful directions for the ordering of his groups, might not write."[17] We shall in what follows ask the unorthodox question whether there is anything in the stage directions that an actor or some other person intimately acquainted with the play on the stage could not have observed.

In several examples, both "foul papers" and performance observation offer explanations. One instance is the listing of a "ghost character," the mercer, in the opening stage direction. It is generally thought that Shakespeare intended the mercer to appear in the first scene but changed his mind and forgot to expunge him from the direction. It is at least possible that in a stage version a mercer did appear. Even in a mute role, his livery would make him an ironic exemplar of feeders on Timon's extravagance. The occasional indefiniteness and permissiveness of the directions need not be attributed to their derivation from Shakespeare's "foul papers." Some indefiniteness is to be expected in a play that required a large number of actors, as large a number as the varying resources of the theater permitted. For instance, the direction *"Enter Alcibiades with the rest"* (1.1.246) may sound indefinite, but it is clear that there should be twenty attendants (240), and the direction presumably indicates that supernumeraries of a number as close to twenty as possible were to appear or did appear. Similarly, such apparently "permissive" phrases as "certain senators" (1.1.39) and "diverse friends" (3.6.1) may merely indicate that the number depended on availability. For that matter, they could have come from an observer who did not remember the exact figure.[18]

Besides indefiniteness and permissiveness, the feature most thought of as characteristic of stage directions in "foul papers" is their descriptiveness. The prompter, it is argued, would have pruned the directions, made them tidier and directly relevant to the performance. Be it said that there is no general sloppiness in the stage directions of *Timon*. The movement on the stage, the visual drama, is rendered in them with an evident knowledge of stage conditions. The entrances of the characters are marked in anticipatory technique (as Chambers noted), that is, the entrances are so placed that the characters have sufficient time to arrive at the points of interaction. (Cf. 1.1.176, 239; 1.2.111, 118; 5.1.29.) We do not know, in fact, how much promptbook stage directions differed from authorial ones, and we may have given prompters too much credit for alterations. According to researches in the sixteen extant Elizabethan-Jacobean-Caroline playbooks by William B. Long, the inquiry into this matter has suffered from two major misapprehensions: first, that the actors needed much assistance from both playwrights and prompters; and second, that the playbooks of an earlier period must be marked in accordance with our contemporary expectations. Much less is changed in the playbooks than we would assume.[19]

For our present purposes, Long's most significant observation is that on authorial advisory directions, that is, directions in which an author specifically instructs an actor what to do or how to do it. Long finds them very sparingly used by professional playwrights. Yet directions of this kind are frequent in the *Timon* text. The question therefore arises as to whether they are really all Shakespeare's. To take an example of one of these directions, that for the first banquet:

> *Hautboys playing loud music. A great banquet serv'd in; and then enter Lord Timon, the states, the Athenian lords: Ventidius with Timon redeemed from prison. Then comes, dropping after all, Apemantus, discontentedly like himself.* (1.2.1)[20]

I do not find convincing Oliver's argument that Shakespeare had to remind himself that Timon redeemed Ventidius from prison. Nor do I believe that the characterization of Apemantus is "at best an indication of what an author would like to see on the stage"; it sounds so much more like what somebody saw on the stage and later remembered. Is it not more plausible that a person who observed the actor of Apemantus would describe him as entering "like himself" than that the author of the play did? It may be significant that almost all the descriptive stage directions are from scenes in which Timon appears. The actor of this role, the text of which is most nearly perfect, one may surmise, had an influence on them.[21]

To add other visually or auditively impressive directions:

Trumpets sound. Enter lord Timon, addressing himself courteously to every suitor. (1.1.97)

Flaminius waiting to speak with a Lord from his Master. Enter a Servant to him. (3.1.1)

Enter Alcibiades, with drum and fife, in warlike manner; and Phrynia and Timandra. (4.3.49)

To these stage directions may be added those that relate a character to the scenery, the kind of scenery created by simple emblematic stage props.

Enter Timon in the Woods. (4.3.1)

Enter Timon from his Cave. (5.1.30)

Enter Timon out of his Cave. (5.1.139)

Enter a soldier in the Woods seeking Timon. (5.3.1)

These directions may have come from Shakespeare's visualizing imagination; but they also could have been derived from an actor's or observer's memory of the play.

Even more impressively worked out than the visual drama in the directions is the musical one: music is a specific and integral part from the beginning to the end. Dramatic points are repeatedly made through music: several trumpets, for instance, announce the first entrance of Timon, only one that of Alcibiades. Everywhere the exact musical instruments are prescribed: the lutes and oboes of the masque, the drum and fife of Alcibiades' march across the stage, the trumpets when he demands the city's surrender, and the drums that strike as he exits in the end. John Long, accepting the prevailing opinion of the unfinished state of the play, surmises that these directions indicate that Shakespeare generally composed his plays with the appropriate orchestration from the beginning.[22] I find it hard to believe that he would not have left some of these details for later elaboration, perhaps after a talk with the musicians. The minimal conclusion to be drawn from the musical directions seems to me that the play has a high degree of structural finish. They have the ring of having been tested or witnessed on the stage. The directions for the masque, in particular, give me a distinct impression that whoever phrased them heard the music not merely in his mind:

Second tucket. Enter the maskers of the Amazons, with lutes in their hands, dancing and playing. (1.2.111)

The lords rise from table, with much adoring of Timon, and to show their loves, each singles out an Amazon, and all dance, men with women, a lofty strain or two of the hautboys, and cease. (142)

If indeed the "Amazonian Masque" in a British Museum

manuscript of court music is the original score for the *Timon* masque, as Bradbrook thinks, we lack nothing for reconstructing the masque.[23] We would then also have evidence that the play was performed in Shakespeare's time. In any case, the burden of proof is on those who say it was not.

It has not been my purpose to advance a new theory of the derivation of the text but rather to ask for an open-minded reexamination of the possibilities. *Timon* presents a special case among the Folio texts since it is a notch below the others. Perhaps we shall never know for certain why this is so. Even in the case of plays where a good and a bad text exist, scholars often disagree about the reasons for the latter's deficiency; the difficulties multiply in *Timon*, where there is only a bad text. If the possibility of an influence on the text by a staged version of the play has merit, as I believe it does, we should seriously consider it. I have sought to go a step in this direction.

When the suggestion of an influence by the actors on *Timon* (or for that matter, on other plays) has been made in the past, this influence has generally been thought as corrupting. Our brief inquiry intimates that this is not the only way to look at it. The performance features of the text, particularly the stage directions, allow us to consider it as a theatrical document. And at least one modern director appears to believe that the Folio text has a special value for producing the play: she tracked down the "directional hints and signals" of the text for a performance.[24] At any rate, we should be careful not to overstate the deficiencies of the text. It certainly does not vitiate a detailed and organic criticism; it does not lack any significant details, nor is it replete with loose ends. Rather, it presents a fully planned play, executed with care in all important aspects.

Date and Sources

      The date and sources of *Timon* concern us in this study because of their bearing on the play's pessimism. We shall ask the following two related questions: when was Shakespeare likely to have written this somber tragedy; and, what earlier or contemporary works inspired or helped him in conceiving it? Arguments by previous scholars will be discussed from the perspective suggested by these questions.

To seek to place *Timon* into Shakespeare's life story, as some early critics attempted, can be nothing but speculation; we shall therefore use literary criteria. We must concede at the outset that no argument that can be used furnishes a definite proof by itself; several such arguments together, therefore, also fail to constitute proof. For tying *Timon* to a specific date, we have only weak links and can therefore forge only a fragile chain. Such as the evidence is, it makes me incline to 1607 as the date of the composition of the play and its first performance; but I would not be surprised if in truth it were somewhat earlier or later. Style and versification are of Shakespeare's later or last tragic period; the affinities with *Lear* (which confidently can be dated between 1604 and 1605) and with *Coriolanus* (which is tentatively put between 1607 and 1608) are evident. Like most recent critics, I have seen *Timon* as closer to *Coriolanus* than to *Lear*.[1] Timon and Coriolanus are placed in similar situations: prominent citizens, they are alienated from their societies because of banishment and turn against their native states. Both conceive of themselves as victims of fortune and ingratitude. (See *Cor.* 4.4.12–26.) In addition, Alcibiades has some affinities to both Coriolanus and Aufidius: a professional soldier turned rebel, he leads an army against his native city like Coriolanus; yet, like Aufidius, he is a pragmatist who resists being ensnared by tragedy. With regard to socioeconomic issues, however, *Timon* may be said to be closer to *Lear* since both castigate the luxury and extravagance of the rich more explicitly than *Coriolanus*.[2] I therefore tend to put *Timon* after *Lear* and before *Coriolanus*. This sequence, I shall argue later, is also made credible by the presumptive relationship of *Lear* and *Timon* to one of the latter play's sources, the comedy often called the Old Timon.

This placement is supported by what seems the most logical relative chronology of Shakespeare's later classical plays. A reawakened fascination with Plutarch, whose *Lives* he had not used since *Julius Caesar* in 1599, may have led Shakespeare to "The Life of Marcus Antonius" and made him write his *Antony and Cleopatra*. Plutarch's story of Timon in this Life in turn may have stirred him to write his tragedy of the misanthrope. His search for materials would then have led him to Plutarch's "Life of Alcibiades" since the general is mentioned in the Timon biography. Alcibiades would have drawn Shakespeare's attention to Coriolanus because Plutarch parallels the careers of the two soldiers banished by their native cities. If *Antony and Cleopatra* was written between 1606 and 1608, and *Coriolanus* between 1607 and 1608, as is usually assumed, *Timon* could then be dated between late 1606 and early 1608. It must be fully admitted that the dates of the other plays are also tentative and that Shakespeare could have followed a different sequence, less logical though it is; he could have dramatized the Timon story before that of Antony, from which it came, or after that of Coriolanus in a delayed reaction.

The plausibility of a date not earlier than late 1606 is increased by the strong probability that Shakespeare was inspired for Timon's mock praises of gold by the dythirambic encomia of Volpone and Mosca in Jonson's *Volpone*. If there is a dependence of one play on the other in these speeches, I have argued that it is Shakespeare's on Jonson's.[3] Jonson's speeches are in a simple eulogistic pattern that points up the naive greed of his characters, whereas Shakespeare's more subtly heighten the mock praise into an accusation of the world's subservience to gold by accentuating the odious metamorphoses it brings about. *Volpone* was first printed in

1607, but as the title leaf and the colophon of the second quarto of 1616 indicate, it was performed by "the King's Majesty's Servants" in 1605. The uncertainty as to what style of calendar is used makes it possible that 1605 may also cover the earlier part of 1606, and some contemporary events that may be alluded to in the play have induced scholars to prefer the later date.[4] Although Shakespeare is not listed in the colophon among the "principal actors" who performed in *Volpone*, he surely saw the play of his competitor when performed by his own company. He may have put this experience to good use in *Timon* soon after that.

Considerations based on the economic and social conditions of England between 1606 and 1608 support a dating of the play in these years. These were generally hard years for the economy. The harvests were poor and prices, which had been rising almost continuously, were particularly high. Borrowing was widespread, but money was scarce. A remark like that of Shakespeare's Lucullus that "this is no time to lend money" (3.1.41–42) would have had a familiar ring to Shakespeare's audience. The conditions that brought about loss of estates would also have been quite topical for Shakespeare and his audience. Shakespeare's own property in and around Stratford was threatened by the enclosure movement, and the 1607 revolt of the "diggers," who squatted on some of the enclosed land in his native Warwickshire, was a reaction to the economic pressures.

There is one possible topical reference in the play that, if accepted, goes far toward proving a date of 1606 or 1607. Maxwell, among the modern editors, notes it but rejects it because of its conflict with his general belief in the precedence of *Timon* to *Lear*. Says the servant who castigates the hypocrisy and villainy of Sempronius:

> How fairly this lord strives to appear foul! Takes virtuous copies to be wicked, like those that under hot ardent zeal would set whole realms on fire: of such a nature is his politic love. (3.3.33–36)

Coleridge suspected here an "addition of the players" during the time of Charles I because he thought the passage was "introduced so *nolenter volenter*, by the head and shoulder."[5] There is no need to assume that Shakespeare did not write these lines; they fit into the theme of the play since they anticipate Timon's later apocalyptic strains. Yet they are still extraneous enough to the immediate context to suspect a topical allusion. In this respect, the note by Maxwell is intriguing: "Per[haps] he [i.e., Shakespeare] was thinking specifically of the Jesuits (rather than, as Warb. [Warburton] thought, the Puritans), whom it was customary a little later to describe as incendiaries."[6] This supposition gains likelihood because of Shakespeare's famous stab at Jesuitical equivocation in *Macbeth* in the "porter-at-hellgate" speech (2.3.8–11), which refers to Father Garnet's trial in the spring of 1606 for complicity in the Gunpowder Plot. The *Timon* passage seems to me to echo the kind of analogies drawn between the plot and the ultimate conflagration of the world at the Last Judgment. King James, in fact, had drawn this analogy, gently, in his speech to the Parliament, arguing that the threatened and avoided explosion was merely a warning and a call for purgation.[7] The Gunpowder Plot made references to setting realms on fire under the pretext of religion particularly topical during the year or two following it, that is, 1606 or 1607. No event ever excited in England so much horror about human degradation. It furnished amunition for the pessimists.

We shall now proceed to the question of what literary sources induced Shakespeare to shape *Timon* into a pessimistic tragedy. There is one clear negative answer: if the inquiry is restricted to the sources as narrowly defined—the story of Timon in Plutarch's "The Life of Marcus Antonius" and Lucian's dialogue "Timon the Misanthrope"—the answer must be that they could have had little part in suggesting to Shakespeare a tragic plot of any kind. Nor was the inducement greater if he also knew, as seems likely to me, the old *Timon*, an anonymous manuscript comedy of uncertain date. None of these three versions takes Timon seriously; none seeks to generate feelings for him deeper than curiosity, amusement, or contempt. Furthermore, none of the three contains any notable criticism of the society that caused Timon to become a misanthrope. Shakespeare, as much as he drew plot details from Plutarch and Lucian or the Lucianic tradition, including probably the Timon comedy, owed very little to them for the character of his hero and even less for the tragic vision of his play.

A solution to this dilemma is proposed by Peter Pauls in "Shakespeare's *Timon of Athens*: An examination of the Misanthrope Tradition and Shakespeare's Handling of the Sources" (Ph.D. diss., University of Wisconsin, 1969).[8] Pauls pays greater attention than do other scholars to two sources of the Timon story that are usually considered secondary or wafted aside as mere analogues, Pierre Boaistuau's *Le Théâtre du monde* (1558), translated into English by John Alday under the title of *Theatrum mundi, The Theater or Rule of the World* (1566, rpt. 1574, 1581), and particularly Richard Barckley's *A Discourse of the Felicity of Man* (1598, rpt. 1603, 1631). Pauls considers these two works not merely for the short and largely traditional accounts of Timon's life they contain but also for their general contents. He argues that when direct sources prove inadequate as they do for this play, we must look for "indirect" ones, for the kind of material Geoffrey Bullough classifies as "subsidiary." Pauls locates these in moral traditions of flattery, friendship, ingratitude, anger, and mutability. I would add to these the traditions of the *contemptus mundi*, of *vanitas*, of the decay of the world, and manifestations of the economic crisis as well as notions on art, nature, and fortune. Of course, these traditions pertain largely to the intellectual background and the sociocultural context of the play; but I think Pauls is right in treating such materials as subsidiary sources. Shakespeare appears to have made up for the scarcity of facts and ideas usable for shaping the Timon story into a tragedy by casting widely beyond the direct sources that gave him most of the plot situations. I shall therefore extend my discussion of sources beyond the usual three; but I shall restrict it to works that make at least a passing reference to Timon, works that provided a counterweight to the comic-satirical tradition. Anything available to Shakespeare in which Timon's misanthropy engenders sympathy or is taken as an at least partially justifiable reaction to the world's wickedness is a potential source of *Timon* and should be examined as such.

We shall look at the sources generally thought to be immediate, that is, those most significant for plot details, first. The clearest case here is the short Timon biography in Plutarch's "The Life of Marcus Antonius." That Shakespeare used it proceeds from his transcribing two epitaphs of Timon, one that Plutarch ascribes to Timon himself and the other that he assigns to the Poet Callimachus (5.4.70–73). Plutarch's account is the primary warrant for the linkage between Timon and Alcibiades and for Timon's association with Apemantus. Shakespeare accentuated two features of Plutarch's story to make them significant for the pessimistic implications of his play. The first of these is Plutarch's suggestion that Timon suffered from the ingratitude of his friends. (This was Plutarch's reason for including the tale since this ingratitude paralleled that of Antony's friends after his defeat.) The second touch lies in the Plutarchian Timon's ominously forecasting here and in "The Life of Alcibiades" that Alcibiades would bring about the ruin of Athens. Shakespeare's Timon echoes this sentiment (4.3.105–30), which may also have been a general incentive for Shakespeare's making Timon call on soldiers and war as allies in the destruction of mankind. But the character of Plutarch's Timon bears no resemblance to Shakespeare's. He is a jester and vituperator, not a great spender and wild hater, and he does not leave Athens. Apemantus is said to have imitated his manners rather than becoming, as in Shakespeare, a kind of model for the later Timon. Altogether, Plutarch's Timon is hardly more than a nuisance, the proverbial "critic Timon" (*Love's Labor's Lost*, 4.3.168) as Shakespeare seems to have conceived him in his earlier years.

Honigmann suggests that Shakespeare drew suggestions not only from Plutarch's biography of Timon but also from "The Life of Marcus Antonius" in general as well as from "The Life of Alcibiades" and its companion biography "The Life of Coriolanus."[9] But Shakespeare could not have found much material for a tragic shaping of the Timon story in any of these. From "The Life of Alcibiades," he could have gained an impression of national decay in Athens; but this was also a familiar subject of the Renaissance Diogeniana, where it was presented as a warning for London and England, and it is this tradition that must have prompted Shakespeare to create a kind of Jacobean Athens for his tragedy. The complicated political and military events told by Plutarch could have provided him with a plot for a tragedy of Alcibiades but were of little use for his tragedy of the misanthrope. However, I have argued in chapter four that although Shakespeare disregarded the external details of the Alcibiades biography, he gave a definite Plutarchian coloring to the general's character. Honigmann draws attention to the fact that both Shakespeare's Alcibiades and Plutarch's Coriolanus are professional soldiers; but I see no similarity in the characters of the two. Shakespeare did not model Alcibiades' reaction to banishment on that of Coriolanus; his Alcibiades does not lose control over himself. Shakespeare possibly may have conceived the idea of contrasting the temperament of Alcibiades with that of Timon from reading Plutarch's comparison of Alcibiades' and Coriolanus's anger; if so, he thought of Timon, not of Alcibiades, as Coriolanus-like.[10] The Shakespearean Alcibiades, like the Plutarchian, subordinates anger to his purpose and reneges when the Athenians repent.

The second most important source for the main plot, Lucian's dialogue "Timon the Misanthrope," presents a peculiar problem: it is impossible to say how Shakespeare knew it. It was not available in English, although Latin, French, and Italian translations existed. He could possibly have had it in Latin in grammar school, as T. W. Baldwin suggests, and remembered enough of the plot when he came to write the play; this would explain the lack of convincing verbal parallels.[11] He could also have read it in Italian or French, although the claims for this possibility are not persuasive. Neither is R. W. Bond's argument that Shakespeare knew and used Boiardo's *Il Timone*; as Bond himself admits, the non-Lucianic elements of the Italian comedy do not appear in Shakespeare's play.[12]

The whole question of Lucian's influence on Shakespeare is bedeviled by the existence of the old Timon comedy, which is even more difficult to date than Shakespeare's play—dates from before 1600 to 1611 have been suggested. If this *Timon* preceded Shakespeare's and he knew it, he could have derived most, perhaps all, of his Lucianic material from it. If, however, Shakespeare did not know the play because it postdated his or was not accessible to him for some other reason, Lucian looms much larger as a source. It is possible to derive most of the material that Shakespeare could have acquired from the comedy also from Lucian, and attribute the rest to accident or other influences, as does Honigmann. It is also possible to suppose with J. C. Maxwell, M. C. Bradbrook, and others that the comedy was written before Shakespeare's play and that he drew on it.[13] It is even possible to suppose, as does G. A. Bonnard, that there was a common source, now lost, on which both Shakespeare and the author of the comedy drew, although this theory is too speculative to hold much attraction.[14]

The evidence, such as it is, points to some connection between the comedy and Shakespeare's *Timon* and to Shakespeare as the borrower. The conviction, dominant in earlier criticism, that the comedy depended on Shakespeare's play rested on nothing better than the feeling that Shakespeare could not have been inspired by what was then considered a very silly product; this feeling was leagued with the belief that he had no chance of seeing the play since it was attributed to one of the two universities. Recently, however, M. C. Bradbrook and James Bulman have associated the comedy with the Inns of Court; if this is true, the chances of Shakespeare's having seen it increase because of his connection with the Inns, where some of his plays were performed.[15] However, Bradbrook's belief that the comedy followed the tragedy and satirized, parodied, and burlesqued it seems to me quite untenable. A drama that satirizes another drama must have allusions to it which an audience that sees the second play after the first can easily grasp, and none of Bradbrook's instances are of this sort. There are many easily understandable barbs in the comedy: against Lucianic satire, Homeric heroism, inflated rhetoric, mytological lore, quiddical logic, lying travelers' tales, Jonsonian comedy, stock motifs of drama, and what not. But there are no recognizable barbs against Shakespeare's *Timon*. It will not do to create them and to claim that the comedy mocks the "extensive Jove imagery" of Shakespeare's play. I discern no such imagery, the one reference to the god being casual (4.3.110); if Shakespeare's Timon impersonates a classical deity, it is Fortuna rather than Jove. The mockery of the comedy is clearly directed against the Jove of Lucian's dialogue. Surely if the comedy were a satire of Shakespeare's *Timon*, one could expect some burlesquing of the Plutarchian materials, some reference, at least, to Apemantus and Alcibiades, and there are none. Bulman, who opposes Bradbrook, strengthens the presumptive evidence for the precedence of the comedy to the tragedy by developing arguments that the comedy burlesques Jonson's "comicall satires," arguments that had been adumbrated by Hart and by Herford, Percy, and Simpson in their editions of Jonson's plays. The last of these satires, *Poetaster*, was produced in 1601, and Bulman opines that the comedy, in order to retain its topicality, must have been performed soon thereafter.

I am not really persuaded that it must have followed very soon. It is true that satirizing Jonson's satires would have been démodé by 1611, the date Bradbrook gives to the comedy. (She puts Shakespeare's *Timon* at 1609.) Contrary to Bulman, I think that spoofing at Jonson's satires may have been appropriate a considerable time after their performance; they must have remained popular reading at the Inns. And even if one accepts Bulman's date of "soon after 1601" for the comedy, his corollary does not follow that Shakespeare's play must have been written soon after the comedy. There is no telling how long Shakespeare may have remembered some details from the Old Timon if he saw it performed or read it in manuscript.

Although I am unconvinced by G. A. Bonnard's speculation that Shakespeare and the anonymous author had a common source, I see merit in one of Bonnard's other claims, namely, that the comedy echoes *Lear*. I believe that he is right when he reads Gelasimus's urging Timon to jump from a rock as a spoof at the Edgar-Gloucester episode at Dover Cliff and when he points out that the servant's disguise as a soldier in the comedy resembles Kent's in serving his old master. To Bonnard's parallel may be added some others noted by Robert Goldsmith, notably the resemblance of cursing speeches by the comic Timon to Lear's raging on the heath.[16] Goldsmith, it should be said, believes that Shakespeare was the borrower (and not only for *Lear* but also for *Timon*); yet his parallels between the comedy and *Lear* could also be claimed for the opposite and, to me, more plausible relationship. In particular, the comic Timon's "All things are made of nothing" (5.2) sounds like the proper academic answer to Lear's "Nothing will come of nothing" (1.1.90), reminding the audience, as the phrase does, that God made the world of nothing. Shake-

speare's Timon's "And nothing brings me all things" (5.1.187),
I shall show, is in a different pattern. If the comedy spoofed
Lear along with Jonson's satires and contemporary dramatic
fashions, a date of 1605 or 1606 would be appropriate for it;
the date of 1607, to which I incline for Shakespeare's *Timon*,
would also be quite apt.

To return to the source question, it seems to me likely then
that Shakespeare knew the comedy and borrowed from it.
But he probably also knew the Lucianic dialogue in some manner since a few details of his plot can be better derived from it.
From Lucian, either directly or indirectly, Shakespeare took
over the notion that Timon's misfortune and ensuing misanthropy were caused by his financial ruin. The comedy was
here the more rewarding source since it dwelled on Timon's
prodigality and pointed it up by a servant's agonizing over
it, a pattern Shakespeare adopted. Lucian, however, seems to
have realized more obviously than the writer of the comedy
that one could be of two minds about Timon's spending habits
and ensuing fall. This passage, which has been claimed to have
influenced Shakespeare, is intriguing:

> Why, if you like to put it so, it was his kindness and generosity
> and universal compassion that ruined him; but it would be nearer
> the truth to call him a fool and a simpleton and a blunderer; he
> did not realize that his protégés were carrion crows and wolves;
> vultures were feeding on his unfortunate liver, and he took them
> for friends and good comrades, showing a fine appetite just to
> please him. So they gnawed his bones perfectly clean, sucked
> out with great precision any marrow there might be in them, and
> went off, leaving him as dry as a tree whose roots have been
> severed; and now they do not know him or vouchsafe him a nod
> —no such fools—, nor ever think of showing him charity or re-
> paying his gifts.[17]

The animal and cannibal images and the identification of
Timon with a tree are at first sight suggestive of Shakespeare's
borrowing; but it should be said that the images were common
for usury in Shakespeare's time, and that the pictures of the
tree of life and fortune were emblematic commonplaces. No
specific resemblance is evident between the animal images
either of the dialogue or of the comedy and the animal imagery
of *Timon*. In neither source is there a systematic undergirding
of the plot by animal and nature images as in Shakespeare's
play. Although Shakespeare may have modeled some individual features of Timon's odious friends on these sources,
he had no incentive in them to portray a whole corrupt society. And though Lucian saw the possibility of depicting a
Timon that might strike some as humanitarian and others as
prodigal, the actual Timon of his dialogue is not ambivalent
but rather an ignorant boor, incapable alike of the generosity
and the apocalyptic hatred of Shakespeare's character. When

impoverished, Lucian's Timon is relatively content with his primitive life in nature. After finding the gold, he becomes a miser and hoards it in a tower. This is much the way Shakespeare's Timon advises his steward to take the gold and "build from men" (4.3.530); but it differs totally from Timon's use of gold for the destruction of man. Lucian's Timon would not make a tragic hero; he was intended to be the vehicle and butt of satire rather than a character to be analyzed seriously.

Some similarities between Lucian's dialogue and Shakespeare's play have no exact equivalent in the comedy. Only Lucian has a character resembling Shakespeare's poet (the comedy has a musician), and only in Lucian are the circumstances of Timon's finding of gold and his reaction somewhat like those in the tragedy; in the comedy, contrary to the dialogue and the tragedy, Timon does not apostrophize gold. On the other hand, Timon's rejection of his friends has some resemblance to the way in which this matter is handled in Shakespeare's play, and, most important, it is crowned by a mock banquet. In both plays, Timon hurls stones (painted like artichokes in the comedy) at his guests, and his guests therefore think him mad, whereupon Timon leaves, cursing Athens.

When it comes to materials that could have helped Shakespeare create a pessimistic tragedy, the comedy seems to me to render as little as the dialogue. Bulman, in seeking to advance the comedy above Lucian's dialogue as a source, goes astray when he calls it "the only source which could have provided Shakespeare with the *De Casibus* tragic pattern of Timon's rise and fall from fortune."[18] The comedy is the only source merely if one forgets Barckley, and I do not see that it really gives any prominence to this pattern. It is certainly not underlined verbally—a *sententia* about the change from riches to poverty and an image of ebbing and flowing mean very little. I also fail to discern that "Timon himself, though the comedy's central character, remains oddly at the periphery of the comic action—a misfit, a railer, whose fall from fortune follows a distinctly tragic curve." Through most of the play, the comic Timon is the main target of the satire, a nincompoop who is taken in by every blatant cheat and liar and is infatuated with a too-obvious little minx. This Timon is ruined not because of his prodigality but because his ships are wrecked (a stock motif of drama); his character and actions have no direct bearing on his fall. Nor is he tragic in his reaction to misfortune. Near the end of the play, he indeed makes a short speech that demands the disruption of natural order as does Shakespeare's hero. But this seriousness is not sustained; presumably the author of the comedy seems to have intended the speech as a satire on the cursing convention of tragedy. Altogether, I find it impossible to believe that Shakespeare gained from this comedy the inspiration for transforming into a tragedy what had been looked upon as a satirical story and was treated here as an excuse for multiple parodies. Bulman himself admits that the comic author's tone is not at all akin to Shakespeare's.

To summarize, Plutarch, Lucian, and the Timon comedy, the works that are usually looked upon as being the sources of any moment, offered Shakespeare next to nothing to suggest tragic possibilities for the character of Timon or to invite writing anything but a comical or satirical play about him. What he needed, first of all, was a Timon who could be taken more seriously than an odd character to be laughed at. Here a passage in Pliny's *Historia naturalis*, often noted by scholars without much comment, is of seminal significance. Shakespeare is likely to have known this fundamental work, some of it perhaps in Latin, since grammar school; it was translated by Philemon Holland in 1601. Pliny mentions Timon among men of strange and peculiar natures and temperaments. Such were the founders of philosophical schools like Diogenes, Pyrrho, Heraclitus, and Timon; the latter was "so far gone in his humor that he seemed professedly to hate mankind." Pliny saw Timon as having "a corrupt, perverse, and froward nature."[19] No matter that he may have conflated here Timon of Athens with Timon of Phleius, a skeptic philosopher and baiter of other philosophers; the point is that he took Timon seriously. Also, he confirmed an earlier brief diagnosis by Cicero of Timon's misanthropy as a sickness of the soul, intense, persistent, and deeply rooted.[20] In the inveteracy of his hatred, Shakespeare's Timon is in the tradition of Pliny and Cicero rather than of Plutarch and Lucian: the senators rightly conclude that "his discontents are unremoveably / Coupled to nature" (5.1.223–24). We should note that the context of Pliny's allusion carries pessimistic implications about the nature of man. Timon is depicted as extreme among a group of serious thinkers whose dislike of man, though constitutionally conditioned in its severity, is at least in part attributable to a reaction to human misery and wickedness. Pliny also provided material for the pessimists by turning an old commonplace about Mother Nature into a troublesome question, asking whether she "hath done the part of a kind mother or hard and cruel stepdame" in bringing forth man naked rather than in equipping him with wool, hide, and feathers.[21] Pliny enhanced the pessimistic applicability of his question by following it with a catalogue of man's miseries that point up his foolish arrogance. Pliny's question and lament provide the *locus classicus* for Lear's speech on "unaccommodated man" and they also echo into *Timon* (4.1.32–36).

Features of the Plinian-Ciceronian Timon, the unbending

hater, appeared in various Renaissance versions of Timon's life. Of these, the most influential was Pedro Mexía's in *La silva de varia lección* (1540), translated into French by Claude Griget (first three books, 1552, and often reprinted with additions. Mexía followed Plutarch's account of events; however, he made Timon live not in Athens but in a hut in the fields. He emphasized his strangeness, isolation, and remorseless hate even beyond death. Timon's burial at the seaside was for Mexía an express gesture of his scorn of men: he chose it to be protected against them by the waves. It is doubtful, however, that Shakespeare knew Mexía's story since it was not in the partial version of the collection translated by Thomas Fortescue (1571). Neither does Shakespeare seem to have owed much, if anything, to the story as told in William Painter's *Palace of Pleasure* (1566), which depends largely on Mexía. And it should be said that neither Mexía nor Painter portrayed a particularly evil society to which Timon's misanthropy was a reaction. Painter, in fact, spoke of Timon's beastliness rather than that of the Athenians.

The two sources of the Timon story available to Shakespeare that took Timon seriously and shifted the emphasis away from the horror of his misanthropy toward a pessimism about human nature were Pierre Boaistuau's *Theatrum mundi* and Richard Barckley's *A Discourse of the Felicity of Man*. Although neither Boaistuau nor Barckley concerned themselves particularly with Athenian society, they spoke strongly in condemnation of their own. Both saw in Timon not a human oddity or a vehicle of satire but an ancient witness to their own pessimism. This pessimism is indebted to old Christian assessments of unregenerated man's depravity, which Calvin and others revived. Shakespeare found here misanthropic arguments he could adapt to the pagan climate of his play, and these might send him to similar works for further materials. The proviso to be made is that Shakespeare did not merely read Boaistuau's and Barckley's brief accounts of Timon's life, which add little new to the facts, but that he was sensitive to the contexts and leafed, at least, through the rest. This is not an unreasonable assumption.

Boaistuau saw Timon in the Plinian tradition. In his Epistle Dedicatory, he recalled that "certain ancient philosophers have framed marvelous complaints against the ungratefulness and forgetfulness of man." On the first pages of the tract itself, he reminded his readers of some "vigorous censors of the work of nature" who called her a "cruel stepmother in the stead of a gracious mother" (shades of Pliny). He gradated these, beginning with those who laughed scornfully, continuing with those who wept, and concluding with those who were not content to "murmur against human nature or to complain of her effects" but who hated man and discharged their "wrath and malediction" against him. "Amongst the which, Timon, a philosopher of Athens, was the most affectioned [i.e., passionate] patriarch of this sect, the which declared himself open and chief enemy to man. . . ." It did not suffice Timon, said Boaistuau, "to have men only in horror and detestation and to fly their company as the company of fierce and cruel beasts, but in forsaking them he sought their ruin and invented all the means he could to extinguish human kind."[22] Shakespeare's contrast of Apemantus and Timon may well owe something to this gradation of philosophers: Apemantus is the murmurer against human nature and Timon the misanthrope who seeks to extinguish mankind.[23]

For Boaistuau, Timon was a pagan who could teach Christians a proper contempt for man and the world. Even though he looked upon him as a strange creature, he applauded his view of man as a miserable, ungrateful, and wicked creature. Boaistuau saw signs of the human deterioration all around him. The pride and deceit of merchants, the amassing of gold and silver, the spread of luxury, the eruptions of war, the increase of murder, treason, fraud, covetousness, usury, and theft—all indicated to him that the apocalyptic predictions of the ancient philosophers were being fulfilled. And this worst of societies was placed in a threatening cosmic setting; the elements as executors of God's wrath had a fearful potential for man. Therefore, as I have suggested previously, Boaistuau could have inspired Shakespeare to create some of the cosmic apostrophes and images of his misanthropic speeches.

One intriguing parallel here is that between a passage in the *Theatrum mundi* which takes its departure from the Plinian commonplace about Mother Nature, and Timon's address to the earth. Boaistuau shifts the point of gravity of the commonplace toward the earth's destructiveness, and so, but much more strongly, does Shakespeare's Timon.

Boaistuau:

> The earth that is the most gentlest and tractablest of all elements, which is our common mother of all, receiving us when we are born, that nourisheth and sustaineth us . . . notwithstanding it bringeth forth all the venoms and poisons with which our life is daily assaulted. . . . And yet it is a thing more marveled at and turneth to more confusion the pride and loftiness of men that the earth bringeth forth certain little beasts that oppress and make war upon him.[24]

Timon:

> Common mother, thou
> Whose womb immeasurable and infinite breast

Teems and feeds all; whose self-same mettle,
Whereof thy proud child, arrogant man, is puff'd,
Engenders the black toad and adder blue,
The gilded newt and eyeless venom'd worm,
With all th' abhorred births below crisp heaven
Whereupon Hyperion's quick'ning fire doth shine:
Yield him, who all the human sons do hate,
From forth thy plenteous bosom, one poor root.
Ensear thy fertile and conceptious womb;
Let it no more bring out ingrateful man.
Go great with tigers, dragons, wolves and bears;
Teem with new monsters, whom thy upward face
Hath to the marbled mansion all above
Never presented.

(4.3.179–94)

Boaistuau, of course, described nature's destructive potential whereas Timon apostrophizes this malignant nature, lending life and horror to his speech by the vividly imagined ferocity. Since we are dealing with a commonplace here, we cannot claim for certain that Shakespeare had Boaistuau's passage in mind when he penned the speech; at any rate, the *Theatrum mundi* is the Renaissance source of the Timon story that anticipates most strongly the apocalyptic ring as well as the decay-of-nature substance of Timon's diatribes.

Barckley's *Discourse* repeats and reinforces many of Boaistuau's pessimistic themes and adds others. It introduces the Timon story at the beginning of the fifth of its six books, the book that deals with the felicity of this life, a felicity to be rejected in favor of the life to come, the subject of the last book. Timon is again the fiercest of the philosophers that impugn human misery and vice—the passage is almost literally from Boaistuau—and he becomes a solitary exile. As Pauls has noted, Barckley's Timon is considerably more sympathetic than that of the other sources—never once is he called a monster or a beast, whereas his friends are dubbed "furious wild beasts." The pessimism about man and society inherent in Barckley's use of the Timon anecdote pervades the whole book, which breathes the kind of mood and enlarges upon the kind of themes characteristic of Shakespeare's tragedy. As Pauls says, some of Barckley's sentences are almost Timon-like in their bitterness. For instance, Barckley uses animal imagery and the beast theme in a much more intense and systematic way than do Lucian and the old comedy, and the associations are quite those of Shakespeare's tragedy: vices such as flattery, hypocrisy, and usury are characterized by their beastliness. If any source can be invoked as inspiration for this theme in Shakespeare, it is the *Discourse*.

Another prominent theme of *Timon* that may have its origin in Barckley's book is the ironic treatment of honesty. It will be remembered that it is initiated by Apemantus's search for an honest Athenian in order to knock out his brains (1.1.192). The joke, of course, rests on the ubiquitous story of Diogenes' search with the lantern for one honest Athenian. Barckley records this anecdote together with a similar one about an order of Marcus Aurelius to register all honest Romans; the censors found none living and ravaged the graves to come up with a suitable specimen. Barckley adds that there would be no better result in these present iniquitous times when "hardly a faithful friend or an honest man is anywhere to be found."[25] Shakespeare may have gotten the idea of making Apemantus imply that an honest Athenian is a dead Athenian from these two anecdotes. Barckley, in any case, pointed the way to apply the ironic honesty theme to the decline of friendship as does Timon. "My honest-natur'd friends," the misanthrope mocks the poet and the painter (5.1.85). Barckley's invoking of Diogenes' censure of the Greeks is in tune with the Renaissance Diogeniana on which Shakespeare drew not only for Apemantus's cynical philosophy but also for Timon's criticism of man and society.

Another strong theme of Barckley's likely to have had an effect on Shakespeare's conception of the Athenian milieu is that of mutability and fortune. Barckley's claim that all human activities except contemplative piety are useless is illustrated by anecdotes that prove the vitiating effect of fortune; many important historical personages are shown to have been ruined by fortune or to have ruined themselves in its pursuit. In this respect, Pauls notes that Barckley acclaims the resolution of the emperor Diocletian, who, on top of Fortune's wheel, rejected rule, honor, and glory and completely withdrew from public life—Timonesque one might call his decision. Pauls particularly notes that Diocletian, like Timon, refused the plea of his native city to come to its aid. When the Romans sent ambassadors to him in their distress and asked him to return to his throne, he denied their request and sent them back to Rome. None other of Shakespeare's sources has a similar analogue to Timon's rejection of the plea of the Athenian senators.

I may add that the *Discourse* is also the most likely source for Shakespeare's making "nothing" into a key word of his tragedy. Timon, who experiences the nothingness of his friends and harps on this theme at the mock banquet, becomes in the wood a preacher on the nothingness of all things. He says to the steward: "My long sickness / Of health and living now begins to mend, / And nothing brings me all things" (5.1.185–87). Now, in the pages preceding the Timon story in the *Discourse*, Barckley entones a veritable hymn to the nothingness of life and also backs it up by a paradox of health and disease resembling Timon's:

> Knowest thou not that the life of man is nothing in respect of the life to come. . . . That which is temporal and comprehended within time and hath end seemeth nothing nor beareth any proportion to that which is without time, perpetual, and infinite. Much less the afflictions and troubles of this temporal life, in respect of the perpetuity of the joys of the life to come, beareth any proportion, but is to be accounted nothing. And who will call him a sickly man that in the whole course of his life hath never felt any sickness, but only a little short fit of an ague, but rather will call him a healthful man? Much less can the afflictions and troubles of this life be called infelicity because between the other is some proportion; between this life and the life to come, none at all.[26]

Shakespeare did not use this or other source themes slavishly, from wherever he got them. Timon's words are phrased to express his utter nihilism. The "all things" death brings to Timon entail no hope of an afterlife; they voice merely his desire to be left alone by humanity.

Barckley, it appears, was of primary importance for the transmission of the moral and philosophical pessimism Shakespeare infused into his drama of ideas, a pessimism that drew on Socrates, Plato, Diogenes, skepticism, Stoicism, the Bible, the Fathers of the Church, and whomever or whatever else was appropriate. To the degree that the *Discourse* can itself be put in a specific pessimistic tradition, it is the *vanitas* literature. The futility of all human endeavor, on which Barckley dwelled, was to point up the need to put aside all the useless strife for the pursuit of holiness, the only true felicity of man. With Ecclesiastes, this tradition said that all is vanity and that man smells of mortality.

The seminal book of this tradition was Heinrich Cornelius Agrippa of Nettesheim's *De vanitate artium et scientiarum* (1530), translated by James Sanford in 1569 (rpt. 1575). It was certainly one of Barckley's sources, as it was that of Thomas Nashe and many another Elizabethan and Jacobean satirist and moralist. Its influence lay in the comprehensiveness of its denunciation of man and his world: it belittled, satirized, or attacked every form of knowledge, every science, art, trade, and human endeavor except absorption in piety. It is hard to say whether Agrippa was serious or merely performed an exercise in paradoxical satire, but he certainly provided an encyclopedia of invective and condemnation for his readers. In all likelihood, not only Barckley but also Shakespeare knew this exploitable book, and I think that there are indications in *Timon* that he did.

Although individual parallels between Agrippa's treatise and Shakespeare's play that belong to the general moral and satirical tradition mean little as such, their number and scope are astonishing. Even a partial catalogue is impressive. For instance, both Agrippa and Timon satirize the commercialism, lying, and counterfeiting of poets and painters, expose the lust and hypocrisy of priests, castigate courtiers for being more concerned with promising than performing, attack the evils of war and equate soldiers with thieves, call the physicians poisoners and slayers, scourge loudmouthed and greedy lawyers, and censure the willful and unjust administration of the laws.[27] The two passages that seem to me to point clearly to Shakespeare's borrowing come from Agrippa's exposure of sexual and societal disorder. The first is in Agrippa's attack on dancing, which parallels in content and general structure Apemantus's commentary on the dance after Timon's masque. Attacks on dancing, it is true, were plentiful in Shakespeare's time; the Puritans, in particular, saw it as a diabolic invitation to sin. But Agrippa's sally, much like Apemantus's commentary, makes the more unusual points that dancing is foolishness, madness, disorder, and vanity, and it does so in a similar arrangement:

Agrippa:

> To music moreover belongeth the art of dancing, very acceptable to maidens and lovers, which they learn with great care . . . and do as they think very wisely and subtly the fondest thing of all other and little differing from madness, which, except it were tempered with the sound of instruments, and, as it is said, if vanity did not commend vanity, there should be no sight more ridiculous, no more out of order, than dancing.[28]

Apemantus:

> What a sweep of vanity comes this way.
> They dance? They are madwomen.
> Like madness is the glory of this life,
> As this pomp shows to a little oil and root.
> We make ourselves fools, to disport ourselves,
> And spend our flatteries to drink those men
> Upon whose age we void it up again
> With poisonous spite and envy . . .
> I should fear those that dance before me now
> Would one day stamp upon me.
>
> (1.2.128–40)

Here as elsewhere, Shakespeare brilliantly adapted what he took to his different purpose. Apemantus contrasts the vanity of dancing, symbolic of the ceremonies of man, with a touch of his cynical philosophy, "the little oil and root." The disorder of dancing becomes an allegory of the whole topsy-turvy world of fortune seekers.

Finally, an anecdote of Agrippa's about the emperor Heliogabalus in the chapter "Of the Whorish Art" is reflected in Timon's treatment of the prostitutes Phrynia and Timandra. The story, it is true, was available elsewhere (for instance, in Barckley); but Agrippa's is, as far as I know, the version closest to Shakespeare. Heliogabalus, Agrippa narrates, amused himself by treating prostitutes like soldiers:

> Sometimes also he assembled together in the common place all the whores from the place called Circus, from the theater and amphitheater, from the exercise, and from all places and bains, and there made unto them an oration as it were unto soldiers, calling them fellow soldiers, and disputed all the kinds of figures and pleasures, and after the oration he caused three ducats to be given each of them as if they had been soldiers.[29]

Like Heliogabalus, Timon offers the prostitutes payment from the gold he finds and treats them as if they were members of an army:

> Hold up, you sluts,
> Your aprons mountant. You are not oathable,
> Although I know you'll swear, terribly swear
> Into strong shudders and to heavenly agues
> Th' immortal gods that hear you. Spare your oaths:
> I'll trust to your conditions. Be whores still;
> And he whose pious breath seeks to convert you,
> Be strong in whore, allure him, burn him up;
> Let your close fire predominate his smoke,
> And be no turncoats.
>
> (4.3.136–45)

Timon's tone, of course, is grim rather than anecdotal like Agrippa's; instead of disputing "figures and pleasures" like Heliogabalus, he uses paramilitary terminology when he enrolls the prostitutes in his imaginary army of destruction and, by the fire image, suggests their potency for sexual contagion. But there can be little doubt that the anecdote is the source for this, the most devastating of Timon's misanthropic sallies.

With Agrippa we have come to the end of the sources as defined in this chapter, that is, works relevant to the spirit and tone of Shakespeare's play that make at least a reference to Timon. That of Agrippa is to Timon as a philosopher who reproves his colleagues for their stupidity and wickedness. This is no great contribution to the Timon repertoire, although—who knows?—it may have provided Shakespeare with an incentive for making Timon's drubbing of Apemantus the ideological climax of the play. However, the significance of Agrippa, like that of Boaistuau and Barckley, does not lie primarily in verbal and plot parallels but in the pointers he provided for Shakespeare's reshaping of the story into a pessismistic tragedy.

Notes

For full references, see the first citation of each work. Where not otherwise stated, the place of publication of sixteenth- and seventeenth-century books is London. The titles of common literary and scholarly journals have been abbreviated according to *PMLA* custom.

Chapter One

1. E. K. Chambers, *Shakespeare: A Survey* (1925; rpt. New York: Hill and Wang, n.d.), p. 268.

2. *Coleridge's Shakespeare Criticism*, ed. T. M. Raysor (Cambridge: Harvard University Press, 1930), 1:85.

3. Andor Gomme, "Timon of Athens," *EIC* 9 (1959): 107.

4. A general account of the play's critical history is by Francelia Butler, *The Strange Critical Fortunes of Shakespeare's "Timon of Athens"* (Ames: Iowa State University Press, 1966). For an overview of modern scholarship and criticism with a bibliography, see Maurice Charney's article in Stanley Wells, ed., *Shakespeare: Select Bibliographical Guides* (London: Oxford University Press, 1973), pp. 224–38.

5. *Johnson on Shakespeare*, ed. Arthur Sherbo, Yale Edition of the Works of Samuel Johnson, 8 (1968): 745.

6. *Characters of Shakespeare's Plays*, in *The Complete Works of William Hazlitt*, ed. P. P. Howe (London: Dent, 1930), 4:210.

7. *The Works of Charles and Mary Lamb*, ed. Thomas Hutchinson (Oxford: Oxford University Press, 1924), pp. 183–95.

8. For German interest in Timon, see Karl Georg Mantey, *Shakespeares Letzter Tragischer Held* (Berlin: Helbig, 1963). I find Mantey's raptures about the hero and the play a little embarrassing. For Schiller, Marx, and the Marxists, see Walter Martin, "Shakespeares *Timon von Athen* im Lichte der Wiederspiegelungstheorie," *Shakespeare Jahrbuch* 100–101 (Weimar, 1965): 227–52. For the Brechtian conception and modern performances from this point of view, see Armin Gerd Kuckhoff, "*Timon von Athen*: Konzeption und Aufführungspraxis," ibid., pp. 135–59.

9. Friedrich Schiller, *Die Schaubühne als eine moralische Anstalt,* quoted by Mantey, p. 13; by Martin, p. 227. As Martin points out, the tribute to *Timon* was in the original version of the essay but not in the later revision.

10. Hermann Ulrici, *Shakespeare's Dramatic Art* (London: Bell, 1876; first German edition, 1839). Similarly, Gustav Rümelin, *Shakespeare Studien* (Stuttgart: Cotta, 1866), p. 248.

11. Georg Brandes, *William Shakespeare* (1896; rpt. München: Langen, 1904), p. 135.

12. Henry Hudson, Introduction to *Timon of Athens* (Boston, 1855), Vol. VIII; rpt. in *The Modern Reader's Shakespeare,* ed. Israel Gollancz (New York: Bigelow, Smith, & Co., 1909), pp. xiv–xv.

13. Edward Dowden, *Shakspere: A Critical Study of His Mind and Art* (1872; rpt. New York: Capricorn Books, 1962), p. 380.

14. E. K. Chambers, *William Shakespeare: A Study of Facts and Problems* (Oxford: Clarendon Press, 1930), 1:483.

15. C. J. Sisson, *The Mythical Sorrows of Shakespeare* (London: Annual Lecture of the British Academy, 1934).

16. Harry Levin, "Shakespeare's Misanthrope," *ShS* 26 (1973): 89–94.

17. G. Wilson Knight, "The Pilgrimage of Hate," in *The Wheel of Fire* (1930; 4th rev. ed., London: Methuen, 1949), p. 221.

18. Chambers, *Shakespeare,* p. 268.

19. F. P. Wilson, *Elizabethan and Jacobean* (Oxford: Clarendon Press, 1945).

20. R. Hugh Trevor-Roper, *Religion, Reformation and Social Change* (London: Macmillan, 1967), p. 72. The quotation is from Gerald Brenan, *The Literature of the Spanish People* (Cambridge: University Press, 1951), p. 272.

21. See below, chapter 5; the literature on the subject is given in n. 25 of this chapter.

22. Richard Barckley, *A Discourse of the Felicity of Man* (1598, ed. 1631), p. 16.

23. Barckley, pp. 634–35.

24. The source is in Machiavelli's chapter 17, with a touch from chapter 15. See Machiavelli, *The Prince,* trans. Luigi Ricci (New York: New American Library, 1952), pp. 84, 90.

25. T. J. B. Spencer, "Greeks and Merrygreeks: A Background to *Timon of Athens* and *Troilus and Cressida,*" in *Essays on Shakespeare and Elizabethan Drama in Honor of Hardin Craig,* ed. Richard Hosley (Columbia: University of Missouri Press, 1962), pp. 222–33.

Chapter Two

1. A. S. Collins, "*Timon of Athens*: A Reconsideration," *RES* 22 (1946): 96–108.

2. Anne Lancashire, "*Timon of Athens*: Shakespeare's *Doctor Faustus,*" *SQ* 21 (1970): 35–44. *Timon* has been compared to *Everyman* by David M. Bergeron, "*Timon of Athens* and Morality Drama," *CLAJ* 10 (1967): 181–88.

3. O. J. Campbell, *Shakespeare's Satire* (London: Oxford University Press, 1943), pp. 185–92.

4. Alvin Kernan, *The Cankered Muse: Satire of the English Renaissance* (New Haven, Conn.: Yale University Press, 1959), pp. 204–5. E. A. J. Honigmann, "*Timon of Athens,*" *SQ* 12 (1961): 3–20, notes similarities in the satirical thrust of *Timon* and *Troilus and Cressida,* and argues that both plays were intended for the Inns of Court.

5. Sylvan Barnet, ed., *The Complete Signet Shakespeare,* (New York: Harcourt Brace, 1972), pp. 63–64.

6. Clifford Leech, *Shakespeare's Tragedies and Other Seventeenth Century Drama* (New York: Oxford University Press, 1950), pp. 113–36.

7. Larry Champion, *Shakespeare's Tragic Perspective* (Athens: University of Georgia Press, 1976), pp. 201–18.

8. M. C. Bradbrook, *Shakespeare the Craftsman* (London: Chatto & Windus, 1969), p. 166. Cf. below, chapter 10.

9. J. M. Nosworthy, *Shakespeare's Occasional Plays* (London: Arnold, 1965), pp. 45, 225–26.

10. Robert E. Morsberger, *"Timon of Athens*: Tragedy or Satire?" *Shakespeare in the Southwest: Some New Directions*, ed. T. J. Stafford (El Paso: Texas Western Press, 1969), p. 58. That *Timon* is a mixture of Renaissance genres is argued interestingly by William W. E. Slights, "*Genera Mixta* and *Timon of Athens*," *SP* 74 (1977): 39–62. Slights distinguishes the forms of masque, anti-masque, satire, and tragedy. But surely not all these elements are of equal significance in *Timon*.

11. Dorothea Krook, *Elements of Tragedy* (New Haven, Conn.: Yale University Press, 1969), p. 14.

12. Arthur Schopenhauer, *The World as Will and Idea* (New York: Scribner, 1950), 1:326.

13. Remarks on pessimism are scattered all over Nietzsche's works. Most notable are those of *The Will to Power*, bk. 1, ed. Walter Kaufman (New York: Random House, 1967), and *Ecce Homo*, in Friedrich Nietzsche, *Werke* (München: Hauser, 1956), 2:1108. Nietzsche's *Die Geburt der Tragödie* had as its subtitle "Griechentum und Pessimismus," and was later accompanied by Nietzsche's "Versuch einer Selbstkritik," which deals largely with pessimism and tragedy. See also J. C. Opstelten, *Sophocles and Greek Pessimism* (Amsterdam: North Holland, 1952), p. 6.

14. John Marston, *Antonio's Revenge*, ed. G. K. Hunter (Lincoln: University of Nebraska Press, 1965), p. 3.

15. Denis Lebey de Batilly, *Emblemata* (1596), fig. 4.

16. The translation is that of Leon Golden, *Aristotle's Poetics*, with a commentary by O. B. Hardison, Jr. (Englewood, Cliffs, N.J.: Prentice-Hall, 1968).

17. Julius Caesar Scaliger, *Poetices Libri Decem* (Geneva, 1561), bk. 1, chap. 26: "Imitatio per actiones illustri fortunae, exitu infelici, oratione gravi metrica."

18. Daniel Heinsius, *De Tragoediae Constitutione* (Leyden, 1643), chap. 3, 1. 26: "Subita in contrarium mutatio."

19. Krook, p. 13.

20. Northrop Frye, *Fools of Time: Studies in Shakespearean Tragedy* (Toronto: University of Toronto Press, 1967).

21. G. K. Hunter, "The Last Tragic Heroes," in *Later Shakespeare*, Stratford-upon-Avon Studies 8 (1966): 11–28.

22. Cyrus Hoy, "Jacobean Tragedy and the Mannerist Style," *ShS* 26 (1973): 49–67. The "alienation" of Timon, however, seems to be an insufficient criterion for calling the play "mannerist," as does Hoy.

23. R. A. Foakes, *Shakespeare: The Dark Comedies to the Last Plays* (Charlottesville: University Press, of Virginia, 1971), p. 85.

24. For the phrase "unsounded self," cf. *Lucrece*, 1819.

25. Honigmann, *SQ* 12 (1961): 15–16.

26. This *catharsis* is similar to the one attributed to satire by Alice L. Birney, *Satiric Catharsis in Shakespeare* (Berkeley: University of California Press, 1973), Birney, like Kernan, considers Timon an excessive satirist.

27. For a discussion of pessimistic modern tragedy, which authors often insist is comedy, and for its affinity with Schopenhauer's and Nietzsche's conceptions, see David Lenson, *Achilles' Choice: Examples of Modern Tragedy* (Princeton, N.J.: Princeton University Press, 1975), chap. 7: "The Other Tragedy."

Chapter Three

1. Mark Van Doren, *Shakespeare* (1939; rpt. Garden City, N. Y.: Doubleday, n. d.), p. 249. There has been much unfavorable criticism of the structure, beginning with Johnson's remark that there is "not much art" in the play. David Garrick, however, defended the structure when he objected to Richard Cumberland's alterations on the grounds that they destroyed the play's "simplicity": "I think that excellent rule for writing as it is laid down by

Horace, *simplex et unum*, was no more verified than in Shakespeare's *Timon*." See *The Letters of David Garrick*, ed. David M. Little and George M. Kahrl (Cambridge: Harvard University Press, 1963), p. 592. When romantic critics, such as Hazlitt, praised the play's unity, they thought of tone rather than dramatic structure, and so do some modern critics.

2. Cf. Ludovico Ariosto's Third Satire: "This lofty Mountain is Hill of Fate." *Ariosto's Satires in Seven Famous Discourses* (1608), p. 42.

3. That the wheel conception does not govern the structure of Shakespeare's tragedies is argued by J. Leeds Barroll, "Structure in Shakespearean Tragedy," *ShakS* 7 (1974): 345–78. Whatever one may think of Barroll's conception of structure (I do not find it persuasive), he effectively refutes Willard Farnham's claim that Shakespeare modeled tragic structure on the wheel motion. Cf. Willard Farnham, *The Medieval Heritage of Elizabethan Tragedy* (1936; rev. ed. Oxford: Blackwell, 1957), passim. My argument is merely that the wheel rhetoric emphasizes the structure of *Timon* (as I think it does that of *Richard II*). This rhetoric also lends coloring to characterization; see *Timon*, 4.3.252–96, where Timon sets himself off from Apemantus through the pathos appropriate for the hero of a *de casibus* tragedy.

4. See Howard R. Patch, *The Goddess Fortuna in Medieval Literature* (1927; rpt. New York: Octagon Books, 1967), p. 164, and Samuel Chew, *The Pilgrimage of Life* (New Haven, Conn.: Yale University Press, 1962), pp. 38–41. Chew notes the Latin tags also in Dabridgcourt Belchier's play *Hans Beerpot* (1618).

5. T. W. Baldwin, *Shakspere's Five Act Structure* (Urbana: University of Illinois Press, 1947).

6. Ruth Nevo, *Tragic Form in Shakespeare* (Princeton, N.J.: Princeton University Press, 1972), Since Nevo does not include *Timon*, the following analysis on the basis of her principles is my own. The applicability of the structural formula to the tragedies, again without reference to *Timon*, is also briefly discussed and affirmed by Clifford Leech, "Shakespeare's Use of a Five-Act Structure," *Die Neueren Sprachen*, N. F. 6 (1957).

7. Knight, pp. 207–39.

8. Maurice Charney in *Signet Shakespeare*, ed. Barnet, pp. 1367–68.

9. Oliver, pp. xliv–lii.

10. Harold Wilson, *On the Design of Shakespearean Tragedy* (Toronto: University of Toronto Press, 1957), pp. 138–39.

11. Bradbrook, *Craftsman*, p. 166.

12. Baldwin, p. 256.

13. Ibid., p. 237.

14. Ibid., p. 256.

15. Ibid., p. 256.

16. Ibid., p. 238.

17. Ibid., p. 296.

18. Nevo, p. 24.

19. Baldwin, p. 256.

20. Ibid., p. 306.

21. Charney, *Signet Shakespeare*, p. 1367. The problem is dealt with wittily by Bernard Paulin, "La Mort de Timon d'Athènes," *Etudes Anglaises* 17 (1964): 1–8.

Chapter Four

1. Oliver, p. xlix.

2. Geoffrey Bullough, *Narrative and Dramatic Sources of Shakespeare* 6 (London: Rutledge & Kegan Paul, 1964): 250. That the character of Alcibiades in Shakespeare resembles that of Plutarch's "Life of Alcibiades" is argued, on grounds somewhat different from mine, by Peter Pauls, "Shakespeare's *Timon of Athens*: An Examination of the Misanthrope Tradition and Shakespeare's Handling of the Sources" (Ph.D. diss, University of Wisconsin, 1969), pp. 99 ff. For Paul's judicious treatment of the source problems, see the Appendix.

3. Plutarch, "The Life of Alcibiades," in *The Lives of the Noble Grecians and Romans.* trans. Sir Thomas North, 1579 (Stratford-upon-Avon: Blackwell, 1928), 2:128. This same saying is also in the Timon biography of "The Life of Marcus Antonius," *Lives,* 6:382.

4. Ibid., 2:159.

5. John Lydgate, *Lydgate's Fall of Princes,* ed. Henry Bergen, Early English Text Society (1924; rpt. Oxford: Oxford University Press, 1967), pt. 2, bk. 3, p. 422.

6. Jean Bodin, *Six Books of a Commonweal,* trans. Richard Knolles (1606), p. 422.

7. Thomas Lodge, *Wit's Misery and the World's Madness* (1596), pp. 3–4.

8. Lodge, *Catharos: Diogenes in his Singularity* (1591), fol. 17.

9. Cf. the greeting of Macro by Sejanus in Jonson's *Sejanus:* "Let me enjoy my longings" (5.324). Here the cordiality is feigned.

10. On the problematic nature of honor in Shakespeare, see Alice Shalvi, *The Relationship of the Renaissance Concept of Honor to Shakespeare's Problem Plays* (Salzburg: University of Salzburg, 1972). Shakespeare's and his audience's sympathy for Alcibiades is argued by G. R. Waggoner, "Timon of Athens and the Jacobean Duel," *SQ* 16 (1965): 303–11. Waggoner is aware of the shifting attitudes toward honor, and he argues well that we cannot be sympathetic to the senators; but it does not follow that we must be for Alcibiades.

11. *Lives,* 2:227.

12. We should say, of course, that there are two epitaphs, both adapted from Plutarch, the one reported to have been composed by Timon, the other by the poet Callimachus, and the two contradict each other. Whatever the reason for this duplication is, it is doubtful evidence for the play's incompleteness. See the Text Appendix.

13. Paul Siegel, *Shakespeare in His Time and Ours* (Notre Dame: University of Notre Dame Press, 1968), pp. 122-62. Similarly, J. W. Draper, "The Theme of *Timon of Athens*" *MLR* 29 (1934): 20–31; and J. C. Pettet, "Timon of Athens: The Disruption of Feudal Morality," *RES* 23 (1947): 321–36.

14. Leech, *Shakespeare's Tragedies,* pp. 115–16. Similarly benevolent views are expressed by David Cook, "Timon of Athens," *ShS* 16 (1963): 94; A. S. Collins, *RES* 22 (1946): 96–108; and Leonard Goldstein, "Alcibiades' Revolt in *Timon of Athens,*" *Zeitschrift für Anglistik und Germanistik* 15 (1967): 256–78. A more balanced account is by Richard D. Fly, "The Ending of *Timon of Athens:* A Reconsideration," *Criticism* 15 (1973): 251.

15. Paul Jorgensen, *Shakespeare's Military World* (Berkeley: University of California Press, 1959), p. 192.

16. Michel de Montaigne, "On Physiognomy," in *Essays,* trans. Donald L. Frame (1957; Stanford, Calif.: Stanford University Press, 1965), p. 796.

17. Sir William Cornwallis, *Discourses Upon Seneca the Tragedian* (1610), sig. Aa. 7r.

18. Barnabe Rich, *The Fruits of a Long Experience* (1604), fols. 3–5, 52–54.

19. A civic procession in Antwerp in 1599 used this symbol. See Sheila Williams and Jean Jacquot, "Omnegangs Anversois du temps de Bruegel et de van Heemskerk," in *Les Fêtes de la Renaissance,* 2d ed. Jean Jacquot (Paris: Centre National de la Recherche Scientifique, 1960): 359–88. This device is also in Jean Cousin's manuscript emblem book, *Le Livre de Fortune* (1568), ed. Ludovic Lavanne (Paris and London, 1883), fig. 119.

20. Barckley, p. 473.

Chapter Five

1. Cook, *ShS* 16 (1963): 83–94.

2. *Leigh Hunt's Dramatic Criticism 1808-1831,* ed. L. H. Houtchins and C. W. Houtchins (New York: Columbia University Press, 1949), p. 135.

3. Timon was frequently referred to as an example of melancholy in the Renaissance. See Lawrence Babb, *The Elizabethan Malady* (East Lansing; Michigan State University Press, 1951), pp. 94–95. Cf. John W. Draper, "The Psychology of Shakespeare's Timon," *MLR* 35 (1940): 521–25.

4. *Johnson on Shakespeare*, p. 745.

5. Timon is a "would-be Saturnian figure, living in an imaginary Golden Age, who is unaware of the nature of the fallen world in which he actually exists," says R. P. Draper in "Timon of Athens," *SQ* 8 (1957): 196.

6. Cf. *Venus and Adonis*, II. 433–50. See Frank Kermode, "The Banquet of Sense," *Bull. of the John Rylands Library* 44 (1961): 68–99; Donald K. Anderson, Jr., "The Banquet of Love in English Renaissance Drama 1595–1642," *JEGP* 63 (1964): 422–33; John Doebler, *Shakespeare's Speaking Pictures* (Albuquerque: University of New Mexico Press, 1975), pp. 148–50. Robert C. Fulton, III, "Timon, Cupid, and the Amazons,"*ShakS* 9 (1976): 283–99.

7. The ancients thought of the friendship of great men as essential for the state, In *De amicitia* (vi. 23), Cicero said that without friendship no house or state would endure.

8. Bodin, pp. 700–701.

9. Robert Greene, *Greene's Groatsworth of Wit Bought with a Million of Repentance* (1592), sig. E4^r. For the background, see T. W. Baldwin, *William Shakespeare's Small Latine and Lesse Greeke* (Urbana: University of Illinois Press, 1944), 1:633.

10. Lydgate, 1:59, 123; 2:503.

11. Gerald de Malynes, *Saint George for England* (1601), p. 38.

12. Morris Palmer Tilley, *A Dictionary of Proverbs in England* (Ann Arbor: University of Michigan Press, 1950), F 688. I owe this idea to John Ruszkiewicz, "Liberality, Friendship, and *Timon of Athens*," *Thoth* 16 (1975–76).

13. Cf. Jarold Ramsey, "Timon's Imitation of Christ," *ShakS* 2 (1966): 162–73; Siegel, p. 52. That the identification of Shakespearean characters with Christ lacks theological justification is shown by Roland Frye, *Shakespeare and Christian Doctrine* (Princeton, N.J.: Princeton University Press, 1963), pp. 34–39.

14. E.g., Malynes, p. 47; Arthur Warren, *The Poor Man's Passions and Poverty's Patience* (1605), sig. B3v.

15. *Johnson on Shakespeare*, p. 713.

16. R. Swigg, "*Timon of Athens* and the Growth of Discrimination," *RES* 62 (1967): 387–94.

17. Hunt, p. 137.

18. See E. Catherine Dunne, *The Concept of Ingratitude in Renaissance Moral Philosophy* (Washington, D.C.: Catholic University of America, 1956).

19. Winifred T. Nowottny, "Acts IV and V of *Timon of Athens*," *SQ* 10 (1959): 493–97.

20. Peter Ure, *Shakespeare: The Problem Plays* (London: Longmans, 1961), p. 50.

21. L. C. Knights, *An Approach to "Hamlet"* (Stanford, Calif: Stanford University Press, 1961), p. 27. See also Knights, "Timon of Athens," in *The Morality of Art: Essays Presented to G. Wilson Knight*, ed. D. W. Jefferson (London: Routledge & Kegan Paul, 1969).

22. Algernon Charles Swinburne, *The Complete Works* (London: Heinemann, 1926), 11:153.

23. Excellent remarks on Timon as a prophet are made by Robert C. Elliott, *The Power of Satire, Magic, Ritual, Art* (Princeton, N.J.: Princeton University Press, 1960), pp. 165-67.

24. See Christopher Hill, *The World Turned Upside Down* (London: Temple Smith, 1972), chap. 6: "A Nation of Prophets."

25. See Victory Harris, *All Coherence Gone* (Chicago: University of Chicago Press, 1949); Paul H. Kocher, *Science and Religion in Elizabethan England* (San Marino, Cal.: Huntington Library Press, 1953); C. A. Patrides, "Renaissance and Modern Thought on Last Things," *Harvard Theological Review* 51 (1958): 170–85; Marjorie Nicolson, *The Breaking of the Circle* (rev. ed. New York: Columbia University Press, 1960); George Williamson, "Mutability, Decay and Seventeenth Century Melancholy," *ELH* 2 (1935): 121–50.

26. Thomas Draxe, *The General Signs and Forerunners of Christ's Coming Judgment* (1608), sig. K^r.

27. Cf. Revelation 6:8. Also, the four words Daniel read on the wall of the king of Babylon; see Daniel 5:24–30. Draxe listed four signs that heralded the approach of the Last Judgment. Stephen Batman, *The Doom Warning All Men to the Judgment* (1581) stresses the pattern of four in the design of the world and consequently in its dissolution: four elements, four evangelists, twelve apostles (three "quadernals"), several sets of four preachers, etc. Calvin comments on the significance of four in Ezekiel 1:4; see *Commentary on the First Twenty Chapters of the Book of the Prophet Ezekiel*, trans. Thomas Meyers (Grand Rapids, Mich.: Erdman, 1948). Timon's "Sun hide thy beams" is in the pattern of a four-word prophecy.

28. Boaistuau, p. 127

Chapter Six

1. The figures, according to Marvin Spevack's *Concordance*, are: Hamlet, 39.128%; Timon, 35.367%; (before Macbeth with 32.191%); Claudius, 13.810%; Apemantus, 9.877%; Polonius, 8.977%; Flavius, 8.553%; Horatio, 6.893%; Alcibiades, 6.614%.

2. Plutarch, "Life of Marcus Antonius," in *Lives*, 6:382.

3. Cicero, *De amicitia*, 23:87, trans. W. A. Falconer (Cambridge: Harvard University Press, 1964), p. 203.

4. Jan Simko, *"King Lear* and *Timon of Athens," Philologica Pragensia* 8 (1965): 320–41.

5. Brian Vickers, *The Artistry of Shakespeare's Prose* (London: Methuen, 1968), p. 373.

6. See John Lievsay, "Some Renaissance Views of Diogenes the Cynic," in *Joseph Quincy Adams Memorial Studies*, ed. James G. McManaway (Washington, D.C.: Folger Shakespeare Library, 1948), pp. 447–55. Lievsay notes the existence of two views of Diogenes in the Renaissance, an approving and a contemptuous one.

7. Pauls, pp. 109–25. Pauls sees Timon even more than Apemantus in the pattern of the Renaissance Diogenes.

8. Warren, sig. D^r.

9. Diogenes Laertius, *Lives of the Eminent Philosophers*, trans. R. D. Hicks (London: Heinemann, 1925), p. 29.

10. For instance, an emblem by Perrière shows a man dancing to the tune played on a flute by Fortuna; the accompanying verse warns that the music will not last, and man should therefore guard himself of its allurement. Guillaume de la Perrière, *La Morosophie* (Paris, 1553), fig. 91.

11. Diogenes Laertius, p. 29.

Chapter Seven

1. Thus Caroline Spurgeon, *Shakespeare's Imagery and What It Tells Us* (Cambridge: At the University Press, 1935), p. 343; and (in spite of observations on the dramatic functioning of the imagery) Wolfgang Clemen, *The Development of Shakespeare's Imagery* (1951; rpt. New York: Hill & Wang, n.d.), pp. 168–76.

2. Charney, *Signet Shakespeare*, p. 1370.

3. *Timon*, with 36 occurrences, is far ahead of its nearest rival, *Errors*, with 19. The role of gold is discussed by Martin, *Shakespeare Jahrbuch* 100–101 (1965): 227-52.

4. Spurgeon, pp. 344–45; cf. Knight, p. 233.

5. Clemen, p. 171.

6. J. C. Maxwell, ed., *The Life of Timon of Athens*, New Shakespeare (Cambridge: At the University Press, 1957), pp. xxv-xxvi.

7. "All" in *Timon*: 0.614%; *Coriolanus* follows with 0.466%. "Nothing" in *Timon*: 0.140%; followed by *Lear* with 0.130%.

8. See Rosalie Colie, *Paradoxa Epidemica: The Renaissance Tradition of Paradox*

(Princeton, N.J.: Princeton University Press, 1966), pp. 219–72. In a neo-Latin poem, the humanist Joachim Comerarius called the idea that we are happy only when we are nothing "a marvelous philosophical trick" (Qui jam nil sumus, hi sumus beati. / O miras sapientiae latebras). *Lateinische Gedichte Deutscher Humanisten*, ed. Harry L. Schur (Stuttgart: Reklam, 1967), p. 31.

9. *Othello*, 0.162%. *Timon* 0.146%.

10. William Empson, Timon's Dog," in *The Structure of Complex Words* (Norfolk, Conn.: New Directions, n.d.), pp. 175–84.

11. See Audrey Yoder, *Animal Analogy in Shakespeare's Character Portrayal* (New York: Columbia University Press, 1947). Yoder, appendix 2, finds *Timon* to have 26 animal references to man in general; *Lear*, which is next, has 8.

12. Willard Farnham, *Shakespeare's Tragic Frontier: The World of His Final Tragedies* (Berkeley: University of California Press, 1950), pp. 68–74. "Beast" occurs 17 times in *Timon;* 8 times in *Hamlet*, which is next; and only twice in *Troilus and Cressida*.

13. "Apology for Raymond Sebond," in *Essays*, pp. 318–57. Cf. Barckley, pp. 374, 663.

14. Swigg, p. 391.

15. Karl Marx, *Early Texts*, trans. and ed. David McLellan (New York: Barnes & Noble, 1971), pp. 181–82; *Das Kapital*, bk. 1, chap. 3, sec. 3, n. 91. See Kenneth Muir, *"Timon of Athens* and the Cash Nexus," *Modern Quarterly Miscellany* 1 (1947): 57-76.

16. Heinrich Cornelius Agrippa of Nettesheim, *Of the Vanity and Uncertainty of the Arts and Sciences*, trans. James Sanford (1569; 2d ed. 1575), p. 101.

17. On the moral background of Jonson's attack on gold, which is also relevant for *Timon*, see Alan Dessen, *Jonson's Moral Comedy* (Evanston, Ill.: Northwestern University Press, 1971), pp. 75-104.

18. Barckley, p. 105. Cf. Thomas Pie, *Usury's Spright Conjured* (1604), p. 35: "Whosoever leaveth the use of a thing which is agreeable to the end and nature of it, and maketh a use contrary to the end and nature of it is to be condemned; but the usurer leaveth that use of money which is agreeable to the end and nature of it and maketh a use contrary to the end."

19. *Timon*: 24 occurrences: *Hamlet*: 21; the other tragedies have much lower numbers.

20. Roger Fenton, *A Treatise of Usury* (1611), p. 4. In the procreation sonnets, Shakespeare wittily compares the reluctance of the young man to marry and to procreate with a usurer's making use of money only for himself: "Profitless usurer, why dost thou use / So great a sum of sums, yet canst not live?" *Sonn.* 4.7–8. Cf. *Sonn.* 2.9; 6.5; 134.10.

21. Fenton, p. 14.

22. Jean l'Espine, *A Very Excellent and Learned Discourse* (Cambridge, 1598), fol. 14ʳ·

Chapter Eight

1. Draper, *MLR* 29 (1934): 20–31. Pettet, *RES* 23 (1947): 321–36. Siegel, passim. Martin, *Shakespeare Jahrbuch* 100–101 (1965): 227–52. A. A. Smirnov, *Shakespeare: A Marxist Interpretation* (rev. ed. New York: Critics Group, 1936), pp. 80, 83. Alexander Anikst, "Shakespeare as a Writer of the People," in *Shakespeare in the Soviet Union* (Moscow: Progress Publishers, 1968), pp. 113–40. Ivan Anisimov, "Life-Affirming Humanism," ibid., pp. 140–43. Kurt Aspelin, *Timon från Aten* (Staffanstrop: Bo Cavefors, 1971). The topic should be treated with awareness of the inseparability of economics from morality in the Renaissance. The connection of these two areas, which we have almost successfully segregated, is explored by John Ruszkiewicz, "Shakespeare's Moral Economics and *Timon of Athens*," (Ph.D. diss., Ohio State University, 1977).

2. Shakespeare himself was later threatened by the possible loss of a major investment in land, the half-interest in the lease of tithes in Wel-

combe and other neighboring hamlets to Stratford. To protect his interest, which he had bought in 1605, he entered in 1614 into an agreement with those who sought the enclosure of the land. This contract has become a *cause célèbre* through Edward Bond's play *Bingo*. That the facts admit of a less-sinister interpretation than Bond's is shown by Samuel Schoenbaum, "Shakespeare Played Out, or Much Ado about *nada*," *TLS*, 30 Aug. 1974, p. 920. See also Schoenbaum, *William Shakespeare: A Documentary Life* (New York: Oxford University Press, 1975), pp. 230–34.

3. Of the number of books I have consulted for the social and economic background, I have been most helped by the following: C. B. McPherson, *The Political Theory of Possessive Individualism* (Oxford: Clarendon Press, 1962); Lawrence Stone, *The Crisis of the Aristocracy 1558–1641* (Oxford: Clarendon Press, 1965); Lawrence Stone, *Family and Fortune: Studies in Aristocratic Finance in the Sixteenth and Seventeenth Centuries* (Oxford: Clarendon Press, 1973); Christopher Hill, *The World Turned Upside Down* (London: Temple Smith, 1972).

4. Francis Bacon, *A Harmony of the Essays of Francis Bacon*, ed. Edward Arber (London: Queen Square, 1871), pp. 374–48.

5. Sir Thomas Elyot, *The Book Named the Governor* (London: Dent, 1907), p. 139.

6. Nicholas Ling, *Politeuphia: Wit's Commonwealth* (1610), p. 139. Ling attributes the collection to John Bodenham.

7. Bacon, "Of Usury," in *Essays*, p. 541.

8. E.g., Malynes, p. 47; Warren, sig. B3ʸ, John Jewell, *Certain Sermons* (1611), in *The Works of John Jewell*, Parker Society Publications (Cambridge: At the University Press, 1845–1950), 2:1043.

9. E.g., Robert Pricket, *Time's Anatomy* (1606), sig. B2ʳ.

10. Malynes, p. 59.

11. *Aristotle's Politics*, trans. [into French] by Louis Leroy [Regius], trans. [into English] by I. D. (1598), p. 52. Cf. *Politics*, I.iii.23. In *Sonn*, 6.8, Shakespeare puns on "breed" in the two senses of increase by progeny and by making making money grow, as does the lord in *Timon* 1.1.278.

12. Francis Trigge, *A Good and Fruitful Sermon* (1592), p. 25.

13. Lodge, *Catharos*, fol. 5ʳ.

14. A distinction between *donatio* and *usuria* is made by Miles Mosse, *The Arraignment and Conviction of Usury* (1595), p. 15: "For *Donatio proprie est qua aliquis dat ea mente ut statim velit accipientis fieri, nec ullo casu a se reverti. . . .* From whence we may easily observe that the usurer gives not forth his money or his goods in as much as he hath no purpose to make them forever the goods of the receiver."

15. Stone, *Crisis*, pp. 158, 524.

16. Ibid., p. 189.

17. Dabridgcourt Belchier, *Hans Beerpot* (1619), sig. D4ʳ.

18. Pettet, p. 321.

19. Draper, p. 20.

20. Sir William Cornwallis, *Discourses*, sig. G3ᵛ.

21. W. K. Jordan, *Philanthropy in England 1480–1660* (London: Allen & Unwin, 1959), pp. 13–85.

22. John Downame, *A Plea for the Poor* (1616), p. 41.

23. "Of Expense," in *Essays*, pp. 50–52.

24. Robert Wakeman, *The Poor Man's Preacher* (1607), p. 17.

25. Aristotle, *Nicomachean Ethics*, trans. A Rackham (London: Heinemann, 1945), p. 109. Cf. J. C. Maxwell, "Timon of Athens," *Scrutiny* 15 (1948): 195–208.

26. Barckley, p. 326.

27. William R. Elton, "Shakespeare's Ulysses and the Problem of Value," *ShakS* 2 (1966): 95–111. See also Elton, "Shakespeare and the Thought of His Age," in *A New Companion to Shakespeare Studies*, ed. Kenneth

Muir and Samuel Schoenbaum (Cambridge: At the University Press, 1971), p. 192.

28. Thomas Hobbes, *Leviathan* (London: Dent, 1914), pp. 43–47.

29. Ibid., p. 44.

Chapter Nine

1. See Jean Hagstrum, *The Sister Arts* (Chicago: University of Chicago Press, 1958); Rensselaer Lee, *Ut Pictura Poesis: The Humanistic Theory of Painting* (New York: W. W. Norton, 1967). Arthur H. R. Fairchild, *Shakespeare and the Arts of Design* (Columbia: University of Missouri Press, 1937).

2. W. M. Merchant, *Shakespeare and the Artist* (London: Oxford University Press, 1959), pp. 171–75.

3. See Hagstrum, p. 70; Lee, pp. 59–61.

4. The text of the passages is faulty; but no more than a line seems to have gone wrong. The Folio reads: "Our Poesie is as a Gowne, which uses /From whence 'tis nourisht." Editors have accepted the ingenious Pope-Johnson emendation " . . . is as a gum which oozes . . . " But I wonder. "Gown" seems an appropriate metaphor for the deceptive art of the poet, and "use" is one of the key words of the play. With the minimum change of "from" to "form," some sense can be read into the lines; poetry would then be a "gown" that acquires its "form" from the source that nourishes it, i.e., the gentle flame of inspiration: "Our poesy is as a gown which uses / Form whence it is nourished." Admittedly this is a very mixed metaphor; but Shakespeare may have intended it to be revelatory of the poet's inanity.

5. Andrea Alciati, *Emblemata* (Antwerp, 1608), p. 104. The emblem shows Mercury, representing Art, sitting on a square base and Fortuna standing on a rolling ball opposite to him. On this general motif, cf. Gottfried Kirchner, *Fortuna in Dichtung and Emblematik des Barock* (Stuttgart: Metzler, 1970), pp. 80–82.

6. John Norden, *Vicissitudo Rerum, An Elegiacal Poem of the Interchangeable Courses and Variety of Things in this World* (1600), stanza 98.

7. See Antony Blunt, "An Echo of the Paragone in Shakespeare," *Journal of the Warburg and Courtauld Institutes* 2 (1938–39): 260–62; Merchant, pp. 171–75; Hagstrum, pp. 66–81; Lee, pp. 56–57. Ben Jonson, it may be said, touches on the issue in *Timber or Discoveries*, ed. Ralph S. Walker (Syracuse, N.Y.: Syracuse University Press, 1953), p. 34: "the pen is more noble than the pencil."

8. Leonardo da Vinci, *Paragone*, trans. Irma A. Richter (Oxford: Oxford University Press, 1949), pp. 54–57.

9. Barckley, p. 6.

10. Seneca, *The Work of the Excellent Philosopher Lucius Annaeus Seneca Concerning Benefitting [De Beneficiis]* (1578), p. 55.

11. Shakespeare may have gotten the idea from Jonson. Volpone calls gold "the world's soul" in the first speech of the play. The connection of the idea in *Timon* with fortune probably glances at the Stoics' identification of the *anima mundi* with fate. Cf. Cicero, *Academica*, 1.7.29.

12. Perrière, *La Morosophie* (Paris, 1553), fig. 91.

13. Paul Rheyer, *Essai sur les idées dans l'oeuvre de Shakespeare* (Paris: Didier, 1947), pp. 562–72.

14. See James G. Rice, "Shakespeare's Curse: Relations to Elizabethan Curse Tradition in Drama" (Ph.D. diss., University of North Carolina, 1947).

15. Wilson, p. 153.

16. Boaistuau, pp. 92, 127.

17. Thomas Gardiner, *Doomsday Book* (1606), p. 8.

18. Sir William Cornwallis, *Essays of Certain Paradoxes* (1617), sig. F.2^{r}.

19. Edward Topsell, *Time's Lamentations* (1599), p. 235.

20. Swigg, p. 389.

Chapter Ten

1. For the Fortuna iconography, see A. Doren, "Fortuna im Mittelalter und in der Renaissance," *Vorträge der Bibliothek Warburg* 2 (1924): 71–144; Howard R. Patch, *The Goddess Fortuna in Medieval Literature* (1927; rpt. New York: Octagon Books, 1967); Samuel Chew, *The Pilgrimage of Life* (New Haven, Conn.: Yale University Press, 1962), chap. 2; Raimond van Marle, *Iconographie de l'art profane au Moyen Age et à la Renaissance* 2 (la Haye: Nijhoff, 1932): 178–202; Guy de Tervarent, *Attributs et symboles dans l'art profane* (Geneva: Librairie Droz, 1958). For emblems, see also Kirchner, *Fortuna*.

2. In relative frequency of the occurrence of "fortune" in all its forms, *Timon* ranks just below the leading *Antony and Cleopatra* (0.162% versus 0.184%). In the occurrence of the plural form, *Timon* is ahead of the latter play (0.078% versus 0.072%). The others are far behind. On fortune in Shakespeare, see Marilyn Williamson, "Fortune in *Antony and Cleopatra*," *JEGP* 67 (1968): 423–29; Paul Jorgensen, "A Formative Shakespearean Legacy: Elizabethan Views of God, Fortune, and War," *PMLA* 90 (1975): 220–33; Bradbrook, *Shakespeare the Craftsman*, chap. 7 [on *Antony and Cleopatra*]; Frederick P. Kiefer, "Fortune and Elizabethan Tragedy: the Adaptation and Transformation of a Convention" (Ph.D. diss., Harvard University, 1972. Too late for consideration in this chapter came Lewis Walker, "Fortune and Friendship in *Timon of Athens*, *TSLL* 18 (1977): 577–600. Walker's argument that the play demonstrates the operations of the goddess Fortune runs parallel to mine, but he reads more allegorically than I do.

3. The performance took place during the 1956-57 season at the Old Vic, with Ralph Richardson as Timon; cf. *ShS* 11 (1958): 129.

4. See Blunt, p. 260.

5. For the background of this conception, see Patch, pp. 123–36.

6. Stephen Harrison, *The Arches of Triumph Erected in Honor of the High and Mighty Prince James the First* (1604), sig. G. The engravings of the arches are reproduced in *SQ* 12 (1961). See also David M. Bergeron, *English Civic Pageantry* (Columbia: University of South Carolina Press), p. 83, and fig. 8.

7. See Martha Hester Fleischer, *The Iconography of the English History Play* (Salzburg: University of Salzburg, 1974), pp. 41–46.

8. Cook, *ShS* 16 (1963): 85.

9. For this figure of speech, see the following anecdote in Lodge, *Catharos* (1591), fol. 19[r]: "Covetous men in hell shall drink molten gold, as the philosopher telleth that Nero, the Emperor, was seen in hell bathing himself in seething gold, and when he saw a great number of comers-by, he said unto them: 'Come hither you wretches that be sellers of your neighbors and bathe you here with me for I have received the better part for you.' "

10. Lilius Giraldus, *De Deis Gentium* (Lyon, 1565), p. 387. Vincenzo Cartari, *Le imagine dei Dei degli antichi* (Venice, 1571), p. 565.

11. Cartari, p. 486. This is not in the abridged English translation by Nicholas Linche, *The Fountain of Ancient Fiction* (1599).

12. Jean Cousin, *The Book of Fortune[Liber Fortunae]*, ed. Ludovic Lalanne (Paris and London: Librairie de l'art, 1883), fig. 67. This book, extant in a manuscript dated 1568, contains two hundred emblems and symbols of fortune, and it is therefore a convenient source of reference. I trust that all the elements of its emblems can be found in printed sources since emblems were by nature conventional. The emblem under discussion, for instance, is also in Cartari, p. 567.

13. Harrison, sig. H[r]. Cf. Bergeron, p. 64, fig. 7.

14. Chew, p. 50.

15. Cousin, figs. 25, 27; Cartari, p. 576.

16. Tervarent, cols. 291–93, 399.

17. Tervarent, cols. 126, 307, 408. Tervarent, col. 307, notes a tapestry woven in Brussels before 1528 (and now in Madrid) that has a blindfold Fortuna lying on roses and holding a scepter in one hand, a cup from which

stones are falling in the other. The motto has a Timon-like dichotomy: "Hinc spargens Fortuna rosas hinc saxa volutans ludit et aribitri cuncta suopte regit" (Fortuna plays by scattering now roses, now stones, and rules everything according to her own judgment.) Surely there were some similar tapestries or wall paintings in England in Shakespeare's time.

18. Tervarent, cols. 395, 401; Cousin, fig. 25.

19. Cousin, figs. 11, 13.

20. Cousin, fig. 59; George Wither, *A Collection of Emblems Ancient and Modern* (1635), p. 182.

21. Werner Habicht, "Tree Properties and Tree Scenes in Elizabethan Theater," *RenD* n.s. 4 (1971): 69–92.

22. Batilly, fig. 13.

23. Nosworthy, pp. 45, 225–26.

24. Honigmann, *SQ* 12 (1961): 3–20.

25. Bradbrook, *Craftsman*, chap. 6. Cf. "The Comedy of Timon: A Revelling Play of the Inner Temple," *RenD* 9 (1966): 83–103.

26. Bernard Beckerman, *Shakespeare at the Globe* (New York: Macmillan, 1962).

27. De Witt, in a note to his sketch of the Swan (1596), said its columns were so painted. Cf. C. Walter Hodges, *The Globe Restored* (London: Oxford University Press, 1968), p. 69.

28. Lydgate, pt. 2, bk. 3, p. 422.

29. Batilly, figs. 77, 91.

30. Batilly, fig. 56.

31. The Folio has "my Masters house," which is accepted and defended by Oliver. But I consider it a printer's error. as do most editors.

32. Perrière, fig. 79. Pierrière has two buildings, one on top of a mountain, the other on level ground, with a Fortuna figure standing on one side; the explanation says that buildings on level ground, like people of less-elevated state, are safer from disasters, such as earthquakes.

33. Batilly, fig. 57.

34. Cousin, figs. 22, 35.

35. Irwin Smith, *Shakespeare's Blackfriars Theater* (New York: New York University Press, 1964), pp. 231–37; this idea is endorsed by Bradbrook, *Craftsman*, chap. 8.

36. The tide and the sea in general are frequently associated with Fortune. Erasmus in his *Adagia* has a proverb, *Fortuna Euripus* (Fortune is like a channel of the sea), and Fortuna is often depicted as standing on waves.

37. Cousin, fig. 153. *Fortuna Philapolis*, says the note, was called the protectress of the cities by Pausanias.

38. Lodge, *Catharos*, fol. 1^r.

39. Merchant, p. 170.

40. Stephen Batman, *The Doom Warning All Men to the Judgment* (1581), p. 53. The source for this legend is the razing of the Athenian walls by the victorious Spartan general Lysander. As Plutarch reports the story in his "Life of Lysander," the walls were torn down to the accompaniment of music.

41. Cousin, fig. 33.

42. Cf. Adolf Katzenellenbogen, *Allegories of Virtues and Vices in Medieval Art* (New York: W. W. Norton, 1964); Chew, p. 52.

43. Cesare Ripa, *Nova Iconologia* (Rome, 1603), p. 169. Cf. Chew, pp. 51–52. The four seasons and fortune are the subject of an emblem by Barthélemy Aneau, *Imagination Poétique* (Lyon, 1552), p. 35: a man in a house with columns is approached by four figures, the Seasons, who offer him their gifts; the verses warn against changes of fortune. The gifts are for those who are rich.

44. Wither, p. 182. Cf. Patch, p. 61.

45. Cicero, *De amicitia*, p. 159. For the proverb "A good friend is like the sun in winter" see Morris Palmer Tilley, *A Dictionary of Proverbs in England* (Ann Arbor: University of Michigan Press, 1950), S 700. For the moral of the servant, see Tilley, S 979: "The rising not the setting sun is worshipped by most men."

46. Cousin, fig. 142.

47. Jean Boissard, *Theatrum Vitae Humanae* (Paris, 1596), fig. 1. Batilly, fig. 4.

48. Richard Alwyn and Karl Sälze, *Das Grosse Welttheater* (Hamburg: Rowolt, 1959), p. 48. Kirchner, *Fortuna*, discusses German seventeenth-century theater from this perspective.

49. Thomas Nashe, *Pierce Penniless*, in *Works*, ed. B. B. McKerrow, 1 (London: A. H. Bullen, 1904): 165.

Stage History

1. The following is a checklist of productions in England, the United States, and Canada from 1816 to 1978.

28 October 1816	Drury Lane, Edmund Kean as Timon.
8 April 1839	Franklin Theatre, New York City; N. H. Bannister, manager, adapter.
15 September 1851	Sadler's Wells; Samuel Phelps as Timon, manager.
6 March 1871	Prince's Theatre, Manchester; Charles Calvert as Timon, manager.
22 April 1892	Stratford-upon-Avon Memorial Theatre; Sir Frank Benson as Timon, manager.
18 May 1904	Court Theatre, London; J. H. Leigh as Timon, manager.
Fall. 1910	Fulton Opera House, Lancaster, Pa.; Frederick Warde as Timon, manager.
1 May 1922	Old Vic; Robert Atkins as Timon, director.
Spring Festival, 1928	Stratford-upon-Avon; Wilfrid Walter as Timon; W. Bridges-Adams, director.
1931	Maddermarket Theatre, Norwich; Nugent Monck, director.
19 November 1935	Westminster Theatre, London; Ernest Milton as Timon; Nugent Monck, director.
Summer 1936	Pasadena Playhouse; Gilmor Brown. director.
January 1940	Yale University.
1947	Birmingham Repertory Theatre; John Phillips as Timon; Willard Stoker, director.
28 May 1952	Old Vic; André Morell as Timon; Tyrone Guthrie, director.
July-September 1953	Antioch Area Theatre, Yellow Springs, Ohio; Arthur Oshlag as Timon; Mary Morris, director.
August 1955	Ashland Shakespeare Festival, Ashland, Oregon; Richard T. Jones as Timon; Robert B. Loper, director.
August 1956	The Marlowe Society, Cambridge, England; Peter Woodthorpe as Timon; Tony White, director.
5 September 1956	Old Vic; Sir Ralph Richardson as Timon; Michael Benthall, director.
Summer Festival, 1963	Stratford, Ontario; John Colicos as Timon; Michael Langham, director.
Summer Festival, 1965	Stratford-upon-Avon; Paul Scofield as Timon; John Schlesinger, director.

Summer Festival, 1971	Delacorte Theatre, Central Park; Sheppard Strudwick as Timon; Gerald Freedman, director.
Summer 1974	Colorado Shakespeare Festival, Boulder; Allen Nause as Timon; Mrs. Ricky Weiser, director.
11 October 1974	Hartke Theatre, The Catholic University of America, Washington, D.C.; Pinkney Venning Mikell as Timon; Gary Jay Williams, director.
Summer 1977	San Diego National Shakespeare Festival, San Diego, California.
Summer 1978	Ashland Shakespeare Festival, Ashland, Oregon; Jerry Turner, director.

The Peter Brook production in Paris in 1974 is also discussed in the text of this stage history. A recording of *Timon* was made by the Marlowe Society (undated), with William Squire as Timon, directed by George Rylands (Argo ZRG 5253–3).

2. *Theatrical Inquisitor and Monthly Mirror,* October 1816, pp. 243–44.

3. Advertisement, Lamb edition, Folger Shakespeare Library.

4. Lamb, p. 52.

5. George C. D. Odell, *Shakespeare from Betterton to Irving* (New York: Scribner, 1920), 2:79.

6. *Leigh Hunt's Dramatic Criticism,* p. 136.

7. John Genest, *Some Account of the English Stage from the Restoration in 1660 to 1830* (Bath: Carington, 1832), 10:586; W. C. Oulton, *A History of the Theatres of London* (London: Martin and Bain, 1818), 1:345–46.

8. F. W. Hawkins, *The Life of Edmund Kean* (London: Tinsley, 1869), 1:396.

9. *The Table Talk of the Late Samuel Taylor Coleridge* (London: John Murray, 1835), 1:24.

10. Oulton, 1:279.

11. See, for example, Odell, 2:79; or Oscar J. Campbell and Edward G. Quin, *The Reader's Encyclopedia of Shakespeare* (New York: Crowell 1966), p. 877.

12. Based on the playbills and seasonal annotations of John Harley (the Lucius of this production), Folger Shakespeare Library.

13. *Leigh Hunt's Dramatic Criticism,* p. 137.

14. Barry Cornwall [B. W. Procter], *The Life of Edmund Kean* (London: Moxon, 1835), 2:162–63.

15. *Leigh Hunt's Dramatic Criticism,* pp. 136–37.

16. *Theatrical Inquisitor,* October 1816.

17. Cruikshank engraving, published by J. Roach, London, 4 November 1816, Folger Shakespeare Library Art Files. The engraving was published with Roach's 1816 edition of the play (which was not Lamb's text).

18. Letter of Harry Stoe Van Dyke, cited in Hawkins, 1:398.

19. *Leigh Hunt's Dramatic Criticism,* pp. 137–38.

20. Ibid., p. 134.

21. *Theatrical Inquisitor,* October 1816.

22. J. C. Trewin, ed., *The Journal of William Charles Macready* (Carbondale: Southern Illinois University Press, 1967), pp. 155 (23 June 1840) and 247 (18 January 1848).

23. Shirley Allen, *Samuel Phelps and Sadler's Wells* (Middletown, Conn.: Wesleyan University Press, 1971), p. 244. Phelps's *Hamlet* had 171 performances, his *MND* had 80, and his *Coriolanus,* 39.

24. Ibid., pp. 131–33.

25. Based on the Folger Shakespeare Library promptbook described in Charles Shattuck, *The Shakespeare Promptbooks* (Urbana: University of Illinois Press, 1965), *Timon* No. 5.

26. Promptbook, Folger Shakespeare Library, Shattuck, *Timon* No. 8.

27. Promptbook, Folger Shakespeare Library, Shattuck, *Timon* No. 9.

28. Ibid., No. 8.

29. Promptbook, Folger Shakespeare Library, Shattuck, *Timon* No. 11. Previous accounts report this sequence incompletely; the promptbooks clarify it and its significance.

30. 20 September 1851.

31. Henry Morley, *Journal of a London Playgoer* (London: Routledge, 1891), pp. 129–30.

32. Ibid., p. 132.

33. *Athenaeum,* 20 September 1851 and 18 October 1856; *Times,* 13 October 1856.

34. 20 September 1851.

35. *Morning Advertiser,* 13 October 1856.

36. *Athenaeum,* 20 September 1851.

37. See Morley pp. 129-30.

38. This and other reviews were excerpted in a pamphlet, Thomas Charles, ed., *Memorials of Charles Calvert's Productions of Shakespeare and the Poetic Drama* (London: Aubert, 1875), pp. 15–16 (Folger Shakespeare Library).

39. Frank Archer, *An Actor's Notebooks* (London : S. Paul, n.d.), p. 131. Archer was Calvert's Apemantus.

40. Letter to Stanley Williams in Williams, "Some Versions of *Timon of Athens* on the Stage," *MP* 18 (1920): 277.

41. *Poet Lore,* 4:374–75, cited in Williams, *MP* 18 (1920): 277.

42. Ibid.

43. Constance Benson, *Mainly Players: Bensonian Memories* (London: Butterworth, 1926), pp. 108–9.

44. Richard Dickins, *Forty Years of Shakespeare on the English Stage, August 1867 to August 1907: A Student's Memories* (n.p., n.d.), p. 109 (Folger Shakespeare Library).

45. 19 May 1904.

46. Alan Woods, "Frederick B. Warde: America's Greatest Forgotten Tragedian," *Educational Theatre Journal* 29 (1977): 333–34.

47. Warde, *Fifty Years of Make-Believe* (New York: Marcy, 1920), pp. 75, 298.

48. Promptbook, Folger Shakespeare Library, Shattuck, *Timon* No. 13.

49. Approximately 720 of the play's 2,254 lines were omitted; Warde's extensive rearranging of the text makes a precise count difficult.

50. The Folger Library promptbook contains two fugitive reviews, one from Charlotte, S.C.

51. Warde, *Fifty years,* p. 302; Williams, *MP* 18 (1920): 284–85. Warde's autobiography carries (p. 273) a photo of him as a darkly handsome Timon, costumed and jeweled in exotic Eastern style.

52. George C. D. Odell, *Annals of the New York Stage* (New York: Columbia University Press, 1928), 4:312.

53. Trewin, *Shakespeare on the English Stage 1900-1964* (London: Barrie & Rockliff, 1964, pp. 89–91.

54. Herbert Farjeon, *The Shakespearean Scene: Dramatic Criticisms* (London: Hutchinson, 1940), pp. 124–125.

55. Ruth Ellis, *The Stratford Memorial Theatre* (London: Winchester Publications, 1948), p. 149.

56. James Agate, *Brief Chronicles* (1943; rpt. New York: Blom, 1971), pp. 163–64.

57. Ibid., p. 166.

58. Trewin, p. 152; Farjeon, p. 125; *Times,* 20 November 1935.

59. Ibid.

60. H. S. Bennet and George Rylands, "Stratford Productions," *ShS* 1 (1948): 110–11; Trewin, pp. 209–10.

61. Bennet, *ShS* 1 (1948): 110–11.

62. Audrey Williamson, *Old Vic Drama 2, 1947–1957* (London: Rockliffe, 1957), p. 95.

63. Harold Hobson, *Sunday Times*, 1 June 1952.

64. *Times*, 29 May 1952.

65. Roy Walker, "Unto Caesar: A Review of Recent Productions," *ShS* 11 (1958): 131.

66. Williamson, p. 95.

67. The sources for this discussion of the text are : Walker, *ShS* 11 (1958): 129–31; Muriel St. Clare Byrne, "The Shakespeare Season at the Old Vic, 1956–1957, and Stratford-upon-Avon, 1957," *ShS* 10 (1957): 466–77.

68. Walker, *ShS* 11 (1958): 131.

69. Byrne, *SQ* 8 (1957): 466, *Times*, 6 September 1956.

70. *Observer*, 9 September 1956.

71. Byrne, *SQ* 8 (1957): 466.

72. *Observer*, 9 September 1956.

73. *Times*, 6 September 1956.

74. In addition to Byrne and Walker, I have drawn here upon Mary Clarke, *Shakespeare at the Old Vic* (London: Hamilton, 1957), unpaginated.

75. *New York Times*, 31 July 1963.

76. Cited in Francelia Butler, *Strange Critical Fortunes*, p. 147.

77. Ibid., p. 146.

78. Peter Hall, "Shakespeare and the Modern Director," in *The Royal Shakespeare Theatre Company, 1960–1963* (London: Reinhardt, 1964), pp. 41–46; Peter Brook, *The Empty Space* (New York: Athenaeum, 1968), chap. 1.

79. *ShS* 19 (1966): 118.

80. *Times*, 2 July 1965.

81. Robert Speaight, *Shakespeare on the Stage* (Boston: Little, Brown, 1973), p. 293.

82. *Times*, 2 July 1965.

83. David Addenbrooke, *The Royal Shakespeare Company: The Peter Hall Years* (London: Kimber, 1974), p. 159.

84. *New York Times*, 11 July 1971.

85. *New York Times*, 2 July 1971.

86. Caroline Alexander, interview with Peter Brook, in *Timon d'Athènes*, adaptation française de Jean-Claude Carrière (Paris, 1974), pp. 107–8; Martine Millon, "Peter Brook: le sens d'une recherche," interview with Peter Brook in *Travail Théâtral* 18–19 (Janvier-Juin 1975): 87–88.

87. Pierre Schneider, *New York Times*, 3 December 1974.

88. Alexander, p. 110.

89. Mel Gussow, interview with Peter Brook, *New York Times*, 10 August 1975.

The Text

1. Charlton Hinman, Introduction to *Timon of Athens*, in *William Shakespeare: The Complete Works*, Pelican Shakespeare, ed. Alfred Harbage (Baltimore: Penguin Books, 1969), p. 1138.

2. Honigmann, *SQ* 12 (1961): 18.

3. Una Ellis-Fermor, *"Timon of Athens:* An Unfinished Play," *RES* 18 (1942): 170–83.

4. Coleridge, ed. Raysor, 1:85.

5. Wilhelm Wendlandt, "Shakespeares *Timon von Athen,"* *Shakespeare Jahrbuch* 23 (1888): 105–51.

6. Cf. Butler, chap. 2. This theory, seldom voiced now, is still advocated in the generally astute analysis of W. T. Nowottny, *SQ* 10 (1959): 493–97. Cf. also Nowottny, "Shakespeare's Tragedies," in *Shakespeare's World*, ed. James Sutherland and Joel Hurstfield (London: Edward Arnold, 1964), p. 48.

7. Chambers, *William Shakespeare*, 1:481.

8. Frank Kermode, Introduction to *Timon of Athens*, Riverside Shakespeare (Boston: Houghton Mifflin, 1974), p. 1441.

9. Oliver, p. xviii.

10. Terence Spencer, "Shakespeare Learns the Value of Money: The Dramatist at Work on *Timon of Athens*," *ShS* 6 (1953): 75–78.

11. Bradbrook, *Craftsman*, p. 166; Bulman, *ShS* 29 (1976): 115. As J. C. Maxwell notes, the Bible would have contributed to Shakespeare's uncertainty about the value of the talent. A low figure is in Matthew 25:14–30; a high one, in Matthew 18:24. See New Shakespeare, p. 97.

12. Stone, *Crisis*, p. 524.

13. K. Deighton, Introduction to *Timon of Athens*, Old Arden Edition (London: Methuen, 1905), p. xxi.

14. For arguments on memorial reconstruction in the quartos, see especially G. I. Duthie, *The "Bad" Quarto of "Hamlet"* (Cambridge: At the University Press, 1941), and *Shakespeare's King Lear: A Critical Edition* (Oxford: Basil Blackwell, 1949).

15. B. Tschischwitz, "*Timon von Athen: Ein Kritischer Versuch*," *Shakespeare Jahrbuch* 4 (1869): 160–97.

16. Thomas Mark Parrott, *Shakespearean Comedy* (New York: Oxford University Press, 1949), p. 305.

17. Chambers, *William Shakespeare*, 1:481.

18. Similarly indefinite stage directions also occur in *The First Part of the Contention* (1594) and *The True Tragedy* (1595), the two "bad quartos" that according to the opinion of most scholars are not the source plays of 2 and 3 *Henry VI* but reconstructed versions of Shakespeare's plays. An interesting theory that the quartos are a memorial reconstruction by a traveling company that left the promptbook at home is by Madeleine Doran, *Henry VI, Parts II and III: Their Relation to "The Contention" and "The True Tragedy*," University of Iowa Humanistic Studies, vol. 4, no. 4 (Iowa City: University of Iowa, 1928).

19. My information about William Long's study of Elizabethan playbooks derives from his talk to the Seminar on Research Opportunities in Shakespeare during the MLA Conference, 26–29 December 1976; see *SNL* 27 (1977): 15. That the distinction between "literary" and "theatrical" stage directions is not always easy to maintain is admitted by F. P. Wilson, *Shakespeare and the New Bibliography* (1945; rev. ed. Oxford: Clarendon Press, 1970), p. 66.

20. I have modernized the spellings of the Folio stage directions.

21. The only "part" from an Elizabethan play that has survived, one for the character of Orlando in Robert Green's *Orlando Furioso*, has several "descriptive" stage directions. See F. P. Wilson, p. 60.

22. John H. Long, *Shakespeare's Use of Music* (Gainesville: University of Florida Press, 1971), p. 421. Cf. R. W. Ingram, "Music as Structural Element in Shakespeare," in *Shakespeare 1971*, ed. Clifford Leech and J. M. Margeson (Toronto: University of Toronto Press, 1972), p. 183.

23. Bradbrook, *Craftsman*, p. 164.

24. The director was Ricky Weiser, the performance that at the Colorado Shakespeare Festival 1974; see *SQ* 25 (1974): 423–25, and Stage History, n.1.

Date and Sources

1. See above, chap. 2, nn. 21, 22, 23.

2. See Simko, *Philologica Pragensia* 8 (1965): 320–41.

3. See above, chap. 8. I have also noted in chapter 5 that *Timon* 3.1–3 appear modeled on Thomas Heywood's *A Woman Killed with Kindness* 3.5. Heywood's play was published in 1607; but according to Henslowe's Diary it was performed in 1603, and Shakespeare could have seen it then.

4. E. K. Chambers, *The Elizabethan Stage* (Oxford: Clarendon Press, 1923), 4:369.

5. *Coleridge's Shakespearean Criticism*, ed. T. M. Raysor (Cambridge: Harvard University Press, 1930), 1:84.

6. Maxwell, New Shakespeare, p. 133.

7. Address of King James to the Parliament, in *The Works of the High and Mighty Prince James* (1616), pp. 500–502. The same analogy is made by Thomas Pricket, *Time's Anatomy* (1606), sig. F4r.

8. I have discussed my treatment of the sources with Professor Pauls, and he has kindly made suggestions. I have also benefited from reading his unpublished article on "Shakespeare's *Timon of Athens* and Renaissance Diogeniana."

9. Honigmann, *SQ* 12 (1961): 3–20.

10. See Plutarch, 2:227, and cf. above, chap. 4.

11. T. W. Baldwin, *Small Latine*, 1:734.

12. R. W. Bond, "Lucian and Boiardo in *Timon of Athens*," *MLR* 26 (1931): 52–68.

13. Maxwell, New Shakespeare, p. xxi; Bradbrook, *Craftsman*, chap. 8. The dating of the comedy before Shakespeare's *Timon* is corroborated by Hans-Joachim Hermes, *Die Lieder im anonymen englischen Renaissance-Drama 1580–1603* (Salzburg: Salzburg Studies in English Literature, 1974), pp. 49–50. Hermes speculates that Thomas Heywood wrote the comedy.

14. G. A. Bonnard, "Note sur les sources de *Timon of Athens*," *Etudes Anglaises* 7 (1954): 59–69.

15. M. C. Bradbrook, "The Comedy of Timon: A Reveling Play of the Inner Temple," *RenD* 9 (1966): 32–103. James C. Bulman, "The Date and Production of *Timon* Reconsidered," *ShS* 27 (1974): 111–24.

16. Robert H. Goldsmith, "Did Shakespeare Use the Old Timon Comedy?" *SQ* 9 (1958): 31–38.

17. *The Works of Lucian of Samosata*, trans. H. W. Fowler and G. W. Fowler (Oxford: Clarendon Press, 1905), 1:33–34.

18. James C. Bulman, "Shakespeare's Use of the *Timon* Comedy," *ShS* 29 (1976): 103–16.

19. Plinius Secundus, *The History of the World*, trans. Philemon Holland (1601), p. 166. [*Historia Naturalis*, 7:19.]

20. Cicero, *Tusculan Disputations*, 4:11. This work was read in grammar schools; see Baldwin, *Small Latine*, 2:601–10.

21. Holland, p. 166. [*Historia Naturalis*, 7: Proem.].

22. Boaistuau, sig. 2r, pp. 2–3.

23. That Shakespeare modeled the Apemantus-Timon contrast on that of Diogenes and Timon in Montaigne's essay "Of Democritus and Heraclitus" is suggested by Willard Farnham, pp. 65–66. But Montaigne viewed Diogenes as a totally sympathetic figure and admired him for not taking things to heart and for not separating himself completely from man, as Timon did. I have argued that Apemantus is an ambiguous figure and is not used to contrast with Timon in the fashion of Montaigne's Diogenes. Farnham is aware of the significance of Boaistuau and Barckley as sources but restricts his discussion to the beast theme.

24. Boaistuau, pp. 172–74.

25. Barckley, pp. 350–51, 360.

26. Barckley, pp. 368–70. Cf. 2 Corinthians 6:8–10.

27. Agrippa, fols. 35–36, 92, 125–126, 114, 149, 166, 167. Cf. respectively *Timon*, 1.1.215–22 and 5.1.79–84; 4.3.157–59; 4.3.74–77 and 5.1.22–29; 4.3.110–30, 417; 4.3.434–36; 4.3.155-57; 4.3.446-47.

28. Agrippa, fol. 30.

29. Agrippa, fol. 93; cf. Barckley, pp. 15–16.

Index to Lines

The numbers of the pages on which quotations or references occur are in parentheses. The act and scene numbers in brackets correspond to the new divisions proposed in chapter 3; otherwise the numbering follows the Arden Edition.

Index of Names and Subjects